RIDING THE TIGER

H.H. the 16th Gyalwa Karmapa
The title means "Action Man." He is the condensed activity of all Buddhas.

Riding the Tiger

TWENTY YEARS ON THE ROAD:
RISKS AND JOYS
OF BRINGING TIBETAN BUDDHISM
TO THE WEST

LAMA OLE NYDAHL

BLUE DOLPHIN PUBLISHING
1992

Other books by Ole Nydahl:
   Entering the Diamond Way: My Path Among the Lamas
   Basic Dharma
   Practical Buddhism: The Kagyu Path (with Carol Aronoff)
   Ngondro: The Four Foundational Practices of Tibetan Buddhism
   Mahamudra: Boundless Joy and Freedom

Copyright © 1992 Ole Nydahl
All rights reserved.
Cover and Frontispiece: His Holiness the Sixteenth Gyalwa Karmapa

ISBN: 0-931892-67-8

Published by Blue Dolphin Publishing, Inc.
P.O. Box 1908, Nevada City, CA 95959

Library of Congress Cataloging in Publication Data:

Nydahl, Ole, 1941-
   Riding the tiger: twenty years on the road: risks and joys of bringing
Tibetan Buddhism to the West / Ole Nydahl.
     512 p. cm.
   Includes bibliographical references.
   ISBN 0-931892-67-8 : $17.95
   1. Nydahl, Ole. 2. Buddhism—China—Tibet. 3. Kar-ma-pa (School)
I. Title.
BQ974.Y3A3 1992
294.3'923'092—dc20
{B}
                                                     92-6605
                                                       CIP

Printed in the United States of America by
Blue Dolphin Press, Inc., Grass Valley, California

5   4   3   2   1

Dedicated to H. H. Karmapa,
whose 17th conscious re-birth
will be disclosed in the autumn of '92.

Table of Contents

Foreword

*T*HIS BOOK RECOUNTS THE HISTORY of Tibetan Buddhism in the West, and its amazing advance into our lives since the early seventies.

I finished it on the day of our protector, Black Coat, on Hawaii in December '91. When all corrections were done, early January '92 in Copenhagen, it was again on that illustrious monthly day.

This is symbolic and expresses my aim: that the fine people awakening to a spiritual life be protected by some healthy common sense.

Nothing benefits our inner growth like a few good laughs at anything stilted, self-important, illogical, puritanical or sentimental. In this guardian role, we Danes have something to offer the world.

Baikal Lake, Siberia
Full moon of January, '92

Hannah and Ole Nydahl

Lama Ole

CHAPTER ONE

Riding the Tiger: Prologue

*E*UROPEAN AUTUMN WAS AT ITS VERY BEST when we landed in Copenhagen on October 7, 1972. The air cleared one's lungs, and colors and light were intense and pure. This day would be the beginning of a saga. After three years in the Himalayas, H.H. Karmapa—the first consciously reborn lama of Tibet—had sent us home with a task large enough to fill several lifetimes: to make the deep wisdom of Tibet accessible to our part of the world and open the minds of the extroverted West to things as unfamiliar as mantras and meditation.

There had been contacts with the East before, but these were mainly a hindrance. Enthusiastic guru-followers had embarrassed many with public and dramatic displays. At least in the press, the openness in free societies to new things was fast changing into cynicism. The new groups promised such rapid results that pragmatic Europeans could not believe them; and buying mantras for money turned most people off.

In fact, things were as always; those who already knew something were keenly aware of what they did not like, and most people weren't interested at all. There were no palm-waving masses awaiting salvation. Our task was to bring absolute insight to a materialistic world, to offer a complete set of methods for developing one's mind to beings whose every conventional need had already been satisfied. While distancing ourselves from jealous, angry, or otherwise tainted gods, we wanted to bring spiritual experience to societies that had become much too linear.

There were also several helpful factors: the good karma and compassion of people in the West, as well as our ability to think clearly and doubt things in a constructive way. Since mature people are in essence Buddhists, freedom and independence would always support our work.

Our first group consisted of friends from the exciting sixties. They were amused to now see me protecting the purity of Tibetan Buddhism. Some years earlier, I had been protecting them. They trusted us because they knew that we had not fled into religion to escape personal problems or avoid decisions in our lives. We were already immersed in every imaginable joy before meeting our teachers. It thus carried weight when we told them that the mind contains unimaginable dimensions of bliss to which our culture gives no access.

The Diamond Way is for people who have something to share, and many conditions favored us right from the start. In the snob-free seventies, one could be someone without having much, and there was great freedom of movement. "Short range transport" was a sequence of rusty VW buses, and for greater distances we had the help of Niels Petersen from the "Pitzner" rental company. They provided transfer-cars all over Europe and paid the gas. We could thus travel freely between Oslo and Rome to teach. In November 1972, after giving my first lecture at a Teachers' College in Denmark, we drove one of their cars to Austria. There, in lovely Graz, I gave Buddhist Refuge to that first group. This became the pattern for starting scores of centers and meditation groups in the powerful heart of Europe. Even when having to hitchhike, we were picked up by people who wanted to learn about their mind.

During the first years, we felt little need to distinguish between Tibetan culture and their timeless wisdom: both were "Karmapa" and "Tibet" to us. Every evening I showed two dozen faded color slides which Hannah had selected from our years spent in the Himalayas. Though photos didn't tell people what to do about their lives here and now, at least they brought them into direct contact with Karmapa's blessing field. Our money we earned at night, cleaning a school for delinquent children in western Copenhagen. While putting together what the little darlings had trashed during the day, we could hardly keep our eyes open, and again and again I marvelled at Hannah's toughness. As more of our friends became students, they came along after meditation to help with the work

The powerfield of the Eighth Gyalwa Karmapa Mikyo Dorje

and, when travelling across Europe, there was always someone to take the broom. We kept our expenses to a minimum, buying everything second-hand while still making sure to get enough vitamins and protein to keep our bodies fit. That had to make up for daily deficits in sleep. On weekends, I often felled trees in Sweden and, later on, dug the holes for swimming pools which a friend sold. In addition to an always enjoyable night life, this made for good health and strength.

One advantage was in a league of its own: our wonderful parents. They were a constant source of inspiration and help. Hannah's mother could see beneath my rough surface even during my fighting days, and she and Hannah's father maintained their confidence also during our police troubles. I have described those events in my first book, *Entering the Diamond Way: My Path Among the Lamas,* which covers our years in the Himalayas and the wild times before that. My parents' unselfish love was greater than words can express. They were intellectually ripened beings who were always behind my brother Bjørn and us. At an age where many allow themselves to stagnate, they only grew.

While the outer conditions were excellent, without inner transmission, they would have only been a shell. Our growth and the ability to help others arose from meditating on Buddha aspects and from our close and continuous connection to Karmapa. The awareness-field of his eighth incarnation, "Mikyo Dorje," always surrounded us, and I constantly felt the presence of our protector, "Bearer of the Black Coat." He is the fearless power of all Buddhas. Other enlightened energies, often white and female and bearing names like "White Umbrella" and "White Liberatrice," would manifest over the years. With incredible power and precision, they ward off death or serious accidents.

CHAPTER TWO

Work Begins

*W*E STARTED RIGHT AT THE TOP. His Holiness Karmapa had sent us home with a letter for Her Majesty, Queen Margaret of Denmark, in the wording of an English nun. Shortly after landing in Europe, the answer came. It was sent to our minuscule $12 a month apartment, the attic of a run-down house in historical central Copenhagen. With a fine view over the famous-infamous hippie colony, Christiania, and my brother next door, it was a place of great freedom till the authorities pulled it down. The invitation lay in our mail one morning when we returned from the woods of Sweden, and there were only two hours until the audience.

After so long in the East, we were not prepared for an event like this. Hannah's best was an antiquated skirt and I had to fix the inner seam of my only acceptable pair of pants with safety pins, hoping that no one would notice my army boots underneath. I found a jacket that must have belonged to a dwarf and a tie worn for pure provocation during my boarding-school days in America. We drove with screeching tires to Christianborg, the seat of the Danish government, parked our rusty VW between sparkling limousines, and entered the building. In the hall stood about fifty gentlemen adorned with sabers and feathers. They were probably waiting to receive a medal. If I sat down, my pants would rip again. Fortunately, however, no one seemed to notice our attire, and after a short time we were called into a neighboring room.

HIS HOLINESS THE GYALWA KARMAPA   RUMTEK MONASTERY
                                                              GANGTOK
                                                              SIKKIM

                                                          VIA INDIA

        Your Majesty
               Queen Margarethe of Denmark,

        By the blessing of the Highest may you and yours be well
and happy.

        The occasion for writing this letter is the return to
Denmark of my trusted pupils, Ole and Hannah NYDAHL of Denmark.

        As a follower of Lord Buddha, and the head of one of the
four great Sects or Schools of Mahayana Buddhism, in old Tibet,
now living as refugees in India, we are specially concerned with
Dharma and what you would call the religious life. Our Sect is
called the Kagyudpa Sect, and includes many great historical Yogis
and saints.

        One of the features of the modern age is the trend of
many young people towards the East, and I get pupils from many
nations who are deeply sincere in their search for the truth. Ole
and Hannah are two such. I have therefore entrusted them with the
task of establishing a Centre and meditation centre in Denmark
where many earnest seekers young and old may learn to meditate and
"look within" according to our old and tried traditions.

        Belonging to a country which always reveres and respects
the "Dharma ruler" as we call the King or Queen, I wished to write
this letter, which I send by their hands, to introduce them to
you, so that they may have your moral support and protection in
this work they are beginning. In essence all religions are one, and
all seek "the good life", not for ministers and priests only, but
for all living beings, all men and women whoever they may be.

        We have had some very remarkable results with young
people who are going through the trials of what might be called a
war-torn and drug-deluded generation. We have our own way of
showing the way to peace, and a natural healthy life.

        Praying that you may make the way clearer for these
young people.   With blessings

What awaited us there was a real experience. Whatever one may think about the institution of monarchy, in any country there is only one person with the karma to hold this highest function. I experienced our queen as radiant and surrounded by intense, good energy. She couldn't take her eyes off our main gift, a statue of "White Liberatrice." It was from Karmapa's monastery in Sikkim and looked exactly like her. Her interest was real, not just polite. Some months earlier, she had been in Nepal herself and had genuinely enjoyed it. She said she was looking forward to reading our book of Kalu Rinpoche's lectures, "Teachings on the Nature of Mind." Though our views on immigration differed then—I think we should support people inside their own cultures and countries—the impression of her greatness is still there today.

In the winter of 1972-73, there were many signs that Karmapa's energy was developing at the places we visited. The spiritual hierarchy of Central Europe was obtaining a new top. One example was when we used our first earnings to paint one of our rooms in Tibetan colors and stripes. Deep in thought and perhaps a bit dizzy from the fumes, I spoke the mantra of our protector Black Coat out loud—something one should never do. Before I had finished, my voice disappeared in an ear-splitting roar. Hundreds of stray dogs from the hippie colony beyond the street started howling for no apparent reason. For a moment, everything stood still and we knew that the power field of our lineage had now fully arrived. It never left, and the humble beginnings of this first mini-group in Denmark expanded into the hundred-plus growing centers we had started for Karmapa when I wrote this in '91. They are primarily between the river Rhine and Vladivostok in Siberia, in the Americas, New Zealand, and Australia.

In December, a trip to the Danish isle of Funen opened up new dimensions. I had been invited to the Teachers' College in the main town there. They wanted to combine ancient Buddhist wisdom with the newest methods of group therapy and sensitivity training. This was easy as they have derived what is useful in their systems from Buddhism anyway. After the course, as so often during the years to come, we filled our VW with a dozen interested people and drove to our cottage in the Swedish woods. Here, we had greetings from our first Tibetan lama,

Lopön Chechoo. For no explainable reason, his picture buzzed loudly and for several minutes.

The most important event of the winter of 1972/73 happened thanks to a professor named Kjell Sellin. During those years he was a major influence on the spirit of the time. A strong, jovial man of Norwegian-Swedish descent, he helped launch nearly every new "spiritual movement" in Denmark, then the testing-ground for most of Europe. Some of our friends who sat stacked in our flat most of the time had heard about him. They knew that he was planning an exhibition called "The Inner Universe," which would run for three weeks from the middle of January. Its aim was to inform people about the new spiritual directions entering the country.

This gave us a difficult choice. Being certain that we had the best of spirituality, period, we naturally leaned towards an exclusive attitude. We felt no desire to exhibit our ancient Kagyu lineage among Hindu sects, Neo-Christians, Pop-Gurus, and new age-hopefuls. But somehow this did not feel right. How could new people meet us if we didn't attend? There would be visitors who had a deeper interest and Karmapa always wanted to benefit many beings. So next morning we walked through the pale grey neo-classicist rooms of the exhibition. Here, a dozen spiritual groups had already set up their booths and were now arguing over a few inches of space. One guru had become many during our years in the Himalayas, and we saw with amazement how psychologically sophisticated and "Western" their presentations already were, including statements by professors and charts of brain waves. The last room the Protectors had apparently held for us. Nobody seemed to have noticed it. The walls were already painted in the red and yellow colors of Buddhism, and we decided that this environment was noble enough for what we had brought.

While Hannah went to see the professor, I quickly positioned our Tibetan scrolls (thangkas) so dominantly that there was no space for anybody else. We brought Kalu Rinpoche's books, some mattresses to sit on, and were ready. The next day, the exhibition opened and things happened as we wanted. People arrived at our room overwhelmed by all the streamlined systems and needed some time to recover. Sitting among all the blessed objects, they gradually realized that this was where they felt most at home.

A healthy interest grew, and a few days later many came to the second lecture of my life. Having never learned how to speak publicly, it came out with more devotion than structure, but people did not want to leave. As always, the transmission came through. I felt under heavy voltage while my conscious mind observed the situation from the back of my head, amazed at all the things I suddenly knew.

Shortly after this, we learned to guide meditations in our own language. It was a technique new to Buddhism, though some yogis explain and then chant sections of a text, a practice called *gom lung*. The merit goes to Jorgen, "the Rabbit." He led the "Scandinavian Yoga School," exhibiting right outside our room. It might be the first case of Buddhism learning from Hinduism, but its value has increased ever since. Jorgen guided the Yoga School's meditations *in Danish*. Though their goal was relaxation and not enlightenment, it was important to use one's own language. The traditional meditations sung in Tibetan are too unwieldy for many Westerners, but this method was a real jewel. It still gave direct access to the blessing of the lineage and people could participate without feeling strange. Soon the friends I empowered were guiding growing groups everywhere.

Between teaching and our night job, I now gave Refuge to the dozen people our car would hold. The group that evening received something extra: the first guided Karmapa meditation in Danish. It was the right decision to come down from our ivory tower. Though most found Tibetan Buddhism a bit "dusty" and cultural, they liked its timeless qualities. Being free people, they enjoyed its absence of sentimentality and were relieved that our aim is experience and not belief. In three weeks, a hundred friends had become involved. Most were of the "spiritually mobile" kind, students or hippies, but there was nothing in the teachings that made them less useful to the more conservative strata of society. Without really noticing, we had become the spiritual anchors of the exhibition. On the last day, I explained the primary Buddhist motivation of reaching enlightenment in order to benefit others. Nobody else had a teaching like that.

The Professor held us in his big heart and let us use a large basement in medieval Copenhagen for free. He rented the fourth floor of the house to disciples of Guru Maharaji. They helped us develop concentration. Still in their proselytizing phase, they would sing their hit song, "Lord of the Universe." Later when they became practical and opened a restaurant, someone would inevitably drop a tray of dishes right when I started a guided meditation. The courtyard greatly amplified any noise, and taking new, stiff, or confused people through an unknown meditation under such conditions develops great strength!

Several friends helped make the center. Tibetan-style pillars already stood in the main room, so most of the work fell to those who could paint. They did a superb and fully traditional job. In the beginning, I thought of myself only as an introductory teacher. My idea was to transmit Karmapa's blessings and lay the foundation for his visit. Now, however, we already had a center in the heart of town with room for 150, where people came to learn something for their lives. After a few months, we had a program almost every evening and I taught continuously.

Since returning from the Himalayas, we had mainly been looking for a center in the country. Our close friends, Tom and Kate, wanted to finance it. Some run-down barracks on a hill west of Copenhagen fit our wildest dreams, but after five months' struggle with the officials—a true purification for all—we received a final "No." Apparently our work still lay in the city.

The Nordic countries are a family, and while the center in Copenhagen took shape, good contacts ripened in other places. We had known people from the Ethnographic Museum in Stockholm since November, 1972, and the circles soon widened to Uppsala and Gothenburg. A hitchhike there became my coldest experience since the army. While standing by the side of the road, some Swedes would stop and explain the way to the next train station, but not offer a ride. Either they couldn't imagine being without money or their last war was so long ago that they had forgotten their solidarity!

Nearly every night, a tall girl from Oslo sat against the wall in Copenhagen. She had friends in Norway who also wanted to learn about their mind, and several visits there brought about a fine group.

Our cottage in southern Sweden soon became too small. Here we had summarized Kalu Rinpoche's teachings into our first and slightly "churchlike" book, *Teachings on the Nature of Mind.* For months, we had spent every free weekend in four-wheel skids on their gravel roads, looking for a larger site, when a Swedish girl appeared. Her name was Maria, and the fact that she brought the much-needed money forced us to forget an otherwise life-long insight: that people who are not happy themselves can rarely do much for others. She was the "spiritual" type and had stayed with the Hindu-Guru Muktananda near Bombay until Karmapa was invited there. With his joyful power, he had cracked open everybody's preconceived idea of what "being holy" means, and now she wished to open a center for him. With her $10,000, suddenly everything was possible. We could sell our private paradise and establish something of benefit to everyone. Within days, we found a wonderful forty-acre farm on a high moor which was part of the century-old border between Denmark and Sweden. Buying it early in December for less than $20,000, we now had a place for "grounding" the many blessings. The friends who bought our old home let us take dozens of its enormous pine trees along.

During the first year, we often visited Holland and Belgium. A strong-willed lady from Utrecht had brought our lineage into contact with the Dutch Theosophical system. Though this looked like a useful bridge at first, it was to cost many a good lama much precious time with little benefit. It took us too long to realize that they already had a religion:

Karma Ling in southern Sweden

Building the Center

Theosophy. They enjoy listening but automatically ignore what doesn't conform to their own view. Not seeking the meditational experience which should anchor any philosophy, many seemed to consider things true only if they sound good—a weak protection against illness, aging and death. Actually, there's no reason to preach to the already saved. One should visit non-Buddhist groups only as a friend, not as a teacher, and allow the people to stay on a level they can relate to. If, later, the spiritual shoes become too tight or they develop more courage, people will come on their own. Much more important than picking up disenchanted guru-followers, however, is to offer something to interested materialists or skeptics.

Work around Europe developed wherever the driveaway cars went, and in Copenhagen, the group in our basement grew steadily. Some merely drifted through to see the "giraffes," while others seriously wanted protection and blessings—like some black women from an embassy who had been cursed with mice and snake energies by scorned West African lovers. Our real joy, however, was the fine people who practiced in order to help others. They gave lasting meaning to the work. Also, the translation of our most central Tibetan texts had begun. With the help of the kind Tarab Tulku who had lived in Denmark since the mid-sixties, Hannah had first translated the Karmapa meditation and was now working on the preliminary practices of the Diamond Way (Ngondro).

Though Karmapa's letters and the expectations of friends were gradually pushing me into the function of teacher, the first in Denmark to teach from a traditional throne was a stranger, and a woman. Gelongma Palmo was a close friend of Indira Gandhi and a strong-willed English grandmother of the old school. On a journey to England in October 1973 she decided to see the first Tibetan Buddhist center founded by Westerners. She was not without experience. First, she had been a personal student of the Dalai Lama, but as she preferred meditation to debating texts, he had sent her on to Karmapa. Living now on the top floor of Rumtek monastery with her nuns, she was our connection to the politicians in Delhi. She also knew several spiritual circles in the West.

Gelongma Palmo visiting Copenhagen

At the door to our house in Copenhagen, she had an unforgettable experience: a real Danish fist fight, not the children's stuff from the warmer countries where people scream and pull each other's hair. On her way up to the attic, the venerable Gelongma had to step over some drunks passed out on the stairs. Worst of all, nobody was there when she arrived. Fortunately, she had my parents' phone number and found the center with their help. The elderly nun was still in shock when she arrived.

We were already good material for Tibetan gossip, and this event added a social dimension: although from good families, we denied ourselves any luxury in order to spread the teachings. From then on, Karmapa frequently gave us clothes.

Some friends found a suburban house for the nun and over the next days she taught on "Wisdom Buddha Riding a Lion," "Liberatrice" and "The Diamond Mind." At the end of her visit, the first and probably last puja was sung in Danish; it simply didn't sound as good as in Tibetan.

Shortly afterwards, our center was put to the test: His Holiness the Dalai Lama visited Denmark. Prince Peter, heir to the Greek throne, had invited him. The invitation went through due to the personal courage of

H.H. Dalai Lama inaugurates our Copenhagen Center

the Danish Secretary of State and left the Chinese in a rage. It was fantastic! Welcoming him on October 10, 1973 at the airport, forty people clearly saw the outline of a hand on the full moon. When he walked the few steps from his limousine to our center a week later, it suddenly and unexpectedly started to snow—in mid-October. While the Dalai Lama joked with us and initiated the center with the name given by Karmapa—Karma Drub Gjy Ling, The Place of the Practice Lineage— the room was so packed that someone accidentally turned off the light switch a few times. The bodyguards, however, were well trained. When the light came on again, they were covering him with their bulletproof briefcases.

H.H. Dalai Lama

CHAPTER THREE

Driving Kalu Rinpoche Through Europe

$\mathcal{F}$OR OVER A YEAR WE HAD BEEN EXPECTING Kalu Rinpoche, but there was good reason for the constant delays. Before such an important teacher arrived, there were things to do. While we burnt gas and rubber, visiting new places every day, our friends in Copenhagen restored rooms in the "Active University" for Rinpoche and his lamas to stay in. We would have liked to work on the whole institute, as we did for Karmapa's visit later, but there was no time.

Our trips through Europe had already planted the seeds for centers in the main German and Austrian towns. Here we built on solid ground. Though many prefer a general and soft spiritual atmosphere, I wanted them to learn discrimination. Above all, people needed to know the differences between Buddhism, drug experiences, and dualistic religions. Otherwise, both lama and students would waste their time.

On May 30, 1974, Kalu Rinpoche finally arrived in Copenhagen. As on his previous tour, he was sent by Karmapa and had received his passport from him. He was accompanied by Gyaltsen and six newly-hatched lamas from Bhutan and Sikkim. He wanted to place them in the West. We hosted Rinpoche for three weeks. On one of the first days he showed a miracle everyone could appreciate.

Coyly placing one foot on the yard-high throne, against all laws of gravity, he simply "walked up" there and sat down. He gave initiations into "Loving Eyes," and "Guru Rinpoche," who had first brought a full

Reception in Copenhagen

Buddhist transmission to Tibet. Many took the vow to obtain enlight-enment for the benefit of all. The teachings were mainly on the prelim-inary practices, called "Ngondro." The room was always well filled, and though some were amazed to see the young lamas promptly fall asleep when a teaching started, the meeting between the cultures was a success.

During the next months, we drove Rinpoche and his lama students first to Stockholm. Then followed the European countries bordering the Atlantic. It was a good tour to learn from. Several strengths and weak-nesses of traditional Tibetan organization became evident as early as that. But, above all, every day with Rinpoche was a great inspiration. What freaked the lamas most, who after all had seen their first radios and airplanes during the last few weeks, was the twenty minutes on the ferry from Denmark to Sweden. Suddenly the iron house, in which they thought we had parked while waiting for canoes, was moving on its own. Escalators were also quite a challenge. Kalu Rinpoche alone kept his balance while his company fell on their noses.

While on a sailboat near Stockholm, a woman without underwear fell head first into the water. She markedly enriched the anatomical knowledge of the lamas who were life-long monks. Later on, she managed the same maneuver in a similar outfit from a teaching podium in town.

Now our Stockholm group was given a name. Though reserved, people had a strong wish to understand. They asked many practical questions. At our farm in the woods, "Karma Ling" as we called it, Hannah and I winced. Kalu Rinpoche wanted to use it for celibate three-year retreats, which would not have been useful for our friends. To prepare for this, the lamas did a day of pujas in the woods. We half expected some lovesick elk to jump out of the bushes at any moment. The sound of the long horns closely resembled their mating calls.

On our way south again, there was no time for the masses in Copenhagen. Instead, we visited an American-Danish couple on the southernmost island of Denmark. They lived there with a half-dozen kids. Every week they had driven two hundred miles to Copenhagen and back for my teachings. This time the huge ferry to Germany only mildly amazed the lamas with the white man's skill. In Hamburg, we "forgot" the addresses of some chaotic people who were only Kagyu by convenience. We spent the night in a bed and breakfast near the TV tower instead and visited it with Rinpoche in the morning.

Next stop was a Theravadan center near former East Germany, "The House of Quiet." Fifteen years later in India, Rinpoche still talked about this visit. Right in the middle of his lecture, the otherwise mature and well-behaved listeners became increasingly nervous. Then they suddenly ran out of the room, leaving only a few brave ones in the first row. We overlapped with a Zen seminar and the old-fashioned teacher beat his disciples when they were late.

We slept at the house of my first German girlfriend, and then with Tibetans in Belgium. In northern France we all jumped to our feet. The owner of a restaurant had suddenly put her broad finger on Kalu Rinpoche's forehead. "I saw a light there," she said.

Paris was already the center of Kalu Rinpoche's activity. His followers served us unbelievable meals. We stayed for a month and, to the dismay of the bourgeois French, another group of wild Danes arrived shortly after, led by my brother Bjørn. On the way to Lyon, we stopped

With Kalu Rinpoche and Lama Gyaltsen in Paris

at a castle called Plaige. We had advised friends to buy it for Karmapa a
year earlier, and they financed it with an art auction. Due to the French
tax system, it often felt like we had more castles than Buddhists in the
country. As long as the buildings were privately owned, one had to pay
yearly levies on all openings (windows and doors), which could get quite
expensive. But when the buildings were used for public functions, these
taxes fell away. The mutually beneficial scenario, however, where a donor
would give most of a building to the local Buddhist center while keeping
what he needed to live well, rarely worked to the satisfaction of both.
Once misunderstandings arose, the straight and up-front style of the
West was no match for the indirect and delaying tactics of the East. If
the owners' intention had not really been to make a gift to the Tibetans,
they wound up feeling betrayed and left.

In Aix-en-Provence, for the first time we heard talk about starting
a center specifically "for Rinpoche." We could hardly believe our ears and
told them that Kalu Rinpoche was sent by Karmapa. All Kagyus must
work together. Also, some monks and nuns were ordained on this
occasion. This center blossomed at first, but fell apart during the early
eighties under the direction of a moody American lama. Right from the
beginning, their whole attitude had made them vulnerable. They had

focused on Buddhist virtue and not on its joy. This tends to attract weak
people and gives little power or endurance.

The Pyrenees were an amazing display of nature. We also learned
much about Christianity and Buddhism there. Dennis, who came from
the upper French bourgeoisie—which really is "upper"—had an invitation from a super-Cardinal who had fallen out with the Pope. For that
reason, the Prelate now intended to donate a piece of land to some
Buddhists. Kalu Rinpoche, however, couldn't use the offered piece of
land. The piece he wanted, the Cardinal would not give. Seeing these two
elderly gentlemen side by side, each the product of a life on their
respective paths, was more instructive than thick books on philosophy:
on the one side, the Christian "high self" where everything is very
spiritual and personal, and on the other, the spontaneous and relaxed
Buddhist "resting in what is."

Then we visited a psychologist named Schnetzler near Grenoble in
the French Alps. Rinpoche's lamas, making associations which were very

H.H. Karmapa blesses Kalu Rinpoche

Kalu Rinpoche and
the Super Cardinal

foreign to Westerners, called his deeply psychotic patients, his "disciples." Probably no one in France has done more for Buddhism than he;
four or five important centers are the direct results of his activity. Here,
Kalu Rinpoche stated that he intended to leave Bhutanese lamas in Paris,
Plaige, and Nice. Although he always advised everyone to be celibate, for
once he spoke very differently about sexuality: if one had the meditative
power to use it correctly, enlightenment would result within six months
to a year.

In a wine cellar near Nice, I had an extraordinary experience. While guiding some rich supporters of the famous Pawo Rinpoche in the "Three Lights" meditation, a dragon suddenly appeared in front of me. He was very angry and about seven feet long. Though transparent, he was clearly visible down to the smallest detail. He attacked by blowing puffs of smoke at me. The situation was complicated: my French is not the best and it would not do to make mistakes when teaching such important people. One puff had already hit my throat making my voice somewhat hoarse. Most important of all, the forces representing the Buddha must never lose. While keeping everything going, on the mental level of our encounter I sent a hailstorm of triangular "diamond daggers" and the chopping knives held by "Black Coat" into the dragon. I turned his long body into a pincushion until he retreated, hissing, into the rocks. Only later did I realize that it was my mistake. I had brought a foreign energy into his territory without having prepared him. As when "Loving Eyes," "Black Coat," or other Buddhas have the kindness to manifest to me, this dragon also looked exactly the way he should. He could have come straight out of a Chinese picture book.

Then came Great Britain. Early in September, 1974, we took the ferry from Ostende, Belgium, to Dover. Driving on the left side of the small English roads was cozy, but I had to take special care when passing. It exposed Rinpoche, at my side, to the oncoming traffic. He really relaxed in England, perhaps because it reminded him of India. People's interest in Buddhism, however, was not overwhelming. They had already seen men in skirts and heard about reincarnation, so Rinpoche let his timeless Yogi mind play instead and just had fun. I will never forget when he slapped my back in passing while I was taking a leak. I just avoided wetting my pants and he nearly fell over with laughter.

London, proud capital of the Empire, was not too impressed. Perhaps they still remembered having conquered India with only five thousand soldiers. There is, it seems, a strange general tendency in the world; cities with more than a few million inhabitants often have trouble keeping their centers going. Smaller towns tend to function well while big ones either think they already have everything or give up trying to get it.

"Kham House," the center of Lama Chime, was situated on a bare field above an idyllic south English village. There, people were asked to push-start their cars to preserve the silence of the monastery. They also had plenty of other rules and regulations. We did not stay long, however, and in Manchester, Rinpoche suddenly announced that I would now continue his lecture. I was deeply thankful. It was a true initiation into his mind-stream, but I had to keep my eyes off a place right in the middle of the hall. There a man—otherwise quite normal looking—shone in a radiant green. There was no chance to investigate the phenomenon, and if I had not ignored it, there would not have been much of a lecture.

Akong Tulku, the lama of "Samye Ling," the first Tibetan Buddhist center in the West, had become Scottish-Tibetan. So had the solid buildings and the economical attitude of the center. Only the weather was still purely Scottish: wind and rain. While Rinpoche had an impressive program there, I gave teachings in Edinburgh and Glasgow. They seemed stuck in the poor '50s, more evidence that Britain now paid dearly for its former colonies. Kalu Rinpoche stayed for three weeks and we even found time for a retreat in a hut near the monastery.

People who lived in the vicinity had witnessed the beginnings of Samye Ling. Among other famous spots, they pointed out a stable down a gravel road. Here Trungpa Tulku had hidden for weeks before escaping to America. At that time he was slim, shy, and dressed in Chinese silk brocades. The police were investigating local use of drugs. Several events from his life were already legends, like when he drove across a bridge, drunk, and crashed into a joke shop. It was an understandable predicament, people said. His girl friend lived to the right and his monastery lay to the left. The story wasn't as funny as it sounded, however. He was badly injured in the accident and remained partially paralyzed from then on.

We had only met Trungpa Tulku once, in September of 1973. A French artist, Xolotl, had insisted we go to Stockholm to see him. There, Trungpa was visiting our friends from the Ethnographic Museum. They wanted to film a series of very detailed thangkas (Tibetan scrolls) depicting the life of the great yogi, Milarepa. We found the famous Rinpoche in a hand-tailored suit at a private dinner with vintage wines. This was new to us. So far we had only met lamas in red robes, sober and poor. The situation required more flexibility than we could manage. Devotion got lost somewhere, but we managed to be polite.

Kalu Rinpoche's next goal was Canada, which had already received many blessings. In 1971-72, he had stayed there involuntarily for a whole year. His wealthy sponsor, Sherab Tharchin, had not treasured some unsolicited advice regarding his love life. He had refused to pay for Rinpoche's return flight. This time, Rinpoche took Gyaltsen and Trinley Drugpa with him, the most popular of his lama students.

While waiting at the airport, there were several auspicious signs for our future work. The Tibetans sat chatting around a table. On it lay a package wrapped in silk. It looked like a traditional Buddhist text. Following Tibetan custom, I touched it to my head. Akong Rinpoche asked me how it felt. We had a good connection already. Some days before, he had kindly shown us some relics, among them pieces of ribs from the fifteenth Karmapa's holiest wife. They had mantras on them which had appeared spontaneously. I answered that it felt like a good blessing, and everyone laughed. The silk contained English pound notes, which were then larger than today. "If you can get blessings even from money, nothing can go wrong," Kalu Rinpoche said. "And if you can bring those two over here, you will be useful to all beings." He pointed to a working class couple, prematurely aged. The man looked like he had been in the mines, and neither appeared to have had an easy life. Sitting down at their table I told them who Rinpoche was. I could hardly understand their dialect, and they had the same problem with my school English, but we liked each other immediately. Within ten minutes, they were at Rinpoche's side and received his blessing.

Just before the plane left, there was a third good sign. While taking leave of a girl from Vienna, I touched my forehead against hers. Suddenly a map of Europe stood out clearly in my mind. It had lots of bright lights on it—mainly in the center and east of the continent—and I knew that these were the sites for our future centers.

During summer and autumn, we had to re-do a major part of our earlier work in Central Europe. During the first years, our close family bonds within the Kagyu lineage actually slowed our growth. Though it was a wonderful feeling to bring Kalu Rinpoche and later even Karmapa to our friends everywhere—and how could one let them travel alone?—still, any prolonged absence cost the groups dearly. In the early years, there was not much lineage-oriented practice when the heads of the centers were gone.

On October 17, 1974, we received Karmapa's blessings in London. He was on his way to America and his plane landed from a sky full of rainbows. Except for that, our time was spent traveling, teaching, answering ever increasing stacks of mail, and earning the necessary money. Unfortunately, Copenhagen was a bit handicapped by a moody Sikkimese lama who was later sent on to Stockholm and eventually ended up in California. Kalu Rinpoche had wished to "give" him to the center, and he cost Hannah a good deal of time.

To my great joy, the most energetic and disciplined Europeans were now catching on. German interest in Buddhism was awakening in the country's north, south, and middle. Though my first contacts in Munich had gone to South America to live in the jungle, there were exciting things happening in several other places. I sensed growth on a wide scale. Like everything else, Buddhism would become strong in this country.

CHAPTER FOUR

Karmapa!

ON DECEMBER 10, 1974, KARMAPA CAME TO EUROPE. The earlier lamas had set the direction and prepared. Now, the active power of all Buddhas arrived to enrich our wonderful part of the world.

At the Oslo airport, everything was already high voltage. We ran to Karmapa through customs and passport-check and were blown away by his blessing. Looking back today, it must have been quite a show. Physically shaking, as always when in his power field, and wearing one of my usual second-hand military jackets, I lifted the honorable guest onto a much too high cushion on the passenger seat of our rusty VW bus. Then we drove at high speed through town with Karmapa's head nearly touching the ceiling, until someone removed the pillow. Lody Sherab, who functioned as his servant, politely commented that "they have good cars in America." He was alluding to the fact that they had been transported with velvet smoothness in enormously long limousines there. In America at that time, they had wealthy sponsors and the organizations were willing to go into debt. We would gladly have taken the former, but debt we would not accept under any circumstances. I answered: "You can neither steer nor brake those lacquer-boxes, but look what this old thing can do!" adding a number of controlled skids on the Norwegian snowy streets in honor of European driving.

The hotel, however, would have satisfied even the greatest snob. It was large, built from logs and situated in the best-known skiing area in

H.H. Karmapa shows the Black Crown

Scandinavia. On top of being a noble introduction to our part of the world, it was free. The owner had wished to show his solidarity with the Tibetan cause.

Dozens of our friends were waiting. Karmapa gave a short blessing and showed his Black Crown, leaving everyone deeply touched. After that, he gave a protection initiation which kept people in the room long after. Many of the mustard seeds he threw on this occasion spontaneously turned into his treasured "black pills" while people held them in their hands. Just as former Karmapas had presented miracles as gifts when visiting China, now this Karmapa greeted Europe.

When everyone left, unable to hold more blessing, our private time with him began. He melted us completely. With Tenga Rinpoche close by, he gave himself to us as never before. Placing on a chair a life-sized picture showing his timeless state of mind, Karmapa asked: "Who of these two am I?" Then he rolled up the picture and gave it to us. What followed was even more fantastic. He told the saga of his clan. In colorful language, he brought to life powerful Eastern Tibet. Describing their meditations, their loves and fights, he dwelled upon the strongest of his seven brothers, the former Pønlop Rinpoche. When riding through the gate at home, he sometimes braced his legs around his horse and lifted both of them off the ground by a ring above. Exploding with laughter,

"Which of the two am I?"

Karmapa pointed to his head and said, "I was the smallest, but I'm the only one who still has hair today."

The three-day program included several of the important Crown ceremonies. An initiation into the second Karmapa, Karma Pakshi, left everyone breathless. It was like a family uniting. The flexibility of the

Karma Pakshi

A laughing Buddha

Tibetans and devotion of our friends led to levels of openness which make true transmissions happen. Something important seemed to take place every moment, and everything had the feeling of growth.

On the way eastward to Stockholm, this cooperation became quite useful. A friend of the Swedish girl who had helped us buy the farm had invited us. His name was Karl Birger and he gave me goosebumps. He claimed to have developed the technique of Kirlian photography before Kirlian, but missed having it patented.

With Karmapa, his lamas, and friends occupying the extra seats in a rented bus, we drove through woods and snow across Norway and Sweden. Customs officials at the border checked everyone except us. Hours later we arrived at Karl Birger's deserted village. It is situated near the town of Mora, where they make cheap and incredibly sharp lumber-jacks' knives from laminated steel. Its surroundings were not attractive, the hills were bleak and all trees had been felled. Here he wanted to make a spiritual center, apparently with himself as guru.

When we arrived, there was absolutely nothing: nothing functioned and nothing was prepared. Despite several invitations to Karmapa in Oslo, Karl was alone in an unheated house with empty cupboards. So our first task was to get food for Karmapa. Because the bus was so slow, we had not made a lunch stop. I have no idea how they managed. Having devotedly served the female principle in former lives, I have now happily come to the age of fifty without ever cooking a meal. Something acceptable was sent upstairs to Karmapa and the rest of us ate stale oats. The geniuses who transformed the substances were apparently Akong Tulku and Lody Sherab.

The following days had more style. We spent them surrounded by the finest of European culture. Nikita Tolstoy, an elderly but vital grandson of the Russian author, and lovely Diana, backed by the money of Volvo, were our hosts. They invited us to their baroque castle, north of Uppsala, a huge building in the middle of a large park. The walls were over a yard thick, there were secret staircases, and suits of armor stood in every corner.

The first night was dramatic. We stayed on the second floor, close to Karmapa's room, down a light-green corridor with heavy oak doors. As the Swedes had sold weapons during the last few wars but stayed neutral themselves, everything was rich and perfectly preserved. In the middle of the night, we suddenly heard a loud scream in the next room and the sound of falling furniture. Grasping a bayonet I always kept near, I ran into the corridor. At that time, a Chinese attempt on Karmapa's life was a real possibility. I encountered no men in Mao uniforms, however, but the otherwise unshakable Akong Tulku. He did not look happy at all. First, he had seen a hand move through his room all on its own. Then a lady had followed, carrying her cut-off head under one arm. I wanted to get in there at once. Such a lady I had never seen, but Karmapa held me back. "I'll take care of this," he said. He entered the room and threw a few grains of rice. The next day in the bus, he asked me: "What was special about last night?" I answered, "Why didn't you let me see the lady?" Karmapa ignored my response and continued, "Akong Tulku was special. After I told him that, everything was okay and he slept like a rock. This is true confidence, and he has that gift because he meditated so much on his Lama in his former life."

Then he blessed me with a meditation which placed five Karmapas in the five centers of the body. It only came up from my subconscious ten years later. He often did things like that, and impressions he planted then continue to be an important source of guidance today.

There was more excitement to come. After a delayed meal, which Karmapa somehow didn't seem to want to end, the bus with our twenty Tibetans drove the wrong way. Our most important program was scheduled for this afternoon and there was no way we could now make it. Somehow I got hold of a Volvo and reached Stockholm in record time. Over two thousand people, well annoyed by the delay, were just rising to leave the hall. Without even discovering the microphones, I kept them in their seats for another hour until our party arrived. By then they knew who Karmapa was and were well prepared for the Crown Ceremony which followed. I experienced the whole situation as his personal gift. This was my largest audience so far. It was a joy to work with so much anticipation and energy, and my Swedish was rarely better.

Also on Karmapa's agenda was a visit with the Bishop of Stockholm. He was a tall, noble man whom we liked immediately. He had much more heart than the Cardinal in the Pyrenees and really wished to benefit others. But even here, the differences between Christianity and Buddhism were enormous. Kindness with and without the awareness of someone being kind are not the same. A fish in a pot of glue swims differently from a fish in the ocean, and only someone who fully trusts the open space of mind can be truly spontaneous.

I made sure our guests visited the sites of our Nordic gods. During my growing years, I had measured myself against the heroes of the sagas. Today, in a period of empty emotionality and deep confusion, their ideal of courage and a stiff upper lip are more relevant then ever.

To the amazement of many, we brought Kalu Rinpoche, Gelongma Palmo and Karmapa to the statue of "Holger the Dane" at the Kronborg castle in Denmark. It is the site of Shakespeare's "Hamlet." Holger is our national protector and deserves only the best. He stopped the Muslim Arabs in the Pyrenees in 998 A.D. The Polish-Austrian generals who beat the Turks at Vienna five hundred years later, again preserving European freedom, belong in the same illustrious league.

While at "Karma Ling" in southern Sweden, a central part of our lives disappeared. On our way up to Oslo, Hannah's mother had asked several questions about death and in the driveway of their villa north of

Copenhagen, Hannah had a vision of her lying dead. In Stockholm, she had a similar dream. While in the room with Karmapa, we heard she had suffered a stroke. She had died without pain. Karmapa arose, walked to the barn where we had prepared a shrine and gave her the Phowa. This means that he contacted her mind and transferred it to a pure level of existence beyond the illusion of ego, a state from which there is no falling down. He saw deep meaning in the time and way she had gone. Some days later, he spontaneously gave an initiation into "Almighty Ocean" in her name. It seeded the awareness of all present with the perfect compassion of that red Buddha and his consort.

The next day Karmapa had again promised to show his Black Crown. Inside the half-open barn, a hundred friends sat huddling in the snow drifts. During the ceremony, the center's tomcat, a true killing machine, walked in behind Karmapa. All forgot about it, but after the ceremony, Karmapa smiled broadly and lifted his shawl. The cat reappeared, reeling as if drunk. From then on he was a vegetarian and stopped hunting. He didn't give up his male pleasures, however, nor did he grow fat as happened to Kalu Rinpoche's cat in 1970 in Sonada.

On the throne in Copenhagen

Copenhagen was well prepared. This time, we had thoroughly renovated the "active university." The professor and our friends were gracious hosts. Karmapa's room was beautifully made up, but the first thing he said was, "What kind of place is this?" All at once, his temperature shot up to 41 centigrade (105°) and a large boil appeared on his thigh. Nobody knew what the matter was and Gelongma Palmo was shocked when she arrived. Apparently Denmark's last executioner—sometime in the nineteenth century—had lived here. Later, rabbits had been killed downstairs for furs. It was not news to us that the house had mixed vibrations. In the beginning, hurrying to one of the difficult-to-lock toilets, sometimes a junkie would fall out, holding the implements of his trade. To our minds, however, the fine new wallpaper had put an end to the building's negative past.

A doctor lanced the boil. Then shortly afterwards, Karmapa showed the transformative power of the Diamond Way. Seating himself on his throne, he changed pain and illness into a warmth that was felt everywhere in the room. On a film made then, after Karmapa's touch, you see me stumbling back and being caught by our friends.

H.H. transforms pain and sickness into a radiant smile

Denmark made good use of the ten days he stayed. The center was always full. Two days before Christmas, Karmapa showed the Black Crown publicly. As he placed it on his head, the whole hall, filled to capacity with two thousand people, simply froze. There was only awareness. At the start of the second ceremony, something huge moved by at the edge of my field of vision. It was my old friend Sigvaldi from Iceland. He stood in front of everyone, seven feet tall, drunk, and with an enormous red beard, gesticulating wildly. There was not a second to waste or the magic of the moment would be lost.

I jumped up, folded him around my fist, then dragged him back to my seat. Everything happened so quickly, hardly anyone noticed. The transmission was not disturbed.

It was all very unusual and un-Danish: while the shops closed and it became impossible to buy or change Christmas presents, people stood in line for hours to receive Karmapa's blessings. Weak on publicity as always, we had forgotten to advertise this first major Buddhist event in Denmark. But even today people come to our center and say: "That man with the Black Crown, he changed my life."

Christmas and New Year '75 were totally under Karmapa's spell. Gelongma Palmo was happy that several monks and nuns would now be ordained. Though they were festive-looking in red robes, I knew them and thought it very premature. Among Tibetans, ordination is often the only chance to have an education and to avoid nagging wives and thankless offspring. Thus vows are often taken by the strong who want to move on in their lives. In the West, however, celibacy is frequently an escape from the healthy give and take of human life. Only a special kind of people are able to last in this group, anyway. None of the ten who were ordained then are still monks or nuns today. It must have been of use to them, however, otherwise Karmapa would not have allowed it.

Across America, Norway, and Sweden, Karmapa always had Tenga Rinpoche at his side, but never asked him to teach until Copenhagen. Here Rinpoche gave the meditation on the eighth Karmapa which is now practiced by many people. I had the honor of translating.

On December 28, Karmapa again showed the Black Crown to two thousand people. It was yet another encounter with the Buddha in us all. The very shape of the crown produces maximum receptivity and enables him to purify and enrich the deepest levels of our minds. Buddha himself prophesied Karmapa in two important Sutras, and the power of transmission is such that whoever attends a "Black Crown" ceremony will reach the state of "liberation" within three lifetimes. Even among the powerful methods of the Diamond Way, this speed is unique.

There were not many formal teachings. Karmapa kept them short. The English nun who insisted on translating did not know much Tibetan. She also lacked the format for communicating his unconventional Yogi-mind, so things tended to become a bit moralizing and stiff. Instead, he gave long blessings and many interviews. He found time for Refuge and initiations almost every day, and many took the Bodhisattva Vow. This is the promise to reach enlightenment for the benefit of all beings.

On several occasions, Karmapa asked to be driven along a street in the classy consular section of Copenhagen. Here lie two patrician mansions which are now our center. He had the kindness to visit my parents twice, once for a big lunch with his entourage and later more informally. While driving him further north of Copenhagen, he suddenly asked Hannah where her father lived. It was half a mile away, so he also had a special visit that day.

Karmapa's relationship to birds is indescribable. As a sensual man who likes to touch things, I had never been drawn to those small and fragile feather-balls. Here, Karmapa provided automatic "re-education." When driving around major European cities he had never visited before, on several occasions he would say, "Park over there!" Taking us by the hand around the next corner, there lay the largest bird shop in town. Once inside, he listened for a moment and then said: "That one tells the finest stories, but the one over there only talks nonsense." Reaching into the cage, the bird he wanted would fly to him. In their amazement, the owners often nearly gave them to him.

What he did with the birds we also know. As his first Western students and, in fact, his adopted children, we could come to him at all times and thus saw many exciting things: he said mantras and blew cold and warm air on them while telling us, "I am teaching them meditation." His bird keeper, Joel, an American who had the good taste to fall desperately in love with Hannah, also had some unbelievable stories to tell. Later, we witnessed similar things ourselves or had them confirmed by Karmapa. "Yellow finches and canaries are often Bodhisattvas," he said. "Look how they care for each other when one is ill. They also do not eat seed with worms in it. They don't want to hurt the insects."

Karmapa had big plans for Germany—that was obvious. Even when there were very few people present, he would show the Black Crown or do other things to build up an energy field. Near the Danish border, an interesting group of doctors and psychologists were finishing their studies. They lived on an old dairy farm and were very open to the teachings. I liked the consistency and energy of most, but several were the sort I today send elsewhere: frustrated types who gossip and destroy the common basis of trust. A good laugh is allowed when things become stiff and unnatural. But there is little yogihood in putting down other teachers to prove one's own way.

If we respect people mainly for the things they don't do or don't dare to do, we attract bores. That is the surest way to make the strong and independent ones leave. Then and there, I decided to live so authentically that such blocked people would run from me screaming.

Karmapa, the "Wish Fulfilling Jewel," as the Tibetans call him, often told me to be "his man" in Central Europe. As always, from the moment he spoke, the connection became magical and has only increased since then. Though my family is Danish-Norwegian, it has strong bonds with Northern Germany. After being in the resistance during the war, my father wrote fifty textbooks to reacquaint the Danes with the German language. Even today, with groups to teach around the world, I spend more than half of every year in intense Central and Eastern Europe. Nowhere are people having better results with Tibetan Buddhism than there.

Near Lubeck, Karmapa made a statement we never heard before or since. He said, "I was here in a former life." There was no doubt he meant it. The thought of Bach crossed my mind. Then we rolled on through Germany, now my field of responsibility, and into the Netherlands, to the Theosophical ladies there.

With strong and often irrational energies to be tapped and transformed, Germany is perfectly suited for the Diamond Way. The Netherlands, however, were then pure "Mahayana," down to earth and sensible. While the Central Europeans came to Karmapa to be touched and inspired, the Dutch and English came to understand things and discuss them afterwards. The treatment was respectful, but there were not many who really wanted to learn. In Central Europe, desire is the main emotion, but in the "border countries" pride and confusion are often dominant.

In the "Kosmos" in Amsterdam, a "cultural" center where they sold hash on the top floor, everything came to a head. At the entrance, Karmapa started to recite the hundred syllable mantra of purification, which was not a good sign. On the way upstairs to show the Black Crown, people were so inattentive or stoned that we had to push them aside to make room for him. During the preparations, it was impossible to get silence; people simply kept chattering. The more dignified members of the entourage, Gelongma Palmo and Akong Tulku, tried to say something from the stage, but no one listened. The situation was getting impossible, yet it would be a pity to take Karmapa away before he had blessed them. Climbing across some barriers and onto the stage, I started to yell at the people. This was language they understood, and soon they were silent. Strangely enough, no anger remained from my less than flattering expressions, and most even stayed for a final meditation. Though the idea was to make direct Tibetan-Western contacts, I was now expected to handle anything that had long hair and was young.

In Antwerp, Belgium, all stayed with Carlo and Brigitte, the leaders of the group we had started there. Many of their friends, delightful people with life experience, were intensely interested in the teachings and in Tibet. A few came along on the first tour we guided to the East in 1976. In Paris large crowds came to the beautiful halls of expensive hotels. The French charged admission, which everybody should have done. In the long run, it is impossible for a handful of idealists—the heart of any center—to carry the expenses. People lose inspiration when they are always in debt. It was fun to watch the French being organized and to see how much of their basic nature came through anyway. Less wealthy devotees we smuggled inside. We had to help those who seldom found work and followed Karmapa everywhere.

The stage for the ceremonies was always the same: a high throne for Karmapa in the middle with the red Tibetan monks to his right and the black Zen monks from the local center to his left. The halls were filled with an older and more consolidated part of the population than in the

Germanic world. Apparently the youth revolution had not penetrated as deeply as in northern Europe. Here even the young generation looked straight. They knew which side of the bread the butter was on. People established themselves with and not against the existing order.

Arnaud Desjardin, who wrote the foreword to *La voie du Diamant,* our first French book, often gave the opening speech. Some years earlier, he had "discovered" the Tibetans and triggered a wave of enthusiasm for them. His timely films and books had filled the Himalayan monasteries of the Kanjur and Kalu Rinpoche with wealthy French, seeking the magic of the East. During the ceremonies, the differences between Japanese and Tibetan minds stood out as clearly as one could ever wish. Sitting in black robes, the Zen monks held their faces serious and bodies straight while the Tibetans looked like moving maroon heaps. If not whispering or laughing, they were probably throwing rice at each other. Or they simply fell asleep, even during the most "holy" moments.

The wide range of Buddhist approaches became starkly apparent at the temple of the Zen teacher, Deshimaru. First, the Tibetans chanted some wishing prayers. Then the Zen people sang the Heart Sutra while bowing in strict cadence and hitting a gong. It looked like an army drill but was impressive, and then they again sat straight. For a while everything went well; everyone was enriched by the deep wisdom of each other's tradition. But then the Tibetans cracked up. When a Zen teacher hit the backs of his students with a board to keep them focused, that was too much: one by one our group pulled their shawls over their heads and rolled on the floor laughing. Only Karmapa managed to keep a straight face.

Master of Buddha activity

Like most Samurai, Deshimaru had European features and was open
to the goodness of women and wine. He offered Karmapa the finest of
Tibetan statues. Among them was a thousand-armed form of "Loving
Eyes," about two feet tall, and several well-crafted "united" forms.

The party drove on towards Lyons, still in the cars of the local people
and our trusty VW bus. The monastery of Plaige was being restored and
many local people came, thinking Karmapa was a kind of Pope. Here he
gave Hannah and me the Mahamudra transmission, and right after, also
an initiation into "Almighty Ocean." These struck like lightning and I
needed hours to get back to a practical level of functioning again.

In mid January, Karmapa flew to Rome for two days. He had been
invited by Pope Paul the Sixth who did not impress the Tibetans much.
With their usual candor, they said he was "a tired old man."

Diamond in Hand—
Father of Black Coat

De Swarte, a well-known couple of character actors, wanted to start a Buddhist library in Central France. We stayed for some days and Karmapa blessed the site with a special Kagyu initiation into "Diamond in Hand." We had never received this transmission before and to my amazement, at first I felt nothing at Karmapa's touch. But then the blessing came on with full power and wouldn't stop. "Diamond in Hand" is the "father" of "Black Coat." He holds all secret teachings and is the power of all Buddhas. Benson, an English genius, was also present. The inventor of the Delta wing and a number of electronic devices, he had come with his beautiful new wife and some of his eleven children. He wanted to donate 100 hectares of a mountain ridge in southwestern France for a center. At the same time, however, he wished to make it into an autonomous state, like Monaco—an idea which made the officials block all developments there for years.

During our stay at the library, we saw Karmapa's "meditating birds" for the first time, the ones Joel had told us so much about. After this, they would ornament many an altar along our route. Akong Rinpoche came running downstairs, radiant with excitement and with a yellow bird on a plate. It was completely stiff and held its bill pointed upwards. "It received Karmapa's blessings," Akong told us, "and he said that its mind will be free tonight." By supper, the bird became the usual small ball of feathers and was buried ceremoniously. "It was a Bodhisattva," Karmapa said.

He often stretched our education and common sense! This event, however, had wide implications. If something with a nervous system as small as a bird's could be a Bodhisattva, our understanding of the brain as the producer of consciousness no longer held. It would then have to be viewed as a kind of transformer, like a radio which selects programs among the infinite possibilities of space. This would prove the timeless existence which all religions ascribe to mind.

Back in Central Europe the millionaire Schulze hosted us for ten days in his castle near Zurich. A powerful man who had helped open Bhutan to the West, much of the country's business passed through his hands. Here, the Tibetans could relax from our journey, and we had time to set up a structure for our area of responsibility. Step-by-step Karmapa had put Europe east of the Rhine into our hands. People came directly to us from their interviews saying, "Karmapa told me to invite you. When can you come?" An exciting future was taking form.

Next stop was Rikon, a Swiss-Tibetan cultural center nearby. In the sixties, when people thought they could help the refugees of the world by inviting them to the rich West, the Swiss had chosen wisely. They took a thousand Tibetans, a talented, tolerant, drug-free, and hard working people with strong family structures. Though they had only obtained a few of the powerful East Tibetans, these independent people would probably not have adapted well to the Swiss millimeter society, anyway.

Our first visit to the Institute had been in '73. Driving down to thank the Dalai Lama for his visit to Denmark, we received an unwished-for initiation into Tibetan political intrigue. Afterwards we learned to differentiate religion from politics. Even today, it sometimes takes rolled-up sleeves to protect the purity of our cause, but it's also a lot of fun.

Karmapa came, saw, and conquered! Immediately on arrival he said, "They make too much politics here." Then a fierce four-day storm broke loose, stronger than anything people there remembered. Tiles flew off the roof and trees fell. It was impossible to make the usual circumambulations. The outer environment mirrored what was happening inside the building. Many refugees had so little education that they didn't even know what a Karmapa is, while others could or would not do as asked. Before the Black Crown Ceremony, people were told not to take pictures, but their flashes continued merrily. When even the third request was ignored, Akong Tulku and I ran through the rows and knocked the cameras from people's hands. Suddenly they understood. It was a joy to see how quickly that method worked.

Before leaving, Karmapa sent us north for a week to start groups. I held my first public lecture in German at a teachers' college, thinking: "I hope I won't cause a new German-Danish war." Everyone seemed satisfied, however. I gave Refuge and blessings in a private house afterwards.

Geneva was Karmapa's last stop before India. Schulze invited us all to stay at the Park Hotel. Here, the visit was rounded off and important future dimensions opened up. A few days earlier, Karmapa had accompanied Benson by helicopter to the beautiful site the latter intended to donate in southwestern France. It was situated a few miles from the caves of the first fully developed humans, the CroMagnons and Aurinacians. Here, between 10,000 and 40,000 years ago, they had painted magical hunting pictures on the walls of their caves. Then they followed the receding glaciers towards the north and probably became the present Scandinavians.

Though it was a bright day in spring, Karmapa had insisted on taking his umbrella. Standing on the land, he picked up an extraordinarily shaped stone, and said, "We found a similar one when we built Rumtek." Suddenly opening his umbrella, it hailed from a blue sky for several minutes. Smiling, he said, "This, too, is an auspicious sign."

In the rush of the following days, things kept happening which made us want our school fees back. While sitting in front of Karmapa, Barry, an American artist with a stiff knee from a fall in India, was able to bend it inch by inch.

Now work really began—work that would require all our experience, intuition and power, night and day. Karmapa had promised to come again soon. By then I wanted Central Europe to be ready for his return. Above all, people could learn the Three Lights Meditation which he had given as the direct link to his powerfield.

Back in Denmark, we delivered the "Pitzner" car we had transferred and then drove to Sweden with our friend Kim Wunsch. We wanted the Scandinavian centers under one roof, but the lawyers of the Swedish girl—now a nun—delayed the transfer of "Karma Ling" to Karmapa. In Copenhagen, Hannah translated texts from Tibetan to Danish, again with the help of Tarab Tulku from the royal library. For her part, she inspired him to write a number of beautiful poems.

Early in April, we returned to Great Britain with Kalu Rinpoche. He visited the north and "Samye Ling." In London he gave a major outdoor initiation into "Loving Eyes," the compassion of all Buddhas. After this tour, there was again much to do in Central Europe, but it was less repetitive than before, however. This time, many had not forgotten the centers after we left. The Sikkimese lama had been sent to Stockholm. Now Copenhagen was free to grow.

Before leaving Denmark in early '75, Karmapa said that our basement center, though free, was not good enough. Three days later, the house's sewage system broke and flooded the rooms. A week after that again, a friend found a patrician mansion which had belonged to my professor of American literature. On my visit there in 1961, a most unusual wave of compassion had hit me. I had a strong presentiment of "doing something important" from this house one day. Situated on a street the beauty of which Karmapa had often praised, we knew that this was the place. Everyone gave what they could, and in July 1975, when the bottom fell out of the housing market in Denmark, we bought this jewel for $100,000. In 1990, we also took over the neighboring mansion. Now over twenty friends practice and live there.

The Copenhagen group worked well. They kept up the style we learned from logging together in Sweden. Though most of the first team started families and then moved out, they provided the foundation for many to meet our lineage. While they renovated our house, I lived on the Autobahn, whenever possible with Hannah. Gradually a first network of centers expanded from the Alps and north.

In June 1975, we drove through Karmapa's French centers and via Milan to Rome. The people in the group there were pleasant individually, but gossiped so badly that there was no basis for a center. In addition, it was difficult to rent a hall in Rome. When the officials learned we were not from the Gelugpa school, the doors closed. Obviously, they and the Church had an agreement.

Our invitation to Greece had been extended since 1972. We took the train to the "heel" of Italy across what is more Africa than Europe. On the ferry, worn out from months of activity nearly around the clock, I fell asleep in the sun. On the bus from Patras to Athens, I nearly lost consciousness from the sunburn, but giving in wasn't acceptable. It would have been a bad sign for our work in a new country. When we saw the group waiting at the terminal, I knew that work in Greece would require endurance. It would also destroy many preconceptions.

We met secretly at the house of a friend. Nothing public was possible at this time. The generals had just been ousted and the mood in the country was oppressive. The police imprisoned followers of the Krishna, Maharaji and other sects that were not well protected. The mentality of the people — Orthodox-Christian with scars from centuries under a bloody Turkish yoke—was new to us. Much happened very indirectly, which took some getting used to. On the first visit to the main museum, I asked the country's ancient gods to help our work and—the halls being empty—tied Karmapa's blessing cords around the statues' necks. There were more personal ups and downs than in most other countries, but those who kept the bonds of friendship have developed amazingly. If one has the courage for the jump into emptiness, one cannot be content with less than the Diamond Way.

Continuing this pattern, activity along the north-south axis of Europe kept expanding. With both pirates and teachers in my ancestry, however, I knew that nothing can replace personal experience. And where else could our students learn more about suffering and its causes, its ending and the way there, than on a trip to Asia? It would enrich a training which had so far centered on hard work and the development of courage. Such a trip would help many mature. In October 1975, all conditions met for our first pilgrimage.

CHAPTER FIVE

Overland to India and Nepal

$\mathcal{M}$Y BROTHER BJØRN HELPED TOM AND KATE buy two second-hand buses in Germany. Niels, a tall and blond medical student, organized the tour. After leaving his body during an accident, he had added the potential of mind to his curriculum. There was room for fifty friends and we would give it six months of our time. In Copenhagen, the buses

Loading the bus in Copenhagen

were loaded with gifts. Thick Norwegian felt slippers were sure to be popular with the refugees in the Himalayas. We also took along bags of protein biscuits and yeast extract, to cut down on time-consuming stops. There were also masses of medicine to distribute. Thirty to forty of the group were Danes, the rest mostly Norwegians. As the next months clearly showed, several had a latent dramatic streak.

This was practically the last chance to get to Asia over land. Soon after, the hatred and frustration of the Moslems broke out as wars and oppression in many places. Even then, their anger was more apparent than on our earlier trips in 1966, '68, and '69.

The rich colors of the German and Austrian autumn were followed by the desolation of Yugoslavia. Two dozen Greeks had come up to Thessaloniki from Athens. They were touching and received two days of teachings before we drove on to Turkey. The prevalent fear and brutality in that country really shocked our friends. It was obvious this was no part of Europe. Observing our more compassionate reactions to events and people on this tour, Hannah and I saw daily how Karmapa had worked

Teaching our Greek friends in Thessaloniki—how small the groups were then

on our inner levels. We frequently didn't notice it because we were so active for him on the outer ones.

Shortly before Iran, we saw an accident—a truck beside the road with a score of men in a circle nearby. Bjørn quickly stopped the bus and I ran over. Having learned how to transfer the consciousness of dead people to a Pure Realm—this is a duty one has. Entering the circle, I felt countless dimensions open up. Existing in the freedom of space, they in no way limited each other. Right in center was the dead man. He must have been about forty years old but looked seventy. Unshaven, he lay on his back, his mouth full of still liquid blood. Around him were other workers, also malnourished and in shock like a herd surrounding a fallen

Nomads in Afghanistan

cow. At his side, a piece of hip bone contained a tiny pool of blood. It was just coagulating and shimmered in the sunlight. Behind everything hovered the beautiful Ararat Mountain. Half-covered with snow, this volcano is more symmetrical than the famous Mt. Fuji. The deep, blue sky above was limitless. Closing the dead man's eyes, the social dimension came very close. A poor family had just lost a breadwinner. I helped free his mind and knew one thing with deep joy: my field of awareness had excluded nothing while my body had done what was necessary.

The Iranians were unpleasant; they had now added pride about their new-found oil wealth to their otherwise uncharming national character. It was one country where no one asked for extra stops, and we had to protect the women even when getting on and off the bus. In the holy town of Maschad, we had to forcibly pull three members of our group from the hands of some Mullahs. By accident, they had entered some especially holy room in the mosque and should now be forcibly circumcised.

All had been looking forward to Afghanistan. Before their great war, it was one place in the Middle East where one could behave almost normally. In mid-October, we crossed the country on the usual route via Herat, Kandahar, Kabul, and Jalalabad, and then left over the Khyber Pass. The landscape was unique. Near Herat, ten tornados tore up the sands simultaneously. We were lucky that Bjørn is so strong and fast. As we drove full speed over a dam, a front wheel exploded. If he hadn't managed to hold the overloaded bus steady, some people would not have felt so good.

In Kabul, our group showed their sympathy for Afghanistan by buying a lot of their useless wares. At the hotel, we first had to rid the mattresses of used syringes. Hepatitis was the danger then, not yet Aids.

I had given the transmission for the "Diamond Mind" practice before leaving Denmark, so the bus was filled with the steady hum of fifty people reciting melodious Hundred Syllable mantras. These have the power to release all negative impressions from the subconscious, rapidly purifying it. It felt like a carpet of negative energy fell on the road behind us and vanished. Near Jalalabad in eastern Afghanistan, we saw the remains of the two thousand-year-old Buddhist Hadda stupas. They had been destroyed by the Moslems more than a thousand years ago, but

Bright heads in the bus

one could still feel their energy field. We also tried camel-riding. It must be the world's strangest means of transport.

Our drivers really proved their skills on the road through the narrow Khyber pass. When we came to the "Tribal Area," a territory which neither English, Pakistanis, nor Russians have been able to control, I insisted on driving through the night. Everyone advised against it. Even white men's heads could easily end up on stakes there, but we had no time to be careful. We did our best, and our protectors had to take care of the rest.

The Khyber Pass

So we drove on around the clock and our four drivers were incredible. All in the large bus had evil backaches from the ruined and nearly vertical seats. They could sleep at the most fifteen minutes at a time. It was great to see our friends grow tough through the ordeal. They learned to see difficulties as purification and the whole process as challenge.

We crossed Pakistan in a single day. At the border to India, the world's tallest man overshadowed the bus. His head alone must have been a half meter tall. The golden temple of the Sikhs in Amritsar was quite a sight. This was before they started fighting there. The northwestern corner of India, going towards Kashmir and Ladakh, was a new part of the Himalayan foothills to us. They contained some really powerful places, like Mandi. This town is blessed by Mandarava, the first main consort of Guru Rinpoche. Both the area and people had a troll-like quality, and the Tibetans often say that snake-spirits live there.

Srinagar lies by a beautiful lake in an idyllic valley, but is intensely annoying. The local men glue themselves to you, trying to bolster their egos by catching your attention or selling you something. As usual in Moslem towns, no women can be seen. We told everyone to check with us before any purchase above a few dollars. But of course exactly the people who always knew better bought the worst imitations of Tibetan art we had ever seen. They returned proudly with a number of scrolls,

Srinagar

apparently painted by non-Buddhists in an asylum for the blind. Only after we threatened to burn down the merchants' house-boats did they get some halfway acceptable carpets for their hundreds of dollars, instead.

Though our drivers were the best, the bus was twice the length of the local vehicles. Even on the road up to Srinagar, it was almost impossible to get it through. The road across the 4.7 kilometer pass into the valley of Leh was even narrower and more winding. So we had to trust the native imitations of Mercedes mini-buses and the local hash-smoking drivers. The region remains Muslim for amazingly long, even when every stone says "Tibet," and there are destroyed stupas everywhere. Only after a dark night in the town of Kargil did we feel the iron grip of Muslim influence weaken. Suddenly, the atmosphere changed. Women appeared, people relaxed and all spoke a funny and antiquated book-Tibetan.

The capital of Ladakh is Leh. It is a sad story, a lost part of Tibet. Its view is dominated by large numbers of ruined clay buildings. Once majestic, these former stupas, monasteries and castles are the remains of a broken culture. The population of largely alcoholic Buddhist farmers

The iron fist of Islam loosens

is increasingly suppressed by better-educated Kashmiri immigrants. These have already taken over tourism and transportation, the lucrative trades there. It was high time to organize some schooling for the locals. Without that, they will remain among the many exploited peoples in India.

Arriving in Leh at dark, these were not our initial impressions. First came the sensation of one's lungs exploding. With responsibility for so many friends in an unknown land, I got off the bus running. This is not the thing to do when arriving at an altitude of nearly four kilometers and carrying a backpack.

Niels bargained the hotels down to reasonable prices. They were amazingly clean. The next morning, our tours started to the sights of the region: fantastic monasteries, often older than the ones in Tibet. Several were built over a thousand years ago while there were still glaciers to make the land fertile. Since then, the most energetic Tibetans had followed the water ever further east. Under an unbelievably blue sky, we moved by bus or on foot across the high desert. First we saw the permitted sites. The exciting lama dances, however, took place at Chamde Monastery in the prohibited area. This is a part of Ladakh where the Chinese steal land from India year by year. The Indian soldiers caught during these excursions are sent to Beijing for "education," then set free again. In Chinese culture, this is true humiliation.

Another reason for going to Chamde was to visit the Drukchen and Dugpa Rinpoches. We knew them from our years in Darjeeling. Hiding on the back of two trucks, nobody official noticed us on the hour-long drive. On arrival, our group of fifty immediately vanished from the road with all luggage.

The way up to the monastery was difficult but worth it. The strong had to carry big loads. Standing on the pastel-colored mountain top and looking out over a moon-like landscape, we were suddenly a thousand years back in time. Everything was magical and had a timeless, self-lib-

Leh in Ladakh

The Drukchen and Drukpa Rinpoches at Chamde

erating feeling to it. Generations of great visionaries had built up their power-circles here. Hundreds of locals squatted on the walls and looked down into the yard where pujas—loud rhythmic invocations with powerful instruments—alternated with dances with protective masks. The collective trance reached a pitch at night, when people jumped on and off their meditation seats for hours or ran in droves through the streets, screaming loudly.

Everyone tasted ancient and unknown powers of body and mind. When it ended, in the middle of the second night, we ran down the

Chamde Gompa

At the dances in Ladakh

Dances

mountain. In the light of a full moon we walked for hours in the direction of Leh. Here lay Hemis monastery, our next destination.

When the Sikhs sacked Ladakh a hundred years earlier, these buildings were not looted. The monastery was situated in a poplar grove, so the conquerors had simply overlooked it. Later, however, tourists had discovered Hemis and the results were obvious. The monks were directly rude. This time, my jovial style barely helped; they just did not like us. They also refused permission to take pictures. They kept opening and closing the front door so our photographer could not adjust his camera to the light. Finally I lifted the busiest of them from the floor and held him up until the work was done. There was no tip for the venerable gentlemen afterwards. They had overdone it; after all, we were from the same lineage.

Later, having a cup of tea near the main road, an intelligent looking but tipsy man kept calling me Gelong. This is the title given to fully ordained monks with 254 outer vows, including celibacy and a total abstention from alcohol. I pointed to Hannah a few times to indicate that my life contained major sensual pleasure, but that did not change his mind. Then I asked him what he was. "Also Gelong!" he said, raising his glass. Apparently they held few narrow views at this place. He was probably the most sympathetic and open-minded person we met in Ladakh.

On the Indus river, between Leh and the Tibetan border, was a refugee camp. The Dalai Lama gave the great "Wheel of Time" initiation here in the late seventies. Nearby, a courageous disciple of Karmapa had built a monastery with a big open yard. He assembled a large number of cheerful monk-children around him, which was especially important here. The camp was the most desolate we had ever seen. The refugees' houses often consisted of thin pieces of cloth stretched above low concrete walls and had neither doors nor windows. Considering their poor nutri-

Hemis Gompa

tion, we couldn't understand how they even survived the evil winters there. We distributed the felt boots to the most needy, but it was sad to see several for sale already before the group left. Either the families were totally in debt, or winter was still so far off that food or alcohol were more important.

The monastery and our group fused immediately. Best of all, His Eminence Situ Rinpoche and the yogi Drubpon Dechen Rinpoche were willing to give a month of teachings there. It was interesting for them, too. We were the first large group of Westerners they had ever encountered. Of the four lineage holders, Situ Rinpoche left Rumtek first, and it has been interesting to watch the progression of his work. He has developed quite his own mandala and style.

As our group arrived, the abbot looked in amazement at our big bones and blue eyes. To fit us into his cosmology, he asked, "Is there a sun and moon where you come from?" "Yes," I answered, "and they are the same color as here." This information was important; it meant that we came from the same universe. He relaxed and soon gave us a beautiful

Western Himalayan stupa near Leh

thangka of "White Liberatrice" which had belonged to the thirteenth Karmapa. Our doctors got out their Western medicines to distribute, while we unpacked dozens of German knives and other useful gifts. Situ Rinpoche taught for two weeks. He gave an initiation into "Wisdom Buddha Seated on a Lion," which all received for the first time. The following night, nearly everyone had special dreams. Ladakh was now getting very cold. Before the group was forced back to the Indian lowlands, we wanted to visit some last historic monasteries together.

The trip to Tikse Gompa became very important. It brought the blessing of the female protector, "White Umbrella." Entering an otherwise plain room, I felt such a strong presence that I forced open a wooden gate to find the source. As I looked inside, sharp sunlight fell on her statue, several meters in height. Her thousand faces bared their fangs and she was beautiful beyond words. Then and there, I knew her presence would never leave me. Some years later, she saved my life in Germany, and her thousand arms protect our friends all over the world.

Tai Situ Rinpoche gives empowerment

We sent our friends down the mountains while the road was still passable and gladly risked getting ourselves snowed in for six months. Situ Rinpoche's teachings were well worth it. We would be the first Westerners to receive the Six Doctrines of Naropa. It was a unique chance to get a deeper understanding of our mind's energy-nature.

The following full moon night was an intense experience for all. Our group had to clear a destroyed truck off the road in northern India and Ladakh was having a collective fit—there was to be an eclipse of the moon and nature-people don't like that at all. Tibetans call earth's shadow "Za" and say that it has two mouths. If it eats the moon with one mouth, it becomes red; but if it uses the other, the moon disappears completely.

Wisdom Buddha on Lion

White Umbrella bares her fangs and is indescribably beautiful

Before the eclipse

The whole monastery was in a state of alarm, ready to blow away the danger of darkness with their huge horns. They had conflicting information concerning the time of the eclipse, however. The official version from Dharamsala stated "half past nine" while an old astronomer from Rumtek, who always recited the mantra "Karmapa Chenno," said "half past two." He was right, and it was touching to watch everyone's joy when the moon reappeared from the other side of "Za."

For the next three weeks we stayed in closed retreat under Situ Rinpoche and Drubpon Dechen Rinpoche. The latter has recently become famous through a film about Tsurphu, the main seat of the Karmapas in Tibet. The German filmmaker, Clemens Kuby, provided expert footage and Lama Yongdu from Hawaii uses it to collect money for his "Tsurphu" project. The Rinpoches taught us body-exercises which are usually kept even more secret than the breathing and visualizations.

Once out of retreat, we caught the very last truck across the pass. Right after, snow blocked it until April. It was a cold trip. Every twenty minutes we had to scrape diesel oil, thick as butter, out of a container. It was necessary to light a fire under the Mercedes to heat the frozen oil pipes. Fortunately, we sat inside the truck and not exposed on its open load as we did ten years later through Tibet.

After Mandi, we stopped at Tsok Pema, the lotus lake. Being on our own, it was easier to make side trips. Tsok Pema is famous. The lake appeared when the angry father of Mandarava, a princess Guru Rinpoche was just seducing, had the couple burnt at a stake. When he returned the next morning, they were still in union, now sitting on a lotus flower. The lake had spontaneously appeared around them and is today an important site for pilgrims.

Here lived Kunu Lama. In 1972 in Bodhgaya, he had given us a mantra that directly activates Buddha Shakyamuni. He wanted to know

Situ Rinpoche with Drubpön Dechen holding the book

everything about Denmark, and I said to Hannah: "We have to be especially careful about pregnancy when he dies. He will surely find Danish parents for his next rebirth." Kunu Lama studied all religions before deciding on Tibetan Buddhism, and was so learned that he had been officially supplied with a tape recorder. Making use of it every free minute, he mainly spoke on the meaning of sound. He knew more than anybody about mantras, but probably died without passing on all his knowledge. In fact, he took rebirth at full moon in December, 1978 as the son of a Danish woman and a Tibetan yogi, and I helped deliver the child. The next day, I drove mother and baby through thick snow from South Germany to Denmark.

With Kunu Lama lived a middle-aged Tibetan woman, Drikung Khandro. As we walked around the corner of their house, she turned and we were all rooted to the spot. She looked like a robust version of Hannah. Even among the famous Tibetan enlightened women or Dakinis, her history is unique. She meditated alone for seventeen years. After the Chinese invasion, they started shooting holes in the yogis' caves. The sudden flash of light blinded many who had stayed in darkness for years in order to better study their mind. Their optic nerves couldn't take the shock. People managed to get Drikung Khandro out in time, and a group took her along on their flight to India. At first, she refused to eat meat, which was often the only available food. When she grew so weak that people had to carry her, however, big tears fell from her eyes and she started eating what was there. Now she cared for the ailing Kunu Rinpoche. We talked for a long time. She gave us tsampa and we gave her protein powder and money. After we put our foreheads together in farewell, her feeling stayed alive in me for a long time. She was a fantastic woman.

In Dharamsala, we had a wonderful audience with H.H. the Dalai Lama. Then we drove to Delhi without stop. Finding the names of our group in the visa book at the Nepalese embassy, we took the train through the Indian masses to Bodhgaya. Here, the big red bus was waiting. Tom and Kate had driven the small one to Nepal directly from the Pakistani border. The tour had been dramatic but Niels skillfully brought them through it all. In Dharamsala the Dalai Lama had been absent, but they managed an audience in Delhi. Here, they did not find him as graceful as they had expected. Although now in exile, the Dalai Lama is both king and highest representative of Tibet. It is a country which has difficulty gaining international respect. It is therefore a good idea to visit him in one's best clothes. Standing in front of him, ungroomed but devoted, our group experienced more education than kindness in his words.

Seven of us soon left Bodhgaya again. We spent three days on trains via Calcutta and Madras en route to Ayang Tulku's new monastery. It lay in a Tibetan refugee camp near the southern tip of India. Once more, the beautiful area became the site for an initiation into "Limitless Light" and the practice of Phowa. The main part of our group was not used to so much travelling. They had wanted to stay and meditate in Bodhgaya. As a result, our small party was fed without stop. The hospitable people had bought food for all fifty of us. Several times on this tour, I had success with a new method of entering Indian trains. One fights his way through the pushing crowd and then pulls friends and luggage inside, sliding them over everybody's backs and heads.

In Darjeeling, Karmapa had sent his Western secretary to wait for us. After a few hours' drive through the Himalayan foothills we reached

With Karmapa in Rumtek

Entering Karmapa's powerfield

Rumtek in Sikkim, our destination. We arrived on December 25. Karmapa phoned Delhi at once and received a two weeks' residence for all. Our friends stayed with the local families or in tents, often on the flat roofs of houses. Only a few got the runs. Seen from the timeless dimension of the mountains, the previous weeks in India had been a necessary purification and toughening. We could now really receive his blessings. We dove into his powerfield and absorbed it through every available sense. Really caring for us, Karmapa gave the great "Teacher as Black Coat" initiation and painted the first letter of his name—a Tibetan "KA"—on our foreheads. We were close to him every day, and he let his lineage holders give initiations. To create a Dharmic contact, even the youngest Rinpoches were told to recite the texts they were only just learning themselves.

During the Black Crown Ceremonies, we received his direct mind-transmissions. He also taught, gave the Bodhisattva Vow, and initiated us into the second Karmapa and our great female protector, "White

Umbrella." From Shamarpa, we received an initiation into "Buddha of
Limitless Light," his own essence. Gyaltsab Rinpoche gave the seed of
his activity through "Diamond in Hand," and late one evening, also
"Diamond Dagger" initiation, right from his bed. From Jamgon Kong-
trul Rinpoche, we received "Buddha of Wisdom Riding on a Lion," and
Thrangu Rinpoche explained the meditation on the eighth Karmapa.

The group then went on to Nepal, while Karmapa asked Hannah
and me to stay in Rumtek. Something important was coming up. An
American disciple of the great yogi, Urgyen Tulku, had built an enor-

At his favorite seat

Our three lineage holders:
Kunzig Shamarpa, Goshir Gyaltsabpa and Jamgon Kongtrul Rinpoches

mous temple near Bodhnath in Kathmandu. The time had now come to initiate it. We were to drive the Rumtek lamas. For transport, the monastery had four or five jeeps, an Indian sedan, and a truck.

Two vehicles were new, gifts from the ever-generous Bhutanese king; the rest were junkyard quality. Hannah got a Nissan military jeep with Thrangu Rinpoche and Sister Palmo as front passengers while I received the oldest and most run-down Landrover in the Himalayas. Next to me, sat Karmapa's servant. The Black Crown in its container was tied to his belly. Everything was bursting with lamas and their luggage, a real family trip! It was thrilling right from the start: Karmapa's new jeep simply accelerated away and everyone had to follow as best they could.

We arrived in Nepal in early January. The southern road, an Indian project, had been completed, but no one had thought of building bridges. We had to pull each other through rivers several times. A good part of the journey would have fit the current "Camel" ads, but somehow we managed to not take any natives, cows, or hens along as hood ornaments. Suddenly on top of the pass on the old road, there was a breathtaking view of the Himalayan snow mountains to the north. Taking his time, Karmapa told us the Tibetan names of the peaks for hundreds of kilometers on both sides of Mt. Everest. He revealed which Buddha energies were active in each of them, where "Greatest Joy," "Lady of Long Life" and other important forms were centered. It was a total flash to hear this from someone who was simply describing what he saw. Never had we been closer to ancient Tibet.

Shortly afterwards, something happened which is now a legend in Rumtek. It could easily have given me a place next to Mao Tse Tung in the annals of the Kagyu lineage and five hundred rebirths as a mole. The brakes of the Landrover had been bad from the beginning, even by Indian standards. In addition, it was often impossible to shift into lower gears. The hand brake had never functioned at all. Now, rolling down the foothills to Kathmandu, the foot brake also went out, and all this with Karmapa's crown at my side! We skidded through the curves at ever increasing speeds until I finally found a gravel heap left by the road workers. Holding one arm in front of Karmapa's servant, so the crown would not be damaged, I stopped us there.

Departure from Rumtek

The jeep was not too damaged, but the Tibetans found the incident very dramatic. They considered my first remark, "The car is bad but the blessing is great," very amusing. My passengers squeezed onto the truck and the other overcrowded jeeps. They wanted to leave the broken vehicle behind, a risky business. They knew it would disappear the same day, dismantled into parts. I thought it was better for the locals to tend to their farming so, with Karmapa's permission, we tied the jeep in front of the truck to brake it. The hemp rope tore twice, and each time I had to drive on to another gravel heap. Then we found a steel rope. During the last few hours to Kathmandu, it was the truck which had the accidents.

In the great temple of Swayambhu, I entered Karmapa's room during an historical moment: as the first Western incarnation was officially recognized. Many beings are born with little ego and possessing a high level of awareness from former lives, mostly in countries with good karma and freedom, but the Tibetans seldom accept them officially unless brought through their traditional system of education. Lamas like Karmapa, who see people's former lives, then give the others private titles and tasks instead. Here, we had the first white incarnation, young enough to go through the mill. His history was interesting. We had known his parents during the hippie-days and later the American details of his discovery were confirmed by two American friends, Barbara Pettee and Carol Aronoff. The latter will here describe what she saw:

"When the Karmapa visited the U.S.A. in 1974, he had been invited by the peaceful Hopi tribe to visit their reservation in Arizona. Among their prophecies was one about their 'true brothers' wearing red hats, who would come from the East when the spiritual forces declined in the West. They saw the Tibetans as these true brothers. When the Karmapa arrived with his entourage, they had just had several years of drought and asked him, 'Can a holy man like you make some rain for us?' The Karmapa replied, 'I will keep this in mind.' The Karmapa was driven to Hopiland in a gold Cadillac with flags ornamenting the hood. Entering the Hopi Cultural Center with his red-robed monks and then chanting before the meal, brought looks of great bewilderment to the tourists sitting there with their grilled cheese sandwiches and coffee. Adding to their astonishment were the students of Trungpa Rinpoche, then still decked out in full hippie garb. This was all in striking contrast to the

Swayambhu

simply dressed and humble Hopis who watched the whole show with
great equanimity. The Karmapa gave them an initiation into a red
standing form of 'Loving Eyes' and blessed them strongly."

While this went on, the sky had been darkening and just as
Karmapa shut the car door to leave, the first rain fell.

The next day, the headlines of the local newspaper said: "Karmapa
Makes Rain in Hopi-Land." In Kathmandu, a copy came into the hands
of Hettie and Angus. Hettie, an impulsive Welsh princess, at once wrote
Karmapa in Sikkim, asking if he had really made rain. She had borne a
son in New England and some years later, the family suddenly developed
the urge to go to Nepal. Settling near Karmapa's main temple of

Swayambhu, they were amazed to see their child crawling up the stairs to the temple, exclaiming: "My monastery, my monastery!" First, they thought he had learned it from the younger monks, but none of them spoke English. Karmapa's answer to her letter was simple: "Your child is the reincarnation of a former teacher. Stay where you are. I will come soon."

After delivering the jeep, I entered Karmapa's room. On his table lay two sheets of paper. One was old and yellowed. It contained his account of the time and place of the child's birth with a hand-drawn map. Next to it lay a map of Massachusetts. Rivers, mountains and other

Sangye Nyenpa Rinpoche

The great stupa of Bodhnath

landmarks were identical. When Karmapa drew the map, his people had asked if they should fetch the child. After the loss of Tibet, they now frequently found reincarnations in Bhutan and elsewhere in the Himalayas. But Karmapa said, "This one will come by himself." Now, there he sat. Blond and blue-eyed, he looked like a little soldier. He was an emanation of the speech center of the great Sangye Nyempa Rinpoche, whose first incarnation had been the main teacher of the eighth Karmapa.

The initiations in the new temple at Bodhnath were fantastic. Karmapa gave "The Treasure of Kagyu Mantras," the transmission Marpa had brought to Tibet over a thousand years earlier. About 150 years ago, Lodro Thaye, the first incarnation of Jamgon Kongtrul Rinpoche, had gathered these initiations into a series. Everyone was there: Rinpoches, Tibetan monks, and Western friends, as well as many from the Buddhist Newari Tribe. The latter were influential but deliberately dressed down. Though suppressed by the Hindu Gurkhas for centuries, they still carried the culture of the Kathmandu valley and Nepal. When the Gurkhas had conquered the country, they prohibited Buddhist monasteries and also occupied many of the holiest sites. Today, they are still guarded by soldiers who keep non-Hindus away.

Some Danish friends from the sixties offered us the best imaginable residence, the only roof apartment in Bodhnath with a terrace facing the stupa. Here, for the first time, I combined a stay in the Himalayas, where there's nothing of interest to the taste buds anyway, with several weeks of fasting. One avoids falling ill from unhealthy food, and clothes fit much better afterwards!

H.H. Karmapa with several high Rinpoches at the Kagyu Ngadzo empowerments

Karmapa created an immense power field, and the three weeks were filled with wonders near and far. He drove all negative energies from the immediate area, but some must have transferred to Kopan, a nearby Gelugpa monastery. In 1968, we had advised the Russian princess who owned it to give it to the Tibetans, but then we lost contact with further developments. Anyway, during the initiations which nobody from Kopan attended, they wanted to carry a Buddha statue from one building to another. Suddenly it became so heavy that they could not move it. It stayed like that for three days, so they came to Bodhnath and asked for Karmapa's help. Their statue immediately became light again and they took it where they wanted.

Toward the end of the initiations, we received bad news. The deadly Swedish nun and her not much fresher brother had sold Karma Ling, the place we jointly gave Karmapa. The lama in Stockholm had been of no use. The nun had come under the spiritual influence of that Karl Birger who in the past had hosted us so memorably. He had told her that she was surrounded by seven angels, should sell "Karma Ling," and buy into his deserted village instead. This was a blow to Buddhism in Scandinavia from which we still suffer today. Suddenly, the site where we had grown together was gone. I have seldom seen Karmapa as displeased as when he received this message. We sent two telegrams from him telling them to delay the sale until we returned, but that changed nothing.

But what was bad for Scandinavia benefited the rest of Europe. The Swedish farm would not have been adequate for the masses in the continent's center. With two expensive ferries and ridiculous Scandinavian speed limits, we could hardly invite larger groups up there. We had to look south, where spiritual interest was already present. Time was now free for the rest of Europe, and we had received enough money from the sale of the farm to stabilize Copenhagen. On April 1, work started on a broad European track.

CHAPTER SIX

No Quiet on the Western Front

*I*N RUMTEK, KARMAPA HAD GIVEN A MAJOR PROMISE: "Now you have traveled so far to see me, I will soon come to you again." This gave great impetus to our work. While Hannah translated texts with Tarab Tulku, my time was spent between the cities of Europe. For months I nearly fell from my throne from tiredness during teachings and I saw too many headlights on the cars at night.

During this period, the Protectress "White Umbrella" showed her powers. She is the thousand-faced form who had so deeply blessed me in Ladakh. It happened in the hills of Kassel, Germany, on a tour back from Vienna. With her picture securely fastened to the car's roof, I steered a transfer BMW through dense fog at 160 kph. There was a lecture to make in Copenhagen. It was early morning and a Danish woman kept me awake. Suddenly, and for no apparent reason, the picture came loose from the roof and sailed to the bottom of the car. Unable to step on a lady, let alone a female Buddha, I immediately took my foot off the gas, reaching at the same time for her picture on the ground. It was uphill, and the large engine quickly slowed the car. We were down to about 100 kph when a traffic sign appeared in the fog directly in front. Turning the wheel, I avoided hitting it head on. It would have been bad, even at this low speed. Instead, it was thrown into the oncoming lane, where we heard the crunch as big trucks flattened it. The car's side was ruined but we were okay. I changed the tire, put plastic across the missing window, and we arrived in Copenhagen right on time. It was the perfect example of a blessing which came neither too early nor too late. Since then, the presence of "White Umbrella" has never left.

It was also during those months that the two obnoxious characters "How" and "Why" began to seriously analyze their relationship to me. They didn't like the way I always act directly and ignore them. First "Why" left, then "How," and once they were gone, immense extra power was available to me. Today, I know where to find them. They are useful for certain functions, but must never be allowed to control behavior or cause delay.

Kalu Rinpoche was already in Europe again. This time he organized the first three-year retreat for monks and nuns in the French monastery of Plaige. He wanted us to take part in their training and to help build the retreats. We took out the month of July for that, working during the day, then learning and meditating at night. As always it was pure bliss to be with Rinpoche, but some of his students who were gradually taking over the organization were not much fun. There was too much "church" for my taste and the thought of spending several years exclusively among members of my own sex gave me the creeps. I thought it could not possibly be good for my constitution. Hannah, though, of deeper virtue, was not as far from the idea. Her mind only became completely settled on this question several months later when Karmapa said: "If you disappear for three years, who will then start my centers? I promise you the same development through your work for me as you would have in a closed retreat—and never-ending energy besides."

Plaige again showed the fundamental differences between the spread of Buddhism in Roman and in Germanic Europe. In France, things had worked themselves into a church-like pattern and followed hierarchical structures. East of the Rhine, however, our central European groups grew like grass, spontaneously, and guided only by Karmapa's wishes, people's different karmas, and our growing friendships. Accordingly, behavior there was bourgeois and sweet, while we were hearty and rough. When the wild Germanics came, the French were often shocked, but this time was the worst when fifty hippies from Christiania in Copenhagen arrived by bus. They wanted to pay their respects to "good old" Kalu Rinpoche. As usual in the world, there was no "coming together" of the

Diamond Sow, one of the main meditation forms of the Kagyu Lineage

cultures. Girls peed with bare behinds in front of shocked monks and nursed their babies during initiations. Also the phones were busy: neighbors called the castle to ask if the foreign men could please hide the big knives dangling from their belts. Though most of those people we hardly knew, Hannah and I suddenly found our good reputation among the French somewhat tarnished: salvation did not come from the North any longer.

To be on the receiving end of the teachings again was a true holiday, and Rinpoche was in fine shape. Afterwards, the fast trips through Europe gained even more in intensity. On one of them, the protectors showed their power-fields. In the Ethnographic Museum in Hamburg, Germany, "White Umbrella" smiled at me. She blushed and came out of her thangkha. The showcase was opened, and when touching the scroll to the top of my head, my teeth chattered. It felt like a cold shock. It was as intense as a blessing by Karmapa. In Cologne, Germany, "Radiant Goddess," consort to "Black Coat," came to life in an art exhibit, and in Munich, "Six-armed Great Black" spread his protective power from the Folk Museum there.

Through our work, done only for Karmapa, these and other enlightened energies now work together in the power field of "Black Coat." This is the form which most directly expresses Karmapa's activity. When people keep their bonds, this central energy ensures that their development cannot be blocked.

It was a great experience to start the Dharma in Poland. On the train from Austria through Czechoslovakia we could hardly believe how the authorities treated their countrymen in that country: like cattle. They were not totally poor, but had no freedom, which was much worse. Poland, in contrast, was almost a romantic experience. People were profound, a little shy and dreamy. They had dimensions one hardly finds in busier parts of the world, and there was no doubt that the country offered a first-class basis for the Diamond Way.

Our invitation was from Wladyslaw Czapnik in Kracow, a tall and warm-hearted man in the country's south. He had heard about our effectiveness from a Czech man and wished the teachings to be spread across Poland quickly. The Karmapa-meditation moved people instantly. Identification with enlightenment was really their approach. I also taught an oral version of the "Loving Eyes" puja with several dissolving phases. Unfortunately, when the "authorized" version arrived later, this created confusion. It was a sign that in the future it was necessary to keep variant practices out of our centers. Even when they have the same goal—in the case of Buddhism, the full development of our mind—one can't walk

With Wladyslaw and Chris

several roads simultaneously. It was a powerful week and never, at least until the events in Russia of 1989, has so much spiritual growth come from the total devotion of a single family. A second visit to Poland followed when Karmapa was in Europe again. When I took leave, he winked at me and asked, "What is your Dharma-name?" I said, "Karma Lody Gyamthso." He went on, "The name of the first center in the communist world will be Karma Lody Gyamthso Ling. Give them freedom and go east as much as you can."

On November 17, 1976, Karmapa was scheduled to land in New York. We bought bargain three-week tickets and flew over. His reception was totally unlike that in Europe: unbelievably long, yet technically obsolete limousines and people standing stiffly around in "serious" suits and ties. It looked like a funeral. There were a few live faces among the penguins, like Barry's, but we couldn't distinguish who was a hired driver, a policeman, or a member of Dharmadhatu, Trungpa Tulku's organization.

Karmapa came through the V.I.P. exit. Seeing us, he called "Ole, Hannah," and blessed us so intensely that our conscious minds didn't return until in a minibus on Long Island. It was Hannah's first visit to the U.S. I had enjoyed the great country in 1958/59 as an A.F.S. exchange student.

Our destination was Seatucket on the north shore and our host was Mr. Shen, a great pillar of Buddhism in America. He came from Hong Kong in 1946 and established a monopoly for freight routes on the Great Lakes with his "American Steam Ship Company." Together with his sweet wife Nancy, he also helped his family in Communist China and supported innumerable Buddhist schools. Then in his mid-fifties, and in good shape, he had just bought a former mental hospital near Ukiah in northern California. It was meant to house the many Chinese monks he now expected to arrive, mostly from Vietnam. In excellent lectures, he always managed to point out the crucial aspects of the Buddha's teachings, and Karmapa treated him like a brother.

Arriving on his land, he gave us a beautiful wooden house to stay in and then took us directly to see Karmapa in an enormous mansion. Apart from the Vajra guards standing stiffly in every corner, there was a lot going on. A yogi-type, obviously drawing on good actions from former lives, came down the wide oak stairs. He introduced himself as Werner Erhard and smiled like Danny Kaye. He had founded EST, a then popular type of group therapy which, lacking style and good taste, never caught on in Europe. He also loved fast cars, probably the reason we began to talk. We discussed a proposal to invite Karmapa for a tour through his centers. It could generate a good deal of money for his work in India.

Upstairs, Akong Tulku, Ato Rinpoche and Dr. Shen sat on the floor in front of Karmapa's bed. When we came in, he joyfully exclaimed: "Now everyone is here." We chatted cozily about developments everywhere until a stocky man arrived. He was dressed impeccably in a dark blue suit and was the only one who sat down on the bed next to Karmapa. It was the Trungpa Tulku we had last seen in Sweden. We didn't think he belonged on the bed. Only later did we remember that he was an invalid after an accident and maybe couldn't sit on the floor. Karmapa talked seriously to him and told him to remove some unfriendly statements about Akong Tulku from his book *Born in Tibet*. Here, among other things, he had described him as being paranoid. The third edition was then printed without this epilogue, but today the book is once again published with a different afterword.

It was wonderful to be surrounded by American nature again and we enjoyed the wide variety of building styles. The area was like a park with idyllic fishing villages. With his usual generosity, Dr. Shen lent us a car and we immediately broke all speed limits. We just couldn't crawl around on roads as Americans do. That would have required a handful of sleeping pills before each ride. Rich and famous people came and went, and it was often possible to spend private time with Karmapa and Jamgon Kongtrul Rinpoche. They had more free hours here than we let them have in Europe.

Full radiance

Karmapa's powerfield was never boring. One night, Lex and Sheila Hixon, supporters of Tomo Geshe Rinpoche, called from the Bronx. They needed their VW bus back. This was a good chance to see New York at night. Hannah wanted to come along, but Karmapa asked her to stay. She should teach the Three Lights Meditation to Jytte Marstrand, a talented Danish businesswoman. It became an exciting drive and I was glad she was not along. In the middle of Harlem, the car's electrical system broke down. I spent hours push-starting it through dangerous neighborhoods. Not until early morning did I finally reach the Hixon's beautiful home on the palisades of the Hudson River. Over breakfast, we discovered that we had an old connection. In 1959, Lex and I had both attended the Hotchkiss Boarding School in Connecticut. He remembered well how wild I had been. Now, he guided a spiritual program on public radio which reached sixteen million people around New York. He offered me an hour to teach Buddhism. It was a full success. Many phoned in and Hannah said that Karmapa had listened and laughed a lot. As long as Lex worked for the station, visits to America now began with a live program and time for questions. In the end, Lex simply gave me the key to his studio and let me do as I liked. Many who practice today in the New York Kagyu centers made their first contact from this radio show. The town is not very spiritually rewarding, however. Today I mainly stop there to pick up drive-away cars, for going across the country. Our closest contacts are lovely Lisa in Queens and our friend Scott.

Karmapa and his entourage came to stay with Lex and again many famous people gathered. Things stayed superficial, however. We didn't reach people the way we did in Europe. Only rarely did anybody make use of the occasion. Few established that best basis for growth: devotion. Most apparently thought that they already knew what they needed. When pride outpaces desire, the basis for strong and close bonds disappears. People here wanted a show, not a teacher.

The following period was spent with the Dharmadhatu. They displayed a lavish style, having rented the top floor of the Plaza Hotel overlooking Central Park. During the next few weeks, hardly anyone could get close to Karmapa, apart from our European friends. We always took them in, not caring how many guards I had to shove aside. It was odd to see a Bodhisattva whose every breath should benefit all beings, isolated like a president. Several times each day, we tricked security. It was like my time in the army.

In the beautiful hall of the penthouse, Karmapa demonstrated his insistence on a proper education. On his invitation, we took part in his formal meeting with the Vajradhatu, Trungpa Tulku's best trained body of students. The time had now come for them to ask their questions. Among the fifty present were several well-known faces, like Allen Ginsberg. He wanted to discuss homosexuality and pollution. We didn't know much about either, so he ordered our first English-language book instead, the teachings of Kalu Rinpoche. Fame or no fame, however, the questions they asked had little substance. They were all up in the air, like a cup of thin new-age tea.

Pei

When things were somewhere between awkward and embarrassing, Karmapa suddenly exclaimed: "I know one thing you have learned: to sit! Now do the full lotus posture." It seemed Hannah and I were the only ones who fully crossed our legs, but at least everyone's back was straight. Loving Karmapa so deeply, I knew what he would now do. Suddenly, he threw his powerful body forward and shouted: "Pei." I rolled on the floor laughing, as Karmapa quickly left the hall. Less than a minute later, Jamgon Kongtrul Rinpoche came in and began: "Buddha was a prince in India. . . ."

Dr. Shen had given Karmapa a large piece of land. It lay about half an hour north of New York, near the town of Carmel. He thought it suitable for a monastery. Walking through the beautiful autumnal landscape, Dr. Shen explained his vision of the area, especially where he would like a lotus pond. This was very dear to his heart. We Westerners were enthusiastic, but it was too cramped for Tibetan taste. They praised everything in more general than concrete terms, a sign they were being polite but weren't really interested.

When Dr. Shen's jeep got stuck on a slope in the woods, my time came. While he kept his foot on the gas, I honored my Nordic ancestors. Pulling up some trees, and breaking others, I made a track through the forest. When the Jeep was back on the plateau, we had shared an experience. In this way, we became friends.

We also visited John, an old colleague and probably the unluckiest of smugglers. He now resided in Federal Plaza, a prison on the southern tip of Manhattan. This time, he was there for money and not drugs. With his karma and papers, he should have been more careful. He was kept on the top of a high-rise building with the really heavy boys. They were very different from what we knew about criminals. In Europe, convicts believe in their roles and play them to the hilt, becoming very dense. Here, the mainly Spanish-speaking prisoners were smiling, charming, and flexible. But if you turned your back, it could easily lead to a quick and uncharming death.

Our only real excursion in America was to Chicago where Karmapa sent us. The Native American name of the town means "cold wind" which fits. Vickie, a girlfriend of John's, had arranged a teaching. Going by bus was too expensive and it was too cold for hitchhiking, but luckily America also has drive-away cars and so we got under-powered limousines for the trip there and back.

The vastness of the American landscape amazed us, as did the way people crossed it. On wide, straight roads they crawled along at unbelievably low speeds. We took the northern route and it rained heavily. The last few hours we floated rather than drove past the cars we overtook.

The meeting was in a rundown house in the center of town. The very mixed group listened attentively. They had strange ideas, however, indicating they had not received much basic education. Later I told Hannah some of Chicago's Mafia past, adding that there might be bullet holes in the windows. Looking, we actually found some. They brought history very close. The ghettos looked like Europe after the war. Often only one house out of four was standing; the rest had been torched. We stayed with friends of Vickie, generous people in Oak Park. This was also an historical area. It had been built by gangsters in the 1930s, and Al Capone's house was on the next street.

The car back to New York was destined for export to Iran. It had no license plates but we were glad to have it for a few days anyway. In a traffic jam on 5th Avenue, we suddenly heard loud noises from behind. They continued through several traffic lights. When we finally turned around, we looked right into the megaphone of a police van: they wanted to talk with us. While showing the papers which proved that the car wasn't stolen, I developed sympathy for one of the policemen. He was red-haired, of Irish descent, and was actually a fresh lad. Every time I patted his shoulder, however, he half pulled his gun from its holster. It was a reflex; he was unaware of doing it. The police in New York had enough to do. A few days before, we had talked to a man from a rural state. He had just experienced a blowout in Harlem. While he changed the wheel, two local gentlemen opened the hood and began removing his battery. Asking what they thought they were doing, they replied: "If you get the tires, we want the battery." Only when he showed his registration, would they accept that it was really his car.

When the three weeks on our tickets to America were up, Karmapa held out a fistful of dollar bills and said: "Fly to Hawaii and teach them

Driving Kalu Rinpoche

the Karmapa Meditation. Make them stop smoking pot." For a moment, the money was in front of our faces. Then he pulled it back, saying: "No, it's more important that you help Kalu Rinpoche."

So we did. We picked Rinpoche and Gyaltsen up in Paris for their second tour through Europe. This time they had his nephew Wangchen along who was later sent to Los Angeles. A temperamental Scottish girl translated. From Holland, the sister and mother of his Darjeeling supporter, Lhawang, joined us in the bus. Though the interest there was still a mix of Theosophy and Buddhism, again the people were generous and I had learned to cherish that: whatever time was not spent earning money, belonged to Karmapa. It was a good, inclusive feeling: the financial donations of others made them full partners in all the good happenings everywhere.

On that visit to Paris, I received money for a teaching for the first time. I didn't know what was in the envelope except that there was paper and also something heavy. The ten Franc-pieces had just been minted and I hurried to Rinpoche and asked what I should do with the offering.

"Keep it, it's yours," he said. "You work permanently for the Dharma, anyway." Since then, the material blessing on our work has steadily grown, with Karmapa's strong support. Not long after, he paid our way to Ireland to start the first center there. Giving us each a blessed banknote, he said, "You will never lack anything from now on. If you keep your motivation pure, all your projects will succeed."

In spite of the Dutch tendency to intellectualize and ride several horses at once, a group was forming. They wanted to do real Diamond Way practice. From the first gentle flowering in Utrecht, soon connections grew in many places. We even had plans for an enormous center: a six-story tower surrounded by a moat.

Belgium to us was still Antwerp. There, driving off after one of his initiations into "Loving Eyes," Rinpoche tied a blessing string around my neck. It felt like a ring of fire. I swallowed and asked, "Whose energy is this?" "That of Horse Head," he answered.

Horse Head

Rinpoche's reception in northern Germany was touching. Our students on the former dairy-farm received him as naturally as if we were in Tibet. Several had already seen the Black Crown or visited Kalu Rinpoche in France or Scotland. His centers are today too monastic for most Germanics, while we are too wild for them. During those years, however, the jump across the Rhine was not so far. Come to think of it, since the eighties, nearly all Central European contacts westward have been with Karmapa's main seat in the Dordogne. Kept in the public eye through yearly courses given by our lineage-holders and strengthened by the

Gendun Rinpoche

culture-transcending skills of Karmapa's representative, Lama Jigmela, this place is the closest we have in Europe to an international institution. The meditation master Gendun Rinpoche has lived and taught there since 1975, when Karmapa sent him. At that time, he had spent thirty years in retreat. When the men came to fetch him, he hid under his bed several times. We welcomed him at the airport in Paris, where many thought he had some eye-trouble. The reason for his tears was not illness, however, but compassion. The heavy physical suffering of Asia he was used to, but the emotional luxury-stuff of the West was something new.

Kalu Rinpoche's visit to the "White Brotherhood" showed his compassion from yet another side. The local guru, an Englishman, had developed a chakra system which looked like a spastic colon. As he obviously feared losing his disciples to the charming Tibetan, Rinpoche taught only on medicine. For a whole evening, he explained things we have heard neither before nor since. Although I don't remember any of it—the topic never interested me—once again we were amazed by how

Tashi Ling in Norway

vast his learning was. I've heard there exists a recording of this lecture somewhere. It really should be published!

In Copenhagen, Rinpoche gave a public talk in a church. Afterwards, we took a ferry through the night to the beautiful new center we had found near Oslo in Norway. Here, for once, there were more men than women. Incorruptible and tough, the way Norwegians are, they kept things on a steady course while several gifted women had stopped practicing. Pressure from husbands and Christian families had become too much. They were old and close friends, and it made us sad. They could do more than cook. The tour went eastward in our unheated VW. No matter how cold it was, whenever we passed an animal in the snow, Rinpoche slid back the window and said "Om Mani Peme Hung," laying the seeds for a good rebirth. In Stockholm, Lama Ngawang and Sonam now guided a small group. It included several Hungarian refugees. They had improved their house and were now building a retreat center on an old farm to the northwest of Stockholm. Rinpoche blessed it.

Next came our two small Finnish groups. In spite of several visits, the teachings had not taken hold. There simply was not much interest in a well-rounded spiritual life in the country. Though we knew them to be either sectarian, health fanatics, or complete materialists, they should at least be exposed to a holy man. Rinpoche and Gyaltsen went by plane, while we took the ferry. The icy roads had been hard on him and we wanted to minimize any stress. At the airport of Helsinki, the capital of Finland, there was no Rinpoche. Gradually we learned that they had gotten out in Turku, one stop early, and were now being held by the police. An unscheduled landing had made their instructions useless. Also, their visas were valid in all of Scandinavia, but not accepted there. A full audience waited nearby. The lecture I gave in Rinpoche's stead was no joy. Though I don't speak a single word of Finnish, which is a central Asian dialect, I knew with every cell of my body that I was being misrepresented. The buxom woman who had jumped up to interpret was making me sound like someone from a sect. No matter what I did, it came out moral, sweet, or indirect. When Rinpoche finally arrived, few people wanted blessings. Since the spring of 1977, nothing has happened there.

From Denmark, we managed to include a week in Greece in an otherwise full schedule. It was a good meeting. Rinpoche's striking outer

They had never tasted anything better

On Acropolis

appearance and traditional style aroused the imagination of the Greeks, while the Tibetans ate local yogurt around the clock. They had never tasted anything better. Rinpoche gave the initiation and practice of "Loving Eyes." The several who started the Preliminary Practices finished them one by one over the following years.

Eastern Europe, then still communist, would also benefit from such fine visitors. We took the ferry from Denmark to East Germany. Just past Rostock our VW bus suddenly shook and bucked like a horse. The suspension of the rear wheels had rusted through and had ripped open the back welding seam. There was no way to save it. The man who stopped to help us had not yet been paralyzed by socialism. He offered to take us to Berlin for about $70 in Western money. First, we had to make the unwilling police remove the vehicle from our passports. Then we stuffed ourselves and the contents of an overfilled VW bus into the man's Russian ZIM-car, an imitation of a '56 Packard. I still don't know how it was possible. Nobody could breathe. A film-camera which Gyaltsen left on a wall was sent after us. It was a very special honesty.

After an uncomfortable and rainy trip to East Berlin, we had to try several checkpoints before finding one that would let us through. Most important was to protect our driver who must not be discovered and questioned by the police. With wonder, Rinpoche and Gyaltsen regarded this "milder" version of totalitarianism. It was the civilized "European" version of that oppressive political system which had destroyed Tibet since 1951. Already then the Chinese occupied the eastern third of the country. All took a deep breath when the Iron Gates slammed shut behind us. We were now back in the free world.

We arrived near midnight, but that was all right. Since they were currently having a wave of esoteric interest in Tibet, Rinpoche's arrival had been announced on local radio as a happening. Most who had come at eight only wanted the show, but whoever was still there at eleven p.m., probably wanted more. Berlin, then Germany's human dump and a city with deep cultural roots, would often have problems caused by confusion. This time, drugs were the topic. While we were out of the room, someone had translated "hash" to Rinpoche as "medicine." Of course, Rinpoche couldn't refuse people the taking of medicine, not even in the center. This became a hot topic shortly after, when *Bild*, Germany's cheapest tabloid, started a campaign against the "new religions." Although we are five hundred years older than the common European variety and proud not to have persecuted others, a drug bust could have finished us. I personally promised every single member of the center a stay in the hospital if they didn't keep this "medicine" outside.

Our friends from the dairy farm supplied another VW bus. It was the first I had driven with a whole windshield and a sliding door. In Hamburg, our next stop, there were some politics going on below the surface. Some rich students of a Gelugpa teacher had invited Rinpoche to their private castle. They wanted to combine their money and influence with the energy and devotion of our friends. The goal was a so-called "Ri-me" center, open to "all" Tibetan Buddhist directions. We already knew that model: within a short time a Geshe, a learned professor, would arrive from Dharamsala, the seat of the state church. Whether open to other lineages or not, he could teach only what he knew. In no time Hamburg would have an intellectual and virtuous center, ruled by monks. Though I wished them every kind of success, I also had to think of our friends. The exciting people are attracted by Karmapa's blessing and my direct style. Suddenly finding themselves in a church, they would quickly leave. I repeatedly warned Rinpoche but obviously not often enough, as time would tell.

In Munich, Rinpoche taught a Russian tribe, the "Kalmucks." As a result, we can now debunk a myth which had always irritated me. Several new-age books mention "three hundred Tibetans" who were found dead in Berlin after WWII. Gifted with more imagination than scientific method, some writers concluded from this that a number of

A teaching situation in Munich

lamas had said mantras for Hitler and his ugly gang. The facts are quite different: fortunately Hitler recognized too late that Germany was not able to do all he wanted. Understanding that he could only beat the Communists by siding with their restive population, the Nazis offered independence to tribes in Siberia and Mongolia if they fought on their side. Since Stalin was exterminating millions of them, they joined. Later, during the battle for Berlin, some of these Kalmucks, serving as auxiliaries for Hitler's army, had been killed. Most were illiterate and of the Gelugpa tradition, hardly a basis for "wild invocations." Their teacher, Bembijef, had died some years ago. While the majority later emigrated to Taiwan and the U.S., the rest now met in an apartment in the north of Munich. Here, they were taught by a Geshe from Rikon. There is nothing more mystical to the story than that.

The Austrian officials were swindlers. At the embassy, they promised that no extra papers would be necessary for Rinpoche and his attendants, but then they suddenly wanted money at the border. We heard things like that happened every day.

Near Mozart's town of Salzburg, Rinpoche gazed a long time across "Moon Lake" and the mountains behind. Here he made the only political statement we ever heard from him: "This is just what my area in Kham looked like, and the people were happy. What have the Chinese done? . . ."

Vienna brought us a life of luxury and many people were interested in Buddhism. What lacked was a structure to hold things together. Our friend Eric Skrleta from Octopus Publishing had already printed Kalu Rinpoche's teachings from '70 and would later publish many of my German books. As "Pitzner" cars were frequently transferred to this city, we made many friends here.

Beyond the Alps, in Graz, was our oldest group. The Austrians allowed themselves more freedom. They adhered less to the Germanic roles, where men are supposed to be unspiritual and deposit their wives in church while they earn the money. Changing combinations of hopefuls tested their powers over the next few years, freeing themselves of sweet illusions. Not until the mid-eighties, and thanks to Tina and Alex, did Vienna really come together. They had been among my first students in Bavaria and Greece, and later when they took the reins into their skillful hands, everything blossomed. Today, we have a large and representative center right in the historical heart of town.

A visit to a country center provoked an age-old dispute. The Theravadan monk who lived there got angry. He felt short-changed by Rinpoche's classification of Buddha's teachings into higher and lower vehicles. Most of it was a question of terminology. Possessing all of Buddha's teachings, Tibetans structured them to permit the clearest possible overview. It was important for future development to point out that all levels of his teachings are beneficial, but to different kinds of people.

The group in Milan was as uncentered as the one in Rome, but there was less personal stuff. Happily, they mixed the teachings of different schools, but at the same time couldn't understand why they were so confused. Worst of all, there were many "upside-down" racists who believed that one needed a yellow skin for good meditation. People like this are a total obstruction. Doubting one's own qualities is an absolute misunderstanding of devotion.

Before returning to France, we spent some days in Switzerland. Near Zurich I nearly burst with laughter while playing practical jokes with some Jungian sandtrays. It was unbelievably amusing to secretly add phallic and aggressive symbols to the sandboxes. They displayed the inner lives of the local pillars of society.

From Plaige, we drove quickly back to Denmark where the famous thangkha painter, Rinzin Lhadipa Lama died in my arms. Being the absolute best, Karmapa had sent him to Copenhagen to paint the walls of our center. Unfortunately, during the following days, we were not sufficiently aware of Sikkimese custom, which often differs from that of Tibet. The sign on top of his head being perfect was enough for me: the Phowa was successful and his mind had arrived in the "Pure Realm of Limitless Light." No one even thought of sending his body back to Sikkim. As his family was Asian-polite, there were some unclear meetings about this which strained our relationship. Finally we realized how important it was to them. So, unintentionally we must have hurt them, though they were really our friends.

We drove Kalu Rinpoche to Paris and then to Great Britain, where there was still not much happening. This was especially embarrassing in

Rinzin Lhadipa Lama at work

London, where he had invested so much energy. The public lectures took place in "Friend's House," belonging to the Quakers. In front of the assembled tulkus, lamas, and hundreds of listeners, Kalu Rinpoche transcended all good manners. With his charming smile, he compared the four lineages of Tibetan Buddhism as follows: "In Tibet, if people wanted to develop virtue, they went to the Gelugpas. If they wanted wisdom, they went to the Sakyapas. They went to the Nyingmapas to learn meditation, and if they wanted quick enlightenment, they came to the Kagyupas." There was a moment of absolute silence while people wondered what to do with this information.

In "Kham-House," there were as many rules as before. We met Sylvia, who had come along from Bombay to Copenhagen in 1972. She now lived near another English center to the northwest of London which a rich donor had given to Lama Chime. It was one of the "Marpa Houses" that would soon vanish again, there as well as later in Hamburg. In

An informal moment

Manchester, I saw no "green man" this time, and there had been some fine development. It was based mainly on a solid intellectual understanding of the teachings.

The longest stay was again at "Samye Ling." This monastery is situated near Lockerbie, in Scotland, where Arab terrorists blew up a Pan Am jet in 1988. We had friends there from many parts of the world. They lived on farms or in campers in relaxed "sixties" style. The groups in Edinburgh and Glasgow were a pleasure to visit again and we enjoyed spring—the narrow, winding roads of Scotland made even the low speeds of our bus exciting.

At Samye Ling, I learned something important about my way. On a full moon, I took part in a vow of silence, obviously influenced by some of Rinpoche's remarks. This was the last time. Rarely have so many people come for help as on that day. Writing my answers on bits of paper, I felt like a complete idiot. To voluntarily restrict one's means of helping others—only in retreats where nobody can speak!

In the beginning of May, 1977, we left Great Britain after Kalu Rinpoche. Two Tibetan friends were to arrive in Copenhagen. Lama Thubten and Lama Lody, leaders of Bhutia Busty Monastery in Darjeeling, would come to teach.

Lama Thubten, Lama Lodrö

CHAPTER SEVEN

Sunrise

*K*ARMAPA'S NEXT JOURNEY ACROSS EUROPE, a six-month extension of his visit to America, was sensed well in advance. It was like the pull back before a great wave strikes. Akong Tulku had the idea to transport His Holiness, Jamgon Kongtrul Rinpoche and their entourage of about twenty Tibetans in a used bus. This would avoid frequent changes of vehicles. Hannah came along to translate and I because of my connection with the people. My brother Bjørn and Joch from Scotland would drive. For this great visit, we had a month to prepare the mid-area, from Oslo to Athens. Fortunately, the French and British did their own organizing.

The most important event that month was meeting Kurt Nubling. Deeply touched by a slide-projection showing Karmapa with the Black Crown, he ran down the aisle past the line waiting for blessings. He spoke excitedly in Swabian, a South-German dialect only few understand. I told him to write me everything, and his letter in High German the next day showed amazing insight and motivation. "Get ready, you will be import-ant in Germany," was my answer. After years of travelling with me and helping set up the groups south of Frankfurt, today he has immense influence from our main center in Schwarzenberg.

In Belgium, we picked up a Dutch bus which Akong Tulku had bought. Though hardly of German quality, our friends in Antwerp had painted it a bright red and explained its quirks to Bjørn before we drove south.

Our bus

On the morning of June 20, he was with us again. Karmapa and Jamgon Kongtrul landed in Paris with their entourage. They greeted people from a V.I.P. room in the airport. New to us was a Khenpo—a kind of learned abbot—whom Karmapa introduced. His name was Tsultrim Gyamtso. Karmapa said he was sending him to Europe because his nose was as big as ours! His task would mainly be to teach philosophy. During the week there, Karmapa held Crown ceremonies in giant halls, and again and again my world exploded into golden light. His blessing got stronger all the time. There were endless meetings with the French, which mainly focused on cooperation. It was his intense wish to hold the Kagyu lineage together, and every day he asked everyone to assist in this.

While Karmapa drove to Dordogne, Hannah and I had work to do in North Europe. We met again at the old dairy north of Hamburg, which was in a difficult phase. The humorless and exotic tendencies I always warn against had struck. Some girls who had missed the youth-revolution of the sixties were the problem. They had created a church-like atmosphere there which was costing us a number of our most exciting and unconventional friends. The worst thing in my life was to arrive somewhere and hear that people like that had left, shaking their heads. In this

The Tibetan travelling team

context, it was important that Karmapa so frequently called me lama. Immature people trust titles more than the evidence of their own eyes, and even the fact that I had started all the centers east of France was not enough for some. I had viewed myself as a lama once the main purifications were over. But it was no secret that this ran contrary to Kalu Rinpoche's work. He removed the title when it was officially proven that his students no longer slept alone. In my own humble opinion, a day-and-night-Bodhisattva must be as good as one who brings joy only during day, and I was glad Karmapa thought the same. This became a reliable method for distinguishing the Romanic and Germanic spheres of influence: in the former, robes and celibacy are highly regarded, while in the latter they often evoke mistrust.

Norway and Sweden received five days each. Near Oslo, Karmapa jumped from rock to rock despite having so much sugar in his blood that a few drops could easily have sweetened one's tea. The doctors could not understand why he was not in a coma. All in all, it was great how "holy" Karmapa was in the true meaning of the word. He was "whole" and "fully functioning."

In Oslo

When work was over at night, and there were no new birds to teach meditation, he often winked and said: "Let's go." Then we would find the winding country roads which beautify Europe. If the car's tires didn't screech on most curves and we didn't at least double any speed limit, it wasn't fast enough for him. He was daily proof that insight into the conditioned "empty" nature of things brings absolute fearlessness, and it was good he showed it. Otherwise he could never have inspired such mushrooming numbers of strong and dedicated people today.

In Sweden, we enjoyed Crown ceremonies and initiations. The nights never got dark and we spent them with many old friends. During a dinner at the Tolstoy Castle, Akong Tulku was suddenly pressed into his chair by invisible hands. The headless lady was there again. She was obviously of the old-fashioned faithful kind.

Since we had made the schedule, lucky Denmark got to host Karmapa for a full three weeks. This sufficed to give such lively impressions of our country's variety that they still joke about it in Sikkim today. Visiting our Danish-German retreat center at Rødby on his way north, Karmapa said that a thousand Buddhas would appear there. He

Without words

liked the potential of this totally flat piece of Denmark and spontaneously blessed it with a Crown ceremony and a Milarepa initiation.

In Copenhagen, all of North Europe came together. Our guests were put up in the center, and also the public events took place in historical halls in the eastern and "finer" part of the city. Here, Karmapa gave Black

Crown ceremonies and initiations, while Jamgon Kongtrul Rinpoche taught the "Seven Point Mind Training." The earlier-mentioned Khenpo, a skillful and humorous teacher who looked like my uncle, explained Gampopa's "Jewel Ornament of Liberation," an important philosophical book. Everyone was enthusiastic about the art of Rinsing Lhadipa Lama, who had just died. His unique wall-paintings in colorful Central Tibetan style have no equal anywhere in the West.

The first two weeks were busy, with private events taking place in the center. Luckily the weather was good, and the garden crowded with people. Many had come because we had taught friends of theirs; so apparently the word got around. Making clear to all just who was

Karmapa in Rødby

In Rødby

In Copenhagen

The master and his work

responsible for Europe between Oslo and Athens, Karmapa sent people to me every day. Gradually, the future took shape. It was an incredible experience. Feeling the potential constantly unfolding in his powerfield beat any drug.

Copenhagen was the meeting place of all of Europe

In the Copenhagen Center

It was the first course here with such high teachers and some strange karmas ripened. We lost a couple of friends who got caught in an upsurge of pride. It was also the beginning of the end for Axel, a healer from the isle of Fyn. At that point, he was both our only sponsor and biggest problem. During Kalu Rinpoche's previous visit, they had been photographed together in Axel's house. Not long after, two of Denmark's cheapest newspapers published articles that caused our center's telephones to glow. They contained a picture of the two together, sitting on a sofa and holding hands, with an even more damaging text: it stated that Kalu Rinpoche had come all the way from Tibet to thank Axel for the "distance" healing of the great teacher Tenga Rinpoche. Soon Kalu Rinpoche's picture also graced the bottles of "Holy Water" which Axel was selling. They cost about $7 for a pint and the government was unable to stop it since it was simply tap water. One can sell that at any price one wants. Now Axel also wanted a close and lucrative bond with Karmapa.

He gave about $700, which was then vital for the Rødby center. In return, he expected a seat among those sponsoring the next Black Crown Ceremony. It is a place of honor. Only Karmapa can do this meditation which brings timeless benefit. Giving direct access to the subconscious, he uses it to liberate beings from countless future sufferings. Most important of all, he plants the seeds of Mahamudra, of knowing our mind. And Buddhahood is nothing but that.

Again, two thousand people crowded the hall, and this time they knew more than in 1974. During the preparations, two professional photographers started walking around and photographing Karmapa and the sponsors from every angle. They were from the most primitive of Denmark's tabloids, and were obviously looking for that good shot we had schemed to avoid by placing Axel in a group. The audience was first surprised, then irritated, but Karmapa calmed everyone with a movement of his hand and a radiant smile. Everything was apparently all right.

It was. Next morning, the healer called and said, "Karmapa tricked me. Both films are black. The photographers say nothing like this ever happened to them before." We were not surprised. Our basement room in the center already contained a photo signed by Karmapa which Kim had brought. It showed the detailed powerfield of our protector, "Black Coat," in union with his partner, "Radiant Goddess." Its history is as follows: In spring 1972, a Canadian woman photographed Karmapa at a public function in Delhi. As the polaroid picture became clear, she had not known what to think. Bringing it to Karmapa, he simply said: "Thank you. All the others photograph my body, but you take pictures of my mind."

As one of his last acts in Copenhagen, Karmapa visited my mother. Hannah's father was also present. They wanted to thank him deeply for guiding their partners through their deaths. My father's passing, the year before, had been one of the most dignified events we had ever witnessed. A brave and loving man had left this life. After many years of living for others, he had now gone to the Pure Realms. The last thing he swallowed was one of Karmapa's "mother" pills. Whenever I keep him at my side in meditations, there is only a pillar of light.

Karmapa's mind

Early in September we packed the bus and went on to Funen, the central Danish island. We had been invited by Axel, but he and Akong Tulku didn't hit it off. First, Axel's nearly cubic shepherd dog freaked out with so many people around. Then Akong pronounced Axel's bed too short for Karmapa. It was too much for Axel, and he asked us to leave. It was a select "first" for Denmark. Only the Mongolians, Mao, and Axel have ever evicted a Karmapa! Fortunately, no one had to go to a hotel. Some of our group had just signed the papers for a big new house. We were somewhat displeased with Akong Tulku, however. His Scottish style had cost us our one and only Danish sponsor.

On the Danish peninsula of Jutland, the leader of the ecumenical Christian Center of Dialogue met Karmapa. They made a bond which still lasts today. Driving south towards Holland from there, Hannah's kidneys received such a draft that she was miserable for days. During the first event in the Dutch tower, a Karma Pakshi Initiation, she could hardly stand. Karmapa pulled her close, blew down her back, and made her translate the Mahamudra Teachings in great detail. It was amazing how that helped, and she still considers this one of her greatest purifications.

During an excursion, a bearded lama gave an interesting demonstration of non-discriminating awareness. At that time, he held Karmapa's Crown during the ceremonies, and today he holds that of Gyaltsab Rinpoche. He had come across an explicit and detailed porno magazine—probably for the first time—and I will admit to checking his reaction: he leafed through it at a constant speed. Some people like those magazines, while others are too busy with their own affairs. Everyone usually

Giving empowerment

takes a closer look at some detail or other, however, or possibly leafs back, but not he. Apparently everything was as pure to him as the united Buddhas on thangkas. There was nothing personal, no attraction or embarrassment.

After a week of initiations, Crown Ceremonies, and lots of exercise—the tower was six stories tall and only had a toilet on the first floor—we drove on to Germany. We spent the night in a hotel with

Giving Refuge in Berlin

Friedel and others from the Ruhr district, and reached Frankfurt the next afternoon. Here a local cultural organization had organized programs with a thousand people, among them a sour journalist from a big newspaper. He did not like the Khenpo's classical teaching style and made him look ridiculous in his article. Though it was a pity that the event was dragged down, it was also funny. Everything ceremonial should be joked about from time to time, and he was a professional. Karmapa also laughed when it was translated to him. Afterwards the Tibetans made

Blessing in Berlin

contacts for the benefit of their exiled countrymen. Then Karmapa and Jamgon Kongtrul Rinpoche flew to Berlin.

While Hannah stayed to take care of things, Kurt and I drove a car full of lamas through then-communist eastern Germany. They were needed for the Crown Ceremony. The monks were quite shocked by the Wall and the death zone, and all took a deep breath when we reached West Berlin. Even the air seemed different there

In this historical town, Karmapa became a hippie guru. The Crown Ceremony took place in an alternative center in the Turkish ghetto where everything was flowers and long hair. Accepting their praise, he gave Refuge to several hundred there. Then he stated very clearly that he wanted no drugs or politics in our centers; this was just the right teaching for Berlin.

Afterwards, Hannah drove the main lamas to Austria. They traveled in a transfer car, a totally underpowered Ford Transit, and Karmapa kept asking her to drive faster, which was physically impossible. Kurt and I took care of some things along the way. Just as we arrived in Vienna, the phone rang. A girl from Hamburg had news for us: Kalu Rinpoche's rich host had invited our North German groups for a meeting. He had a letter from Kalu Rinpoche asking him to establish a "Ri-me" Center in his house. I had already warned Rinpoche against doing that, and when the host and his wife had stayed totally away during Karmapa's visit, I was certain they were up to something. I immediately ran to Karmapa and asked if his students were now meant to aspire to a higher social status. Should they weaken their bonds with him to receive a beautiful new house for practice? "No," said Karmapa, "stop it!"

Jumping into a car, I drove through the night to Hamburg. Next morning, I arrived just in time. Our friends, who were not yet informed on Tibetan politics, were about to say "Yes." "Students of Karmapa don't take part," I said. A cold breeze went through the room. Our hosts were angry and wanted to discuss it, but I said: "They are Mahayana and can mix everything, but we must keep our Kagyu transmission. Those who follow Karmapa, accompany me into the next room." One by one they came, digesting their non-sectarianism. Only three or four stayed. It would take a while for some people to understand that the popular term of "Ri-me" means doing your thing while respecting others.

At Scheibbs in Austria

The center where the Theravadan monk had been angry with Kalu Rinpoche had not improved in vibrations. Some strong good energies were needed and I felt responsible, having given the first course there some years ago. Also, it was a pet project of my Austrian publisher. Of course, Karmapa lifted everything in no time. On a bright autumn day, he initiated all into "Liberatrice," held a Crown Ceremony, and swept away all troubles.

The next morning Karmapa, Jamgon Kongtrul Rinpoche, and their attendants left for Munich. I drove them since there was no time to take our bus. We were expected by Graf von Durkheim, a well-known Zen teacher, along with a number of interested people. They were waiting in an enormous mansion on the outskirts of town. Instead of conversing with the chosen few, I skipped dinner and taught people the Karmapa Meditation instead. On that occasion, I made both good and mixed connections in Munich. Whether I had run off with their girlfriends or horses in former lives I don't know, but for some years jealous people in that town brought extra spice to my life.

Our destination was near Zurich in Switzerland. Some valleys there were now home to about a thousand exiled Tibetans, some of them Khampas. Like Karmapa himself, they belong to that famous East Tibetan tribe of warriors who are often Kagyupa. The German borders were closed. A few hours before, the terrorist group "Bader-Meinhof" had killed some pillar of society. We were in a hurry, so our best bet was to try all crossings in a westward direction. It would bring us as close to Zurich as possible before leaving fast Germany for slower Switzerland. Karmapa made sure it didn't become boring! While approaching an unlit fork in the road at over 160 kph, he poured two pinches of brown powder onto the back of his hand and invited me to sniff it. Suddenly two icy hands gripped my brain. With screeching tires, I went the wrong direction. When I stopped to check if my head was still all there, Karmapa was shaking with laughter. It was the Indian snuff which Kalu Rinpoche also used, apparently a mix of dynamite and ground boxing-gloves.

The reaction of the South German farmers to Karmapa was touching. They felt his power directly. When we stopped at a pub to ask the way, they left their beer and cigarettes and came for blessings. Though the sight of a portly Tibetan in robes was new to them, his warmth and directness melted any cultural barriers.

After four or five attempts, we finally reached a checkpoint early in the morning where they let us pass. Then we skidded through idyllic Swiss villages to a town near Zurich. The Tibetans there had very red eyes; they had been waiting the whole night through. After delivering my valuable freight, I met the bus with Hannah, Bjørn, and the others at the border.

Unfortunately, there were only Tibetans to bless. Our well-functioning Swiss city centers and many close friends were still in the future. Karmapa also spent two days in Rikon, this time without causing a storm. Some rich people came, but of the exotic rather than the useful kind. They adored Tibetan Buddhism as a great enlightened system in Asia, where it hardly stands a chance of survival, but closed their minds and wallets to our friends who give their lives bringing it to the West. They did not feel that even the most idealistic and well-educated Westerners were "cultural" enough. The understanding that the teachings can only be preserved by giving them roots in practical life is far above most people's horizon. It is usually only found in the humanistic middle class, which has little financial power.

Karmapa was definitely no snob. If invited by people who were interested in having an exotic visit or showing off their wealth, he regularly said things like: "These people have no devotion and bad taste. They only invited me so they can tell their friends I was here." It was then up to the poor translator to keep a straight face and come up with something like: "His Holiness is deeply moved by your interest in the Dharma, which is most important of all. He thinks your house is very beautiful and will include you in his prayers." The last point Karmapa never forgot, of course, and even the slightest contact with him brought wondrous results. We had miracles every day.

Once a big check passed us by in Los Angeles. The newly rich inventor of some gadget wanted to demonstrate his cultural standing by inviting the lamas to a Japanese tea ceremony. When he had washed baby-sized cups and poured water from one minuscule vessel to another for half an hour without any tea appearing, one by one the lamas collapsed with laughter. Even Karmapa had to cover his face with his scarf. Our hosts were not pleased, and no check was signed. But what to do? Not everyone understands the fine arts.

After Geneva, Hannah and I had Karmapa, Jamgon Kongtrul and a few attendants to ourselves for three wonderful weeks. Akong was a red flag to the French, so Karmapa sent him ahead to the Dordogne. It was evident that the southern French centers took their direction from Kalu Rinpoche's monastery in Sonada and not Rumtek. With every visit they became more "church-like" and bourgeois. I did not want to even consider the possibility of a split, but it was strange to observe the lack of real openness to Karmapa which many displayed. Somehow, they expected someone to further explain his already clear and simple words. Economically, however, they were well off. The male role in Roman cultures allows for a spiritual interest. What we missed was the "flash," the limitless possibilities one experiences when people are directly linked to Karmapa's power.

In terms of oddballs, the Riviera nearly beat California. On the way to Nice we were invited to "Mandar-Om," an organization of baldies. Singing "OM" before and after every sentence, their shiny heads gleamed

With Lama Jigmela

on a hillside among oversized animals made of papier-mâché. In Cannes, their leader received Karmapa's blessing, and I taught him the Three Lights Meditation.

Another variety was less strange but proud: disciples of Bhagwan Shree Rajneesh, the late Rolls-Royce Guru. He had just published a book with a few humble claims that were new to us: that Karmapa had pronounced him the greatest Bodhisattva of all times, the man to bring Buddhist Tantra to the West. Karmapa, who did not even know him, was as diplomatic as possible, but the guru's disciples were not very pleased with his reply. Once again I could only shake my head at the enormous naivete of people in spiritual matters. It is shocking how readily they give up both discrimination and common sense.

In Nice, Karmapa and Jamgon Rinpoche stayed in a hotel on the beach. We shared many memories with the lamas. They had been in France since we drove them through Europe with Kalu Rinpoche. In St. Tropez a very rich disciple of Bhagwan Rajneesh waited. He wanted to offer the Tibetans a few days in luxury. Wondering how he became so rich, we immediately got an answer: we were expected to pay for the lunch

The site of the empowerment

he had invited us to. After this, we again switched to eating directly from the supermarket. We could not afford too many fine invitations like that. Karmapa soon decided that he would be more useful elsewhere and ended the visit prematurely. After three weeks at his side nearly around the clock, we arrived in his main French Center for the great initiations planned there.

The Dordogne is exquisite. Not far north of the Pyrenees, it has knobby French oaks, mountains of red-brown limestone and wonderful winding roads. They are a joy for people who can drive. Mr. Benson had given a true gift. Everyone had come but him, and we needed him to finish the formalities. Only then could the invocation of "Greatest Joy" and the inauguration of the area take place. All we had was the phone number of a man in New York, but Jytte Marstrand flew back there anyway. "We will now bless the land," she said to him, "and we hope you want to take part." That worked. During the speeches I praised the generosity of a man who had eleven children and still donated something so great to the Dharma. Already then, the blond heads of our Danes and Germans outnumbered even the French, a strong indication of the future international status of the place. This was Karmapa's wish, and I was glad our friends brought him that joy.

My teaching there was on how impersonal pain can be. Pawo Rinpoche, a very important lineage-holder, had a broken vertebra and could not get on his throne. As I lifted his two hundred pounds, his pain reached into me. For one moment a white flash hit my back. Letting it pass through, I placed Rinpoche on his pillow. The pain was gone at once. When I later asked him why he had been so fidgety, he replied: "I was

In Dordogne, France

Mr. Benson

afraid of getting my feet higher than Karmapa's." So the cultural patterns still functioned on the highest levels.

Some of Karmapa's statements there picked up the thread from an earlier interview in Copenhagen. The tallest woman I had ever seen, a journalist from one of our best newspapers, had waited for hours to see him. She wanted to know what was special about people's consciousness today. "I actually shouldn't say anything," Karmapa answered, "it will only bring confusion. But since you really want to know, here it is: modern people are overstimulated. Their concepts increase steadily and they have little access to their timeless nature." The sequel followed in the caves of Lascaux, a few miles from the center. Bjørn and I had seen the famous stone age paintings there before, with our parents. Just before they were permanently closed to the public, we now visited them with Karmapa. I pointed out how much of the art was hunting magic, that the aim was to control animals so one could more easily kill them. Coming up through the shaft, I returned to Karmapa's statement from Copenhagen which was still irking me. Though I would never doubt his ultimate insight, the vision disturbed me and in no way fit my experience. I saw people and their minds as ever more exciting and pure day by day, and of course my friends were most fantastic of all. "But we are at least better than people were then, aren't we?" I tried again. "No," Karmapa replied, not looking like he wanted to say another word.

Some South Africans wanted to start a center and Karmapa told them to invite me down. Naturally, I agreed. Next, an important meeting was scheduled in a castle near Paris. Karmapa wanted the French Kagyu to cooperate. This was the chance to remove all causes for future splits. Unfortunately, only the "already saved" attended. Those involved in starting an organization directly under Kalu Rinpoche had smelled trouble and stayed away. So there was little to unite, although some friends promised to avoid friction between the groups.

The center in Antwerp provided some juicy stories. Scottish and French influences had clashed. Some old friends had not liked the lama Kalu Rinpoche had left there. Taking the donation-box to Brussels, they had made a down-payment on a stately house for a center under Akong Tulku instead. Once again, we were confronted with the factional tendencies which Karmapa disliked so much. It was the dark side of individualism and made cooperation between England and Scotland difficult for

With Geoff from Johannesburg in France

years. Many idealistic people seemed unable to think impersonally or in larger contexts. With a wry smile, Karmapa gave the Brussels center a twin name to the Antwerp one, made good wishes, and traveled on.

Soon after reaching England, Karmapa sent me to Munich to organize a German Karma Kagyu Trust. They chose me for president and Karmapa's representative. It was great to bring Karmapa the message that at least in Germany, all stood together.

Returning to London, the vast halls of the dignified "Buddhist Society" were impressive. They brought together a wide range of Buddhist traditions, and we enjoyed the richness of it all. First Christmas Humphreys, their president and the author of several well-known books, taught on suffering and the evils of the world. Then Karmapa continued on with the ultimate purity and Buddha nature of all things. Showing how samsara and nirvana are states of consciousness, he said that enlightenment manifests as our true nature, when all veils are removed from the mind. This did not contradict the first teaching, but rather completed it. They chatted joyfully during lunch afterwards.

Driving past the "Marpa House" which had now dissolved, we went on to "Samye Ling." Karmapa would spend Christmas there. Shortly after arriving, he asked some people to drive to a deserted farm nearby and open a window for three big birds trapped in the attic. Although he had never been to the place, he described it in accurate detail. They freed one owl and two crows that would otherwise surely have starved. As he had already done similar things in France, no one was overly astonished.

One pleasant day, Karmapa put a fistful of pound notes into our hands. He wanted us to go to Ireland to start the Dharma there. It was an exciting tour by ferry and train through familiar/unfamiliar countryside. During lectures in hotels, a group formed which is still practicing today. They do not have an easy time. Although the population is Catholic, as in Poland or Spain, the step from people's general level of consciousness to Buddhism is somehow much larger. Those who decided to practice were unshakable, however. As most were geared to a traditional practice and it was expensive to bring me over, after some years I advised them to rely mainly on Akong Tulku. Today, they help him a lot.

New Year, 1978, we celebrated in Wales. Here, an American horse specialist gave the top of a mountain to our lineage. Hannah learned from the Khenpo. Afterwards, we flew to Athens, where she translated for Karmapa and served as his secretary. We met Barbara Pettee there, straight from California. She organized the western third of America and had visited the Hopi Indians with Karmapa. Listening to one of my teachings, she became enthusiastic about the directness of the transmission. Declaring me a Western incarnation on the spot, she insisted that I teach in America more often, which was also Karmapa's frequent wish. "You must go there every year," he said, "give teachings in my centers and start new groups. Promise me this."

Dorje Stone in Delphi, Greece—one of the only signs of
Buddhist influence found in Greece

Only a few could stay in the Athens center. Though it was a majestic house, centrally located, it was not laid out practically. It was a period when everybody spoke well of each other. The Greeks provided inspiration and our Swedish friend Magnus gave perseverance; things were in balance and grew well.

Two dozen Danes arrived, kept on the move by my mother, a dauntless energy bomb. During an initiation into "Diamond Mind," she experienced what had happened to Hannah and I at our first meeting with Karmapa: she saw his State of Joy. Wide-eyed, and pointing at him, she exclaimed again and again: "But he shines, he shines!" She was completely gone for several hours and never forgot that golden light.

After six months of fruitful work in Europe, Karmapa made a last stop in Paris. His birds and piles of gifts had been gathering there. Then he flew to India with Jamgon Kongtrol Rinpoche and his entourage. Leaving in the middle of January, they would be in time for Tibetan New Year in Sikkim. Europe had been thoroughly blessed, and its central-eastern part was now our working area. As always, he had given clear

Diamond Mind

His Holiness
The Gyalwa Karmapa

14th January 197C

For the attention of all the European Dharma centres
especially those in Germany and Scandinavia.

Ole and Hannah Nydahl are followers of the Kagyupa Lineage of
Mahayana Buddhism and they are linked to me by the Samaya Bond
of Lama and disciple.

They established the first Buddha Dharma centres in Denmark
and elsewhere, and have arranged for visits of many highly
accomplished and learned Lamas, thereby making it possible for
many to receive the precious Teachings for the realization of
the true nature of the mind.

During my second visit to Europe, I was highly encouraged to
see the new houses bought and centres established by members of
Karma Drub Djyling and elsewhere by the help of Ole and Hannah's
ceaseless efforts and encouragement. All the Dharma activities
were most beneficial and successful.

Furthermore, I have reappointed Ole Nydahl as the Head of
the Dharma centres of the Karma Drub Djyling Association and I
have reappointed Hannah Nydahl as his deputy; I have authorised
both Ole and Hannah Nydahl to continue to be Instructors to the
people who are first entering into the understanding and practice
of the Buddha Dharma and also to continue to help to establish
new Dharma centres.

I pray that all beings may be liberated from the sufferings
of samsara.

His Holiness The XVI Gyalwa Karmapa.

The Seats of His Holiness the Gyalwa Karmapa

Dharmachakra Centre	Tashi-Chöling	Karmaraj Vihara
Rumtek, Gangtok	Bumthang	Swayambhunath
Sikkim, India	Bhutan	Kathmandu, Nepal

Cable: Dharmachakra Centre, Sikkim   Phone: Gangtok 363

instructions on what to do. It would be exciting to make things grow
without the boss directly at our side.

Our task was to pass on Karmapa's gift, to translate his blessing
into spiritual growth in everyday life. People should feel comfortable
doing the Three Lights Meditation on him, not cultural or personal. With
this one powerful source of contact to their timeless essence, they would
avoid much confusion. True practice is acting fearlessly, joyfully, and
lovingly until we become like our teacher, and this identification matures
us fastest of all. It is the essence of the various Karmapa meditations of
which he made me holder. The function of our centers would be to
strengthen this confidence through teaching and traditional meditations.
They are as effective in removing neuroses today as during the last 2,500
years.

But even the best methods are useless without friendship and trust;
this was obvious. Our friends needed to know that there is only one goal,
human growth. When we are independent and in control of the outer
and inner worlds, our Buddha-nature will manifest. Since the methods
of the Diamond Way are so strong and efficient, people go through many
changes, and it is never boring.

Hannah's qualifications are her deep, stable trust and love. Mine
come from liking people, finding them attractive and exciting. These
qualities combined with my delight in action and the removal of obstruc-
tions—the greater the better—we had given into Karmapa's hands. We
did exactly as he said: I was to travel as lama and establish centers in his
name. Hannah's job was to help the lineage-holders and other Rinpoches
from Rumtek. She should organize for them and translate on their tours.
She had yet another important function: she communicated "upwards"
and calmed the frequent rumors caused by my yogi style. As we are often
together and always in contact, the bridge between East and West
functions well.

Most wonderful of all was that Karmapa never left. Already from
his first visit, his powerfield stayed on and it is growing even today.
Wherever people keep their bonds to Karmapa, their lives grow in
meaning, year by year. His activity, expressed by the power circle of
"Black Coat" is everywhere and protects all. When my students start
telling how often they have felt his help, they are not easy to stop.

Hannah first interpreted for the Khenpo in Great Britain. In Denmark, she began compiling a central work of Buddhist philosophy, Gampopa's "Jewel Ornament of Liberation." During a later course in France, she finished this work and today her excerpts are used by many. From the end of July, she traveled as translator for Ayang Tulku from the Drikung lineage, a famous master of Phowa. He gave the first courses in Copenhagen and Rødby. After that, she drove him through Europe. It was the time when the second batch of good karmas matured in South Germany—mostly through the activity of Kurt. After having started an especially hopeful group in a Bavarian health resort, it was time to write my first major book: *Die Buddhas vom Dach der Welt* (the first and German edition of *Entering the Diamond Way*).

Karmapa had already suggested this in France in 1976, and Kurt and others picked up the idea. The experiences of years spent so close to Karmapa belonged to everyone. We already had the publisher, and time and place were easy to agree on. Whisked away so abruptly that even the most determined ladies couldn't follow, suddenly my world was a basement in Davos in the Swiss Alps. I had three weeks in June for writing and an excellent editor for improving my German. It was hard work at first. Living so intensely in the moment, there is hardly any time for remembering. The countless boxing gloves my head had stopped, the drugs, and a serious motorcycle accident in Munich had done nothing to enhance my memory. Gradually, however, in the vacuum of nothing happening, things came back that were important and soon there was nothing else. I no longer ate, and worked from seven in the morning until three the next. Stacks of paper were soon piled high. When Kurt picked me up, he claimed I was transparent. I had lost twenty pounds.

Thanks to the excellent work of my editor, and another, less private week near Munich to revise the text, the first edition was soon complete. This book (now in several languages) is still the bridge to Buddhism for half the people entering our German-speaking centers today. After a warm goodbye to hundreds of close friends, I set out for South Africa.

CHAPTER EIGHT

South Africa

SOUTH AFRICA IS UNUSUAL AND EXCITING. Everyone is on his own. There are three white "tribes": the Jews who handle gold and diamonds, the English who take care of administration and most cultural matters, and the Boers who own the land. Then there are mulattoes, Asians and black tribes who frequently fight, though not in Western style: their favorite victims are civilians. The blacks are all afraid of the Zulu. In the middle of the last century, they decimated the other tribes under their king, Charka, a military genius. His power lasted until ten thousand of his soldiers clashed with three hundred strong Dutchmen with long bayonets at Blood River. Losing innumerable men against the Boers, he retreated and was killed by his brother shortly after. Much that bewilders the world today about South Africa simply continues this tradition.

The plane departed from Paris and made a stop somewhere in the middle of the continent. In Johannesburg, the Hardacres waited in the airport. Karmapa had blessed our contact in the Dordogne. They were of strong North English stock and Geoff, then in his fifties, had worked for the police in Hong Kong. He had been riddled with bullets there several times, preferring to go first when cleaning out a gangsters' nest. His revolver had a notch for every man he had sent on. For some quaint reason, he cast his own bullets in his garage.

In Hong Kong, a Buddha statue had deeply impressed him. He found a female Buddhist teacher, and by the time he settled with his

Zulu village near Johannesburg

family in South Africa as an insurance agent, he was already a Buddhist. Though overweight and with the many physical ailments which a life of violence brings about, he was a lion of a man and I was glad to stay with them.

There already existed some small groups of very individualistic people. My most important task would be extracting what is Buddhist from the more or less confused spiritual traditions which had arrived there. It involves constantly stepping on peoples' egos, but if one neglects it, all future work will be built on sand. Because of pressure from the church, it was rarely possible to use universities or other public buildings for lectures. Therefore most of our meetings took place in private homes.

Some fixed ideas we probably all have about South Africa gradually vanished. When I asked about the social distance from the blacks, the answer was that the Europeans had arrived there first, which seems to be historically correct. The aboriginal inhabitants had died out before they debarked. When I wanted to know about slavery, which Danes were the first in the world to abolish, they told me that the black tribes had taken one another prisoner. They had sold their captives to the Arabs, who brought them to the coast. Here European skippers gladly loaded them onto their ships. Concerning the emergence of apartheid, they explained it like this: the Boers had seldom taken white women with them on their travels, and in the second and third generations this became very apparent. Seeing their gene-pool disappearing among masses of blacks, they established the impossible system to protect themselves. Today, its ill fame mainly arises from having become law. Light skin means a higher status everywhere—but no one talks about it. One thing was clear: if one wanted to teach Dharma here, politics were not the right approach. Once again I understood why Karmapa always insisted: "No politics in my centers!"

The landscape was impressive and wild but with a brutal and monotonous streak. The wind carried cyanide-treated dust from the gold mines and many had sinus troubles. Johannesburg looked like a miniature New York. It had similar, but smaller, skyscrapers and antique intersections: everyone had to stop to find out which car would cross first. One day we drove to Drakensvaal, possibly the most ancient mountain range in the world. On the way we stopped in Pretoria, the capital, and stood on the steps of Parliament while the Boers made history. They basically told the rest of the world to get stuffed, throwing out a handful of serious United Nations resolutions within an hour. I often thought that if these few million people ever got really angry, the rest of Africa's inhabitants would soon swim in the Mediterranean. They had an immense, obstinate power, rarely softened by any humor.

In the afternoon, I wanted to climb an exciting mountain face. I had already discovered that it must be a mountaineer's delight: the rock was so hard that any single point could support a climber's full weight. This meant one could move upwards very quickly. Some hundred feet up, there was no hold for my hand above, and also not right or left. "I won't go down," I thought, "that would be weak." But then I realized I had no chance to climb down, even if I wanted to. Going up, I had jumped to catch the next hold a few times, and on the way down I would inevitably

Drakensberg Mountains

slide past them to the ground. This was real excitement. There was no place to move to, and slowly I began to tire. Only people from flat countries like Denmark get into stupid situations like that. I also remembered somebody saying one must never look down, but thought: "If you don't do that, how will you learn about your mind?" So, I imagined how much space I would occupy on the boulders down there, and wondered whether animals or men would find my body first.

My strength was just giving out, when there was suddenly the presence of immeasurable love. It was bright and feminine and mild, and felt like a soft breeze. The energy pressed me against the mountainside and up, maybe a few inches, to a hold for my fingers which was not visible from below. The rest was easy and I willingly admit: when I rolled onto the plateau above a few minutes later, my eyes were wet. "I promise to

work harder," was the only thing I could say. I promised this again and
again.

I knew "White Liberatrice" had intervened and afterwards, walking
around on the ancient plateau and reciting her mantra, she also blessed
my mind. The sky took on the color of rose quartz, and when looking to
the ground, the stones changed into bells, dorjes, and lotus flowers,
powerful symbols of Tibetan Buddhism. I must have spent several hours
there in her Pure Land.

Returning to ordinary consciousness, I was so happy that I invited
a university class of mulattoes to our hut for a cup of tea. The local farmers
disliked them intensely. It was their custom to tear plastic bags and throw
the pieces into the air. The Boers' cows liked plastic but couldn't digest
it, so some died every year of constipation.

A journey to Rhodesia (today Zimbabwe) was another memorable
experience. Here Salsbury (now Harrar), held some interested people. The
anchor there was George, another Hong Kong policeman now working

*The presence of
immeasurable love*

The mulattoes I invited

in insurance. One day Geoff confided his Buddhist interest to him and
George nearly gave his old friend up. Driving along in his battered
Peugeot weeks later, he was suddenly struck by a mass of golden light on
the hood of his car. It was a Buddha who shone so brightly that George
drove off the road. While still wondering what had happened, a bus full
of locals hit a landmine. It had been planted for him a hundred yards
ahead. That was his introduction to Buddhism!

The day after the guerrillas—now freedom fighters—had shot
down a civilian plane with a SAM-rocket and massacred the survivors
they could find, Geoff and I flew to Salisbury. We had hoped for a cheap
ticket, but instead we had the plane to ourselves. Over Rhodesian
airspace, two ancient English Hawker Hunter Jets appeared and flanked
us, taking turns switching their engines on and off. This was to make any
rockets, which are much faster than planes, fly a zigzag between them
until they burn out and crash.

As far as architecture was concerned, Salisbury was perfect northern England. Its people were brave. They maintained the famous "stiff upper lip" and always had style although the world was arming their enemies. At the airport, Geoff greeted an old friend who had just lost an arm. His primitive, locally built machine gun had jammed while he was plucking some superbly AK 47-armed rebels from the trees. His only comment was, "Things like that happen."

The luxury of Rhodesia is its spaciousness. Houses in the residential area stood at least a hundred yards apart, which felt great. Whites and blacks had a much more relaxed relationship here than in South Africa. Divisions were not underpinned by laws but came from people's varying abilities. An astonishing number of people, mainly big-boned Northern English types, came to George's house after a small newspaper ad and a short lecture on the radio. They hung their primitive "Stenguns" on the wall and sat down. Then we learned why so many had come. Walking

Geoff and George in Salisbury

down the streets of Salisbury, some had "seen" three men in red robes following me. As in many cultures off the beaten track, quite a number of people here had unusual powers. They were also practical. Several army vehicles were built on stilts. These collapsed when hitting the mines which came in thousands from Russia and China. After a few simple modifications, they drove on as ordinary trucks.

Back in Johannesburg, I gave Refuge to three medicine women. Though deep, they earned their living by sprinkling water in rich people's houses with a cow's tail. The servants then believed they would be cursed if they stole anything. A major part of their training consisted of fasting, and they also knew something about powerfields, though not enlightened ones. Their main work was cheering up difficult gods, and my teachings on the "empty" nature of things made their eyes rolls. This was a notch too abstract. They feared they'd vanish into nothingness or a black hole.

In Johannesburg, some weeks' work had produced a well-functioning group. Goal and way were clear. As invitations kept piling up, it was now time for a tour across the vast country.

The high semi-arid steppe ended shortly before Durban, where the landscape suddenly changed into a lush green. Here, in a hilly area near the Indian Ocean, lived the Souters. They had also been with Karmapa in the Dordogne. Durban was more open than Johannesburg. Many teachers came and went. At that time, a fine hotel housed representatives from the "Findhorn" community in Scotland, people who talk to their plants to make them grow. It was exciting to swim in the lagoons. At any moment, the huge waves might deposit a shark there. Also, the view of Charka's Rock added spice. He had had other chieftains thrown from it for weeks till he held all the power himself. Then he had militarized his whole people with equipment very similar to that of the ancient Romans, not forgetting shields of such soft leather that the opponents' weapons got stuck. Up to thirty-six years of age, men were prohibited from having women. A soldier who has just made love doesn't kill well. On their expeditions, their offer to other tribes was always equally charming: "If you surrender today, we will kill nobody. Tomorrow we will kill one out of ten, the day after tomorrow, two out of ten and so on." Those who defended themselves were completely extinguished. The Zulus had just conquered a large part of Rhodesia when they were stopped

in a day and night battle at Blood River by three hundred determined
Dutchmen.

While I was there, a medicine man became my student. His name
was Jonathan and he looked about forty-five. One morning, he stood
fidgeting at the garden gate of the house. He said he had returned from
Johannesburg by bus last night. Entering his hut, he had found one of
the very poisonous Mamba snakes on his bed. This animal was his totem,
and it meant that he would now receive a dream from the "ancestors," as
he called his spirit contacts. The dream came, and his spirits had told
him to go to house number 4 on Haven Road and learn from the white
teacher there. Although it is very unusual in South Africa for a black
person to just come visiting, he was brought to me in the garden. His
English being good, we could talk about many things. I gave him Refuge,
the Karmapa Meditation, and we talked about energy fields. He was
amazed to meet a white man who was not a Christian and didn't
automatically tell him to exchange his own tradition for a foreign system.
Never before had anyone said: "Let's see what you have and whether we
can add something to it." Deeply thankful, he threw an oracle for me.
Asking me to blow three times into a sack filled with bones, feathers, and
stones, he emptied it on the ground in front. Of course, I was eager for
him to succeed, but actually most of what he said was correct. Later, when
asked to find out something for a neighbor, he was also on track until the
latter made an ironic remark. There was no leeway for that in his system,
and his concentration broke. When I heard from him last, he was
meditating on Karmapa every day and was doing well.

After semi-tropical Durban we drove through a "homeland" into
the dry high plateau again. I was to bless an area called New Behesda.
The Van Loon family had given it to Lama Anagarika Govinda for a
retreat-place. Here we saw some of the oldest plants in the world,
man-size, palm-like growths with fern-like leaves. They have hardly
changed for fifty million years. The hard coal of the world mainly consists
of their predecessors and, though freaky-looking, somehow they carried
a real vibration.

Port Elizabeth shone in clear pastel shades, exciting and hard at the
same time. I stayed in an artists' colony with the Fugards, today famous
anti-apartheid authors. His novels and plays focus on the relationship of

With the Haracres and Van Loons at the retreat center

Port Elisabeth friends

black and white, which was not popular with the authorities. Like many psychologists and other intellectuals, he claimed that to white people, blacks represent the feminine, subconscious and irrational—the uncontrollable part of the mind which disturbs them. To the black people, white people are the masculine, cold and rational, the impersonal and abstract which they cannot relate to.

Fishing was our host's passion and he made a point of how un-Buddhist it is. He wanted to provoke some reaction, but I just blew on his rod and wished him good luck. When he came back three hours later, for the very first time in years he had caught absolutely nothing. In my heart I thanked all Buddhas, but outwardly I behaved as if such miracles happen every day, which they actually do. The group in Port Elizabeth was like most in Central Europe: blessed by wonderful and generous women. I thoroughly enjoyed not having to play any moralistic games, and looking back today, after over ten years, landscapes and names come up when remembering Johannesburg and Durban. In Port Elizabeth, however, I recall fresh shiny faces and experiences that touched me.

View of Cape Town

Cape Town, my next stop, must be seen to be believed. The town probably has everything. Since Phoenician times, its flora has been a rich mixture of European and African plants. Table Mountain, a huge broken rock, dominates the landscape and sometimes one feels the winds of the Antarctic straight south. Here the Atlantic and Indian Oceans meet. Spiritual life was dominated by Theosophists and a few Hindu gurus. Nowhere in the country were the audiences more mature, and many took Refuge. Rosemary Vosse, who still today sends her Ko-Eksister pamphlets around the world, was a very important influence there.

Since whites and Malays had been living together long before the blacks came, racial relationships were much more relaxed than further north. A few newspapers published interviews, and I held some well-attended lectures in the halls of the Theosophists. Then I gave the work into the hands of Rob, a Rhodesian professor who was already studying Buddha's teachings. He had sensed dimensions beyond the intellect when I spontaneously told him which car he had bought.

The plane back to Johannesburg landed at the Kimberly Mine. This is an unbelievably big hole in the earth where they extract diamonds. Hundreds of men and machines moved around it. Strangely enough, the biggest profit is said to have been made by a man who had received permission to hunt the area's ostriches. Like other fowl, they eat stones to digest their meals and the ones not destroyed during the process were of course the diamonds. He simply cut the birds open and left the country with a fortune.

In Johannesburg, the group had practiced well. They gave "Krugerrands," big gold coins, which I later offered to Karmapa. He placed them with "Black Coat" in Rumtek. It was touching how they didn't want me to go, but letters from Europe had been piling up. I had been away for nearly two months and now it was again time for activity in that powerhouse of a continent.

Hannah and Ayang Tulku arrived in Paris a few hours later. They also had not been bored. Now they came from Greece, had given the Phowa many times, and were a good team.

During the rest of 1978, activity was in Europe. After Ayang Tulku returned to the East, we received the gift of the year: wonderful Tenga

Rinpoche had accepted our invitation. He would cure the TB in his foot with us. We could hope to have him in Denmark all through 1979.

Though he was to rest and not work, his very presence would keep the powerfield in Central Europe strong. This made our second pilgrimage to Karmapa possible. Once again it was time to add some practical flesh to the bones of theory. I wanted the teachings to be confirmed by direct contact with the world's sufferings and the methods which dissolve them. This was exactly what our pilgrimages offered.

V. Tenga Rinpoche
with two translators
in Copenhagen

Cable : Dharmachakra Sikkim.
Phone : Gangtok 363

Main Seat
Dharma Chakra Centre
Rumtek Monastery
Gangtok Sikkim India

HIS HOLINESS XVI GYALWA KARMAPA

10th December, 1978

My Desciples Ole and Hannah,

I am highly encouraged to hear all the
wonderful Dharma work that both of you are performing through Achhi
and through your encouraging letters. It is my constant prayer to
the Buddhas and Bodhisattvas that by Their boundless Blessings both
of you will be furthered strengthened to spread the Kagyu Dharma.

The hair of the devoted group of Polish
practitioners have reached me and I accept them as my desciples.
I am enclosing four names for each of the Dharma Centres. Kindly
inform them that they all are in my prayers and Meditation. I am
to receive some of their photographs.

I presume that you have already applied for
the Inner Line Permit into Sikkim. I am looking forward to having
you all during the 'Gharcham' and 'Losar'. You should arrive in
Rumtek by the 24th of February, 1979 as the Sacred Dances will take
place on the 25th and 26th of February, 1979 and 'Losar' is on the
27th of February, 1979.

During your stay here I will do everything to
help you all in your pactise of the Kagyu Dharma.

Both of you are in my mind and prayers.

With Blessings,

(His Holiness XVIth Gyalwa Karmapa.)

The Karma Kargyu Society
P. O. Box 5399
Postal Station A
Toronto Ont. M5W 1N6
CANADA

Karma Triyana Dharmachakra
Mead Mountain Road
Wood Stock, New York-12498
U. S. A.

Dhagpo Kagyu Ling
Leon-sur-Vezere
Montignac 24290
FRANCE

Kagyu mDo Ngak Cho Ling
P. O. Box 364
Manly NSW 2895
AUSTRALIA.

Letter from Karmapa

CHAPTER NINE

Visiting Karmapa

ONE HUNDRED AND EIGHT HOPEFULS CAME ALONG, and many are
our closest friends also today. This time, most were German. It made
things more orderly than with Danes. I taught them in Copenhagen for
a few days, while our protectors were busy. They prevented the owner of
the travel agency from leaving with our money. He had already received
full payment for the tickets, but vanished a few weeks later instead. Today
he lives in South America. Though we prefer not to support the Arabs,
who invest so heavily in war and suppression, this time there was no
choice.

We landed in Delhi a few days behind schedule, to the relief of Kurt
and others who had been waiting there. While Niels rented buses, the
group had a first taste of the Indian chaos. Our first destination was Tsok
Pema. We had collected the best of TB medicines for Drikung Khandro.
Unfortunately for the world, however, she had died some weeks earlier.
Soon, we were again up the mountain and the yogi caves lay in snow.
Today, for some reason, the Indians try to keep both Tibetans and
Westerners away from these sites. Several times when meditating, the
reed islands on the lake moved towards us. The locals notice that. It is
considered a true sign of blessing. On our arrival, all nine islands had
docked for hours in front of the temple we moved into.

The place is great and we spent hours walking around the lake,
reciting the mantra "Karmapa Chenno." In the evenings, Hannah some-

Tsok Pema

times translated the lectures of a local lama, or I taught. The bus drivers were dishonest to the core like most members of India's transport industry, but a bit of shaking up secured our return to Delhi as agreed. On the way, we spent two days in Clementtown, further west in the Himalayan foothills. Here, the great lama Dilgo Khyentse Rinpoche gave six months of initiations, an important cultural event.

Apart from a few of the important initiations, Clementtown gave a shocking insight into the tortures the communist Chinese impose on the Tibetans, still today. In an isolated room on the top floor of the beautiful monastery, we saw Mindroling Rinpoche, the true head of the "Old" or Nyingmapa tradition. He was in bad condition. With a heroic face which would have delighted any sculptor and an immense blessing filling the room, he lay on his bed, alternating between conscious and unconscious states. He had been thoroughly destroyed, and repeatedly called the Chinese, who had beaten him through the streets of Lhasa, his "teachers." Dudjom Rinpoche had taken over the leadership of the School in his place, and after his death, Dilgo Khyentse Rinpoche passed it on again.

We also visited Gelongma Palmo's nunnery in Tilokpur. It is right above the great yogi Tilopa's main cave. Here, the local Indians often run ahead of the visitors and occupy the holy places. When one arrives, they start making loud noises and then they offer peace to meditate in return for money. I had little sympathy for that style and gave them free flying lessons out of the cave, instead. We left Delhi in rented train wagons to experience full moon at the Taj Mahal, which was Niel's idea—and then went directly on to Bodhgaya. At that time, there was not yet a fence around the stupa and one could hardly sit anywhere without collecting a swarm of beggars.

Afterwards, we took buses to the eastern Himalayan foothills. In Sonada we were initiated into "Loving Eyes" by Kalu Rinpoche. Then we headed for Rumtek, where Karmapa showed his influence. In a country where telephones hardly ever function and no one dares take responsibility for anything, he simply phoned the government in Delhi. With a few words, he provided a month's stay for our one hundred and eight friends.

This was the greatest of gifts and we would use it well.

The last two days before Tibetan New Year the lamas danced. Then all stayed up, and early in the morning Karmapa and the lineage holders gave their blessings. The next day it was our turn to entertain, and the athletic jumps we learned in Western schools were especially appreciated. The locals had never seen anything like that before. The doctor of Chinese medicine, Claude, broke a stone with a karate chop, and a psychologist from Munich performed some avant-garde mimics, which aroused little interest. Tibetans prefer more action than that.

After the festivities, we received a thorough education. Karmapa himself

Lama dances in Rumtek

Goshir Gyaltsab Rinpoche as Vajra Master

taught on the nature of mind. He gave Crown Ceremonies and initiations nearly every day. Several were of the kind one only rarely receives. For example, he sowed the subconscious seeds for seeing one's teacher as inseparable from "Black Coat," the activity of all Karmapas. This is the main awareness I pass on when blessing.

Shamarpa's subject was the Pure Land of Great Bliss. Being the emanation of the central Buddha there, this was the logical topic.

Visiting Karmapa

Teachings by Shamar Rinpoche

Giving a Diamond Dagger Empowerment

Gyaltsab Rinpoche, another of the four lineage-holders, is "Diamond in Hand," the energy of all Buddhas. He explained some verses by Shanti-deva in a "lighter" vein than usual. The text easily lends itself to joyless moralizing and should be kept from people who already have that

Sangye Nyenpa Rinpoche

tendency. Sangye Nyenpa Rinpoche and Ponlop Rinpoche, still children
at that time, shared what they were just learning in school, and even the
youngest, the Garwang and Gyaltrul Rinpoches, established a Dharma
bond with our group. They read Buddhist texts aloud. We had been
present when Karmapa found them in Nepal and Sikkim, in 1969. It was

great to share Rumtek with our closest friends. We meet far too seldom, and though we cooperate as smoothly as the parts of a German engine, time spent together remains the most valuable of all.

One day, Karmapa's foreign secretary brought us a document. In it, Karmapa pronounced Hannah and me his official Western disciples. We were the only ones he gave this title to. The letter was touching and warm, omitted formalities, and pronounced us direct holders of his activity. When Hannah saw it, she became insecure. "Now there is no reason to send Rinpoches," she said and wanted the phrase inserted, "in the absence of fully educated teachers." Karmapa was astonished but went along. I should have listened to my inner feeling, however, and not agreed to any "improvement" on Karmapa's letter. This addition later became ammunition for people who had problems with my free yogi style.

The month in Rumtek ended with a big party on the flat roof of our hotel. The next day, with everybody already in the bus, Niels and I were called back. He and our other medics had treated half the village and were now immensely popular. We were led to the house of the Bhutanese royal family, situated behind the monastery. People looked very serious. Gyalyum, the late king's stately main wife, sat on a chair. She held her head in her hands and blood dripped from her nose. This was the butter-and-salt-tea's revenge—a serious stroke which Niels considered deadly. Karmapa did not take it so seriously, however. While he walked around and jokingly threw herbs on her head, he talked to Acchi Pema Dechen, the lovely younger queen. He asked her to invite us to Bhutan when the group went back. What he did to save her, we don't know, but on our travels we frequently meet Gyalyum, who is like a mother to us. While writing this in 1991, she is still in fine shape.

Then followed some wonderful weeks in Nepal with Lopon Chechoo Rinpoche, our first teacher from 1968. When our group returned to Europe, Hannah and I went on to Bhutan. In 1970 we had secretly entered the country twice; first alone, and then hidden under Karmapa's luggage. This time we would go there legally.

At the border town of Puntsholing, a new jeep waited. There were great views along the small winding road leading into the mountains. Here, shortly before Thimphu, the capital, stood our castle. A minister, a son of Pema Dechen, had invited us. Everything was prepared to offer

With Lopon Chechoo—Buddha Laximi and Niels are to the right

the white guests a luxurious stay, but things worked out differently. Instead of catering to our every worldly need, four stately servants, two chauffeurs and various cooks saw the temples of their country. Every day, we walked up mountains for hours. There were amazing places no Westerners had seen before and which can no longer be reached today. During that visit, the most blessed sites of the Thimphu and Paro valleys were put into our hands and their power has been with us ever since. The monasteries had names like Chiri, Tago, and Jowo. I mention them because of the good energy these names evoke.

Late in April, we parted in Calcutta. Hannah went to Nepal to meet Niels and Shamarpa. She would translate at his first course outside Rumtek. As always, I was burning to get my hands on Europe, to share joy and growth with so many friends again. So much was clear: the second pilgrimage would not be the last. They benefited everybody.

My first stop was Stavanger in Norway. Then life went on in second-hand but fast cars, now with German license plates. However grateful we were to the Pitzner rental company, full-time vehicles were needed now.

CHAPTER TEN

America

*J*ULY 1979 SAW THE FIRST SUMMER COURSE with Tenga Rinpoche. It took place in the Danish retreat center and was a great experience for all. Hannah translated, and I taught at night. Then it was time to leave Europe again. After pulling his jeep out of the woods north of New York, I had promised Dr. Shen to return. Now he had sent a ticket. Hannah stayed with Tenga Rinpoche, whose bone TB had healed well. He could now teach some hours every day. Our European network would bring an increasing number of people to him. With everything nicely on track, it would be a luxury to now awaken numerous karmic connections in exciting North America.

The site Dr. Shen had offered was too cramped for Tibetan taste. So he had given them a big old hotel instead. It lay on a mountainside near Woodstock in New York and had a breathtaking view. The original piece of land was just right for the Chinese however, and now he wanted to build temples for "Limitless Light" and Kuan Yin there, a Chinese "Liberatrice." My job was clearing the land of trees. He truly had style and wasted nobody's time. Two brand new Homelite chainsaws were waiting. I had a jeep, a bulldozer, and could buy whatever was needed on his account. As an added benefit, the house had a telephone so I could organize my way across the country. Then he returned to New Jersey where he now lived. The lovely place on Long Island had been sold.

Tenga Rinpoche in Rødby

What freedom! It was total joy. All day, I felled low-quality trees.
There was no one to give suggestions or become frightened when I tried
out some new exciting technique. Whenever one chainsaw got stuck, I
could free it with the other, a luxury we never had in Sweden. As soon as
it was too dark to see, I jumped into the jeep. An hour south lay New
York where I taught in the centers of Khenpo Karthar or Lama Nohrla.
After that followed some disco, and wherever I awoke in the morning, at
eight a.m. sharp I was on the stairs down to the jeep. This quickly became
second nature. I had heard enough about the local towing companies:
once your car fell prey to one of them, it took much time and money to
free it again.

Lex gave me another two hours on his radio show and again I filled Khenpo Khatar's center with people. I really gave my very best in that city, day and night, but despite all efforts, people grew more zombie-like by the year. It was like an incurable disease, and I suspected Trungpa Tulku's Dharmadhatu organization of being its origin. When the land was cleared—and bulldozing the stumps in the end was special fun—Dr. Shen came and said, "Thanks for your contribution, but I think you're overqualified for this work. Here is some money. Please come the day after tomorrow and teach at our Chinese temple in the Bronx." This was a stylish building in an otherwise ruined neighborhood where we had been honored guests before. Here we had recognized how highly Karmapa esteemed Dr. Shen.

My lecture pleased even the very traditional Chinese. But despite their donations, I still lacked money for all my plans during that beautiful autumn. So I took a job with the ex-monk Sherab—now Barry—who renovated old houses and then rented them at New York rates. His knee—healed on Karmapa's last day in Geneva in 1974—was still perfect. Besides worldly work, he did low-budget but eye-catching exhibits which called public attention to the Tibetan cause. Remembering how our money for spreading the Dharma came from shoveling holes for swimming pools, Karmapa once said to Barry, "If you ever hire Lama Ole, pay him well." "Of course," Barry had answered. Winking, Karmapa replied: "You couldn't pay what he's worth, anyway." I was totally satisfied, however. Ten dollars an hour was not bad for the fun of tearing down walls.

We worked on an old, giant mansion. It lay on 168th Street in Harlem, directly opposite the Presbyterian Hospital. The sledge hammer was well balanced and there was no reason to waste time. While walls fell and we emptied basements filled to the brim, I learned a lot about America's material culture over the last seventy years. In Europe, where we always recycled materials for war efforts, there is much less stuff. While Gregg, Stanley, and I worked like horses, Barry frequently came by in his red Cadillac. On the other side of the street a lot was going on. They must have been waging a gang war somewhere. Howling ambulances arrived every fifteen minutes and some of the wounded only had half their heads left.

Invitations from other parts of America were becoming more insistent, and it was time to move on. I chose a classic American way of traveling, the Greyhound. At that time, two weeks in a bus across the country cost one hundred dollars. One saw a lot and could get off wherever one wanted.

The first stop was Columbus, where the group was as focused as in Europe. After that, Chicago had all new faces. They had organized some really good events, however. As I learned when giving interviews, an amazing number of women there had problems with anger. In New York, the main disturbance was jealousy.

Vicki, who had invited us last, had moved to California, and our hosts from Oak Park only drove by. Since winter was rapidly approaching, it would be wise to do the northern part of the West Coast first.

The route went via Denver and Salt Lake City, which I didn't especially like. Its oversized public buildings seemed designed to make people feel small. On the way to Portland, now on a Trailways bus, we passed a car lying upside down in a ditch. I asked the driver to stop while I checked if anyone needed help, which was not the case. Turning to the bus again, it moved majestically away with all my luggage. Fortunately, a car picked me up right after, but at American speeds, it was many miles before we could overtake the bus and stop it. The driver looked like a ghost. After my co-travelers had also given him a piece of their minds, I felt sorry for him. I wondered how much suppressed anger a person must have to leave someone in shirt-sleeves in a freezing desert.

There was a special light over Antelope in Oregon. Here, Bhagwan Rajneesh later assembled his ninety-nine Rolls Royces. His thousands of followers gave enemies of Eastern spirituality a lot to attack. After the fascinating rain forests before Portland, Nancy Wangmo was waiting. She is a powerful woman and opened up the northern half of the West Coast to me. She was glad to have found a teacher she could deal with honestly. Cultural barriers had badly blocked her idealistic work for the Tibetans, and she was relieved that I didn't pretend to be a monk. At that time, it was already obvious that this was not easy in the West. The teachers whom Kalu Rinpoche insisted be celibate in order to retain their "lama" title had great difficulty keeping up their expected lifestyle. Outside their traditional communities, they were often very lonely. The frequently angry rumors were not caused by the question of celibacy, however, which is no big deal in the West, but by an inability to respect women. This had been evident from the arrival of the first Rinpoches in America. Except for Portland and Santa Fe, there were enraged ladies to calm nearly everywhere, and the higher the status of the non-monastic teacher, the worse were the stories in circulation. The Tarthang and Trungpa Tulkus were positively miles ahead of everyone else.

Nancy organized lectures in Portland and in Aberdeen, which reminded me strongly of Port Elizabeth in South Africa. A strong Finn was the main force here, while Seattle was led by lovely Ann Robben. For a while, it looked like the area would produce and not only consume Buddhism, but then the tendency to mix and intellectualize the teachings put an end to that.

The Canadian border officials' thirst for knowledge could barely be satisfied, but the beautiful countryside and the center outside Vancouver reconciled us to the country. During 1971, Kalu Rinpoche was here, and Karma Trinley Rinpoche had represented Karmapa for years. Whoever had the karma for traditional Diamond-way Buddhism was well served in Canada.

What always amazes me in America—both North and South—is how different people look, and how few young faces there are in the groups. Ninety percent of my European students could pass an army physical or do a fashion show, and they have no problem spending their nights celebrating and working hard the following day. Among those Americans who had not experienced the fresh winds of the sixties, spiritual interest was strikingly low.

In Vancouver, an invitation was waiting. Some people I knew from Woodstock had sent an expensive ticket to Whitehorse. It is a pioneer town near Alaska far in the north. We bought warm second-hand clothing, and after some fine shared weeks, Nancy drove south to Portland and her son.

The Yukon territory is breathtaking. Most fixed ideas are useless where permafrost and King Winter reign. On the way from the airport, I didn't stop asking questions. At first sight, everything appears amazingly well-organized. The trees, small pines, all have the same height and stand at equal distance from each other. They have not been planted by some perfectionistic super gardener, however, but grow naturally like that. It is the only way they can survive. Cars stand parked for hours with their engines running to avoid freezing, and if one tries to run somewhere, like I did a few times in the beginning, the cold air feels like flames in one's throat. The nights are beyond any description: the northern lights move like transparent flowing veils of ever changing color. It is impossible to take one's eyes off them no matter how cold it may be.

The people were like the land, rugged and individual. Many came to my lectures which astonished me—I was badly behind on P.R. Right next to my plain-looking posters hung the picture of a superbly dressed gentleman from New York. He advertized every spiritual experience from clairvoyance to healing and astrology, while I could only offer the possibility of gaining some insight into the workings of our mind.

The first few days, I stayed at my hosts' house. Together we cleaned the local supermarket at night. When my constant visitors became too much for them, I moved in with Francine where nothing was ever cramped. Monica from Austria let me teach from her beautiful house. Many people in the area came from Germany. This must have been the reason they so insisted on quality in the lectures, and I was happy to give all I had. Any movement across the vast landscapes took enormously long. One day, we drove to Carcross, a pass for some kind of reindeer, where I was to bless a planned retreat center. It was an old wooden tower from the gold-digging days. Everybody slid on the icy surfaces up the hill, and at the ridge the freezing wind was so strong that one could lean right into it without falling down. It was at least as cold as when we received the "Six Doctrines of Naropa" in Ladakh. On the way back, we stopped at some hot springs. It felt very Scandinavian to roll in the powdery snow and then jump into the warm water again.

In Vancouver, the teachings were at a house with a beautiful view of the harbor, and in Seattle I stayed with Ann. She had a nice basement apartment and, like so many of the yogi women in our centers, earned her living cleaning houses. She was super loyal and sweet, and showed me Seattle after my lectures. Nancy drove me back to Portland where I called people's attention to Lama Trinley Drukpa. He was truly worth supporting—a humble, kind and nonpolitical lama. He had flown with Kalu Rinpoche to America five years earlier, following our first drive through Europe. Down the coast on local buses, I visited several smaller groups. The chillums were seldom empty when I arrived, nor the joints cold, and people were mostly hair and beards. But they were honest. They trusted their basic nature and wanted to learn so they could benefit others. Compared to the smooth "Me" generation that was then just being hatched, they held oceans of depth.

Vicky from Chicago was now working on an Indian reservation in northern California. A day spent there was very instructional. It extinguished any residue of Indian romanticism I might still have harbored. During these months, I met several Indian tribes. From Alaska to southern Mexico, they were all a sad sight. Alcohol was the great destroyer, and as with the blacks, everything was the white man's fault. Only some years later, when meeting a number of their medicine men and women, did I get a glimpse of their former culture.

Since New York, I had stayed in contact with Barbara Pettee. During Karmapa's visit in Greece, we had become close friends. It was her wish that I concentrate my American activity on the West Coast. Many said that the cultural gap to Tibetan teachers was too big there, but I was changing my opinion on that. In the modern world it is not important what clothes people wear or what they eat. But teaching highly educated and independent men and women like they were Tibetan children will not work. Carol Aronoff, a highly qualified university professor who used to lead our Marin group, and now travels and teaches the Dharma, makes a point of telling this to all visiting Rinpoches. My own recipe for teaching is simple: do and say the same, so you avoid

Barbara Pettee on left

rumors. Tell people what you consider important yourself, and don't be afraid to let them share your joy. Never forget the main point: that mind is like space: open, clear, and limitless, and that all good qualities are only natural. Be clear on both way and goal. Allow time for questions and consider those asking your partners in the work. Only set limits when someone tries to be unpleasant, and refer those with heavy vibes to private interviews. Finishing with a meditation which gives the blessing of the lineage to everyone, the teaching will go deeply into their minds.

This style would now be tested on the most informed, spoiled and confused audience in the world: the spiritually interested people around San Francisco. Here gurus seldom manage to stay long. From there and down the coast to Mexico, there would be the added joy of working at places where many had already seen Karmapa.

First I stayed at Barbara's center, a beautiful house on a hill a half-hour southeast of San Francisco. It lay only a few minutes away from California's computer region, the so-called Silicon Valley.

Since even success in high tech takes time, I could at the most teach twice a week. Santa Cruz, however, was the Mecca of leisure. The city had been built in the thirties for retired Mafia members and was a beach paradise until the earthquake in '89. Soon I spent most of my time there, doing manuscripts and sharing countless joys in the carefree atmosphere of that time.

Happy days in Santa Cruz with Richard Krivcher

The center moved several times. A short while before I arrived, there had been enough interested people to start a very big place. But then they had a visit from one of Kalu Rinpoche's lamas whom I have mentioned earlier. In broken English, he told the hip audience a story from the Indian professor Asanga which few Westerners can stomach. The compassion of licking worms out of a dog's wounds was badly off the track in sunny surfing California! People left in disgust and never came back.

At the university there, a big event was planned. America's spiritual chieftains would meet in the largest hall. It was called "Psychology 2000" and totally changed my idea of spirituality. I was to represent both the European avant-garde and Tibetan Buddhism. Running up the stairs to the hall, a little late as usual, I first thought I had entered a farmers' convention. All the books exhibited dealt with plants. Then I saw what kinds of plants: there was everything about the better growing of pot, mescaline, and psilocybin. Maybe I was at the right place, after all. These were the carriers of spirituality in the sixties. There was lots of celebrity. Some were only outrageous, but others had high ideals. Stanislav Grof only quoted statistics. There had just been a major spiritual scandal near San Diego and he seemed concerned about not being accepted scientifically. Most interesting of all was the LSD "pope," Timothy Leary. Slim, white-haired, and dressed in white, he entertained the audience for two hours with an unbroken stream of jokes. Not once did he repeat himself. The clarity of his mind was amazing, but I didn't see much compassion. If you were untalented, black, awkward, or poorly educated, that was your bad luck. His constant point of reference was the brain, and anything romantic was ridiculed. The bumper on his car carried the message: "Intelligence is the best aphrodisiac!"

The hall was filled with about two thousand listeners. They were mostly well-known psychologists who made out big bills to their patients every day. So I decided to give them something useful for the expensive time they spent and aimed directly at their taboos. I gave one of my introductory lectures with special stress on the points which everyone else had thoroughly left out: the necessity of finding values which can carry one through sickness, aging, and death. The audience froze while I spoke, and there were no "clever" questions afterwards. At the party the same night, however, dozens came to thank me. "This was the only lecture with depth," they said, and I answered that I had enjoyed seeing their faces grow longer while I spoke. Then I advised them to read Milarepa and other Buddhist literature. There were several of those present who write thick books, and maybe in this way I helped bring about the next psychological movement in America: the focus on death and dying. On this occasion, many must have understood that death is not an inexplicable black hole.

A Mexican friend in Santa Cruz gave me a demonstration of "white magic." She had spent four years in prison for smuggling hash. From behind her door, she had overheard American policemen teaching their Mexican colleagues ways to interrogate. One popular method is to hold people's heads under water until they nearly drown and keep repeating the process. It is said to be very beneficial to both memory and cooperation. Tough as she was, she had shaken off these experiences, and now she lived near the local center. When out of Santa Cruz, I was amazed how often she appeared in my mind. When I told her this, she smiled, opened a little box and showed me a knot of her hair and mine. "This we learn at home," she said.

Oakland and Berkeley also had small centers, though most disliked going to Oakland. Not receiving much support outside of my rare visits, unfortunately these brave attempts folded after some years.

From San Francisco I flew to Mexico City, invited by Cesar and inspiring Yoshiko from Japan. He had been secretary in the Mexican embassy in Athens when we started the center there. I had given Refuge to both, and they had seen Tenga Rinpoche in the Danish Retreat Center. Now, they wanted to bring Buddha's teachings to Mexico. They were touching. After a night drive through town, we entered his family's patrician home, a u-shaped classical building in the city's center. All had stayed up, and I sensed a bond between them like in my own family.

That night I was visited by both humans and gods, and next morning, at the sun and moon temples of the Aztecs, I already knew them. Cesar was a perfect guide. He showed Yoshiko and me the legendary sites. Very famous was the stone where captives' hearts, still beating, were cut out with a stone knife and offered to the sun. At a different place, they were said to have played a kind of basketball, often with a former team's heads. On the one hand, they had calculated the movements of most planets until sometime in 1988, and on the other, they were said to have killed thousands during their rituals. Like other cultures with little compassion, they had not lasted long.

Cesar translated my teachings very well. A really wealthy American family there supported the Gelugpa lineage, but most people were the same as everywhere. They wanted to discuss everything, but wouldn't do anything consistently. When everything possible had been done, we raced a well-balanced VW Rabbit down the picturesque stretch to Vera Cruz on the eastern Mexican coast. It takes time to get out of Mexico City. Its altitude is 2,4 kilometers and with over twenty million inhabitants, it is the largest city in the world. Its heavy exhaust fumes being enhanced by human waste and cement dust, this was air you could both taste and feel.

In the beginning it was not easy to concentrate on the traffic. Never before had I seen such a sky—such clouds and colors. Soon the mountains became just as exciting and we had a fantastic journey. Fortunately, my three companions were fearless and there were no police. Behind Puebla where the highway ended, it was great to do four-wheel skids through the curves in a car which held the road so well. I don't think many reach the Gulf of Mexico faster than we did. The city's fort was alive with energy. It dated from Cortez' days and seemed fully preserved. In the clear light, it looked like history one could step directly into.

We spent the first hours of the night in a disco. Discovering the skyline of New York painted on a wall, much to my surprise, my eyes turned wet. I thought of Wendy and so many friends, and wished them the happiness which is so difficult to find there.

The next day, we saw some recently discovered Mayan sites. They were accessible only by plane, being in the depths of the jungle. If the Aztecs were cruel, the Mayans were bizarre. They are proof of the proverb, "Whom the gods want to destroy, they first make crazy." For centuries, they had lived in southwestern Mexico. Probably most of the damage they did here was to their own genetics through constant inbreeding. In the end, the old Nubians and Persians, who had similar customs, must have looked quite normal compared to them. Pictures in their temples show people of very irregular shapes. Then one day, they suddenly left their area. Turning cannibal, they went east to the Yucatan peninsula,

With Caesar and Yoshiko in Palenque

arriving just in time to be massacred by the Spaniards. It was a trip to walk through their ruins and feel what they may have been up to. The only building one can enter, a royal tomb, felt very strange. Like most civilizations this culture had been a dead end for human development, and I am sure I never lived there. Some people, however, like beautiful Adriana of Bogotá, are sure they were sacrificed at the place. Whoever wants to fathom the range of associations open to the Mayans, need only eat some of the slim, tan mushrooms growing on the mountainsides. They are very popular with hippies. Containing active psilocybin, they bring effects very similar to LSD.

At the border to Guatemala, my passport fell out of a pocket. Here Cesar had to fly back to Mexico City. On our way north, Yoshiko and I visited some Indians in their village. Again it was all very interesting, but hit no living nerve in me, which Eastern Tibetan and Nordic cultures always do. These were different karmic circuits, different people.

Our next trip was to Acapulco on the western Mexican coast. The pot grown here had inspired American youth in the sixties. A teacher family, idealists working among the poorest of Indians, took Refuge. Driving to Mexico City a few nights later, we did not need our lights. Constant lightning lit the winding mountain road, while we slid along on a thick carpet of rain.

An American in Guadalajara had invited us. We found this second largest Mexican town both warm and pleasant. Again, the mere driving was a pleasure. This time we had an eight-cylinder American car. It was uncastrated by automatic gears, soft springs, sloppy steering, or a cata-lyzer. I had no idea they built things as precise and powerful as that, and we did some fine speeds. Cesar pointed out the special views; they had exciting old cities in this part of the country. Many people came and we slept in an historic flat. Here Maharishi, the founder of "Transcendental Meditation" had made his "Worldplan." Holding his original notes in my hands, I wished that my work be highly effective without losing the timeless depth of what Buddha gave.

Mexico is a culture all to itself and unforgettable. Leaving the plane in Los Angeles meant entering the whole world. Not the mild and humanistic atmosphere of San Francisco, however. This vast city was clear, one-dimensional, and strong-willed.

I came at the right time. Karmapa's bird keeper, Joel, a devoted fan of Hannah's, had died in his car some days before. This is something which usually doesn't happen in the closer family. Naturally, at the outset of their practice, friends and students still have some accidents. If one has yet to purify some dead Chinese soldiers or stolen horses from one's last life, one may occasionally smash one's vehicle, but after Refuge there is rarely bodily harm. In Joel's case, however, there had been special conditions. Karmapa had told him seven things he absolutely had to do: stop working in a bar north of Los Angeles; stop driving drunk; make a puja to Liberatrice every day; visit Karmapa in India, and some other things I have since forgotten. He did none of it, and one fine morning he wrapped his car around a palm tree on the coastal road. Rumtek already knew. A Tibetan lama had been there, and I was happy to also send some good wishes after Joel. Everybody liked him, but like most people, he had taken himself much too seriously.

Barbara Pettee flew down to introduce me to her contacts in L.A. The first lectures were to a group of wealthy people there. Unfortunately, most had only a passing interest in their minds and the leaders moved to Seattle shortly after. It was the old problem of society people wanting to be important but not cooperating. Working with young idealists had more meaning. As friendships deepened, so did the benefit from the teachings.

Some hours west of the shining city, the spirit of the sixties was still vibrant. The snowy mountains there held some dope-smoking but motivated people. They wanted to learn something real and even hoped to invite Karmapa. Here I met Robin, already with a number of fine offspring. Whenever she wanted to leave, her car broke down. As so often in America, the group's members soon scattered, but today several live near the centers I visit.

Robin moved to Fallbrook later. It is the world's avocado capital, inland between Los Angeles and San Diego. She opened it for the lineage, and the weeks I spent there on my yearly visits are the closest I have come to a normal family life. This area housed some interesting individualists of kinds seldom found in Europe. In former lifetimes, they must have been my tribe's traders, while the more group-oriented Europeans were my soldiers. Fine yogis and wisdom-holding women were everywhere.

One day Barbara and I drove to Perris, an area southeast of L.A. in the California desert. Here a sponsor had offered Karmapa a deserted farm for retreats. We wanted to have a look first. The previous gift had been a mountain top further north where everything needed to be brought in by helicopter. The owner of the mountain's base was difficult and shot at people. Now we wanted to see what was possible here. Lovely Marina took care of the place. Today, she supports our centers on Hawaii. Nothing has happened with the retreat place up until now. We still don't have enough people in that area.

Santa Barbara, the first stop north, had a mature group. It was led by Janice Chase and consisted mainly of retired people. Over the years it became a second home to us, no matter how large the hordes travelling with me. Most there were well educated and had time. The social pressure was less, or they simply didn't care. Our task here was making them one-pointed and getting them interested in a practice, not just in words. This last point was not so easy. They were strongly influenced by Krishnamurti's main center in Ojai, not far away. For years, he had talked about "the Absolute" in the most beautiful words, but without giving methods for experiencing it. So I had to convince them that it was not enough to see the goal, that one mainly has to reach it. It was a difficult message to digest and I had to repeat it; hopefully, I did so with enough humor.

Back in New York, I stayed with Wendy for some days. It was not easy to find a publisher for the first copy of *Entering the Diamond Way*. Then came an invitation to Canada. Cynthia from Toronto, a close friend from our second pilgrimage, had organized things brilliantly. Up until now, I have not again had three live TV broadcasts on a single day. Visits to the surrounding towns were also very beneficial. Several people who today support the two local lamas, took Refuge then.

In a high security prison, it was interesting to teach pacifying meditation to a group of mainly murderers. My last impression of North America was in an antique shop which Jytte Marstrand ran in Toronto. Here I saw with a shudder how much money rich people spend and on what.

It was wonderful to see Hannah, Central Europe, and so many fine friends again. The time had been well spent. In three and a half months, I had opened an exciting new world to our lineage. From Guatemala to Alaska, people now meditated on Karmapa. With close friends in many places, the stage was set for big developments.

During 1979, and especially the second half of the year, Tenga Rinpoche blessed Europe. He traveled through Scandinavia and Germany and then again stayed in Copenhagen for some months. Many people became his students then and he truly supported our activity and friends. Among the many Rinpoches we had the honor of introducing to Europe, our bond to him became especially close. One simply could not get enough of him.

This autumn also saw our first serious split. Up to this time, work had been without borders, a real source of strength. People felt united, and wounds from centuries of wars and divided homes were healed. This

state of affairs could be upheld as long as no one carved out private
territories from Karmapa's cake. Naturally, there were always differences:
some groups listened more to one teacher and some to another. We all
studiously avoided asking Kalu Rinpoche's groups who their ultimate
authority was, while they went out of their way to praise and invite
Karmapa. Really all had done a good job of damage-control, papering
over difficulties, pacifying impossible people, and generally keeping the
lid on.

Now, on an otherwise beautiful morning, this united front crum-
bled. It was going to cost many good feelings and some of our most
idealistic people, though not the ones who had fully received Karmapa's
blessing. Sweet Bernadette's letters from Port Elisabeth contained a copy
of the South African Trust. The decisions taken during or after Akong
Tulku's visit there—I hope after—were pure block-politics. They were

*Tenga Rinpoche
in Copenhagen*

far from Karmapa's wish that all work together under Rumtek and himself.

From then on, Europe crystallized into three zones of influence. Akong Tulku now controls England-Scotland-Brussels with Barcelona, leaning heavily on the Situ and Thrangu Rinpoches. Kalu Rinpoche has France (except the Dordogne and its branch centers), Antwerp, and Madrid. Hannah's and my region is from the Rhine to Vladivostok. Karmapa's nephew, Lama Jigmela and I represent Rumtek there. We involve the other three lineage-holders, Tenga Rinpoche, and other Rumtek lamas as much as we can. For us, who work with the most powerful and unspoiled people, it was a real gift. But since Karmapa was against partitioning, we struggled on for some time to keep things together. Apart from Spain, however, the structures have remained, and on a deep level Akong Tulku was right: it is only natural that Germanics, Slavs, Romans, and Celts each find their own approach to something as many-sided as the Diamond Way; that Rationalists, Logicians, and Empiricists think and organize themselves differently. Our common mistake was not meeting somewhere to structure the new "order." As friends sharing so much blessing and responsibility, we would surely have done so if it hadn't been such a "touchy" topic. Instead, things were left to the students to decide, to seek out the teacher most clearly expressing whichever aspect of Karmapa they wanted to identify with. Thus, winter and spring of 1980 slowed the pattern of growth. For the first time, we had to protect our work against influences from within the lineage.

CHAPTER ELEVEN

Taking Leave of Karmapa

*I*N MAY 1980, KARMAPA STOPPED IN LONDON FOR A DAY. He was on his way to America. It was his first longer journey after an operation for stomach cancer. Most who welcomed him had travelled over from Central Europe, and all were deeply touched by his blessing. Driving into town, I joked, "When Karmapa is here, there must be a rainbow." Turning the next corner, there it was. Wide and radiant, it arched across the street right in the heart of London.

Karmapa stayed with Joe, a big and strong American who was lots of fun. We knew him from earlier visits. Of the whole group there, he took Karmapa's wishes most seriously. He had done what he could to activate the lazy English. His latest suggestion for a London center had been buying a deserted police station, but again nothing happened. It was wonderful to be with Karmapa. As always in his energy field, things automatically perfected themselves for whoever held their bonds.

The monks and nuns of Kalu Rinpoche's first three-year retreat had just come out. Curious, I looked for signs of remarkable personality changes, power of blessing, or something like that—after all, I had known them well before they went in. I saw exemplary humility, good education and cooperation, but not the raw power that breaks down people's egos. I missed the "roaring lions" that can protect people and give them the deepest trust.

Upstairs in the stately house, the Tibetans discussed Karmapa's next visit to Great Britain. Just as Joe and I enjoyed a good bout of arm wrestling, Lama Chime came downstairs. He was crying. "Akong Tulku got one whole month," he said, "and once again I only get him for a few days." Since Chime Rinpoche always made a point of promising to protect Karmapa's activity and not starting his own organization, I decided he deserved to meet our central Europeans. For the friends who hold Karmapa's centers there, this moment of compassion brought heaps of trouble later. Misunderstanding the invitation for some "divine right," he quickly became the focal point for dissatisfied people during their phases of purification. What was worse: he tried to introduce different ways of practice into existing centers and told people already engaged in work for Karmapa to make "study" groups under himself. With the power

Black Coat,
main protector of
our lineage

of his title behind it, the result was endless discussions at first. But then people learned to trust their own eyes, the very goal of our work. None of this made Chime Tulku a bad person, of course, but it made cooperation impossible.

Our friends basked in Karmapa's presence and blessing. They would have travelled any distance for that. After a Crown Ceremony he gave on the idyllic banks of the Thames River, he clearly enjoyed a boat trip with us all. Sitting next to him in the airport the next day, my body was in that state of controlled shaking which was its usual reaction to his presence. Looking at me very seriously, he pointed and said to the others: "This is Bearer of the Black Coat." Of course. That was it! Suddenly everything fit. Now I understood which power works through me.

In May, we went to see Karmapa in America, also bringing my dear mother. From New York, we drove to Woodstock where we stayed with friends. Karmapa lived in a beautiful house in the woods, accompanied by Jamgon Rinpoche, Ponlop Rinpoche, and the colorful former Secretary of Rumtek. We could of course visit Karmapa whenever we wanted, but

*With my mother
in America*

In Woodstock

the security net around him was tight. Whenever we brought some friends—even for a short blessing—there was quite a fuss.

Karmapa's visit to the West Coast hadn't been organized yet, so I thought: "Better be useful elsewhere than disturb people here." Telling Karmapa this, however, to our amazement he did not look glad. Taking us by the hand, he led us through the house to a balcony surrounded by a light wire mesh. Here, we could be completely alone. We must promise to meet him in Boulder, he said. This was very important. Then he told us his wishes, as he had done since we became his students in 1969. Following these meticulously is surely the reason that all things go so well. His parting gift was a direct experience of his mind. Looking into his eyes, time stood still. And when we left him, we had no idea where we were. We knew, however, that we would now be certain what to do and when.

After a last Crown Ceremony, an explosion of power and radiance, we drove a Nash Rambler to California. The car had terrible economy— one could hardly fill it while the engine was running. It looked like an aquarium and was approximately as fast.

In Pennsylvania, the power of Karmapa's relics manifested. A bird, either too young or accustomed to the local speeds, got hit. Picking it up from the road, it looked bad. Its neck was broken and there was only bone on one side; muscles and tendons were all gone. I put my round box on its head, the one which transfers Karmapa's blessing to thousands every year. While I built up the pure realm of highest bliss above it, the bird's body stiffened and its head moved up. This was unexplainable by any science we knew about. Only an inner energy could bring about an alignment like that, a muscular cramp would invariably pull the head to the side where the muscles were. Putting it in the grass, small, stiff, and straight, I promised myself never to be lazy in giving blessings— Karmapa's power is simply too valuable for that.

Stopping at the Mesa Verde ruins on the way was instructive. It became clear that noble savages had not been roaming America before

Time stood still

Mesa Verde in New Mexico

Columbus arrived. We alternated between awe and compassion as we fathomed what their lives must have been. Though the beauty of nature was incredible, already around the year 1250, tribes had been scalping one another. Their skeletons show diseases we can hardly imagine today.

I was to teach in Colorado, at the headquarters of the Dharmadhatu organization. But one or two hours before, when we were already in Denver, they canceled the program with no official explanation. Instead, we drove to a giant ranch near Crestone. It had been given to Karmapa by Hanne Marstrand's husband, Maurice Strong. They wanted me to help create a good relationship with the local people, to show in clear language how Buddhism is meaningful to our life and not some exotic sect. Arriving at the Grand Canyon at sunset, the deep river valley was about the most fantastic we had ever seen. The shapes of the rocks, their age and overwhelming colors impressed us deeper than the ever-grey Himalayas.

In Los Angeles, the lama had just fled Kalu Rinpoche's Pasadena center. Coming from the mountain air of Sikkim to the most polluted part of the area, he had thought he would die. Today, he guides the center in Santa Fe with one of the largest Stupas in the Western world. On my drives across the U.S., I nearly always stop there to teach. He is a fine friend and it is a relief to be able to recommend him without the slightest hesitation.

North of town, it had rained for seven days without stop. All went okay during the first six days, but then the earth slid. Many houses were only half, and the driver of a Greyhound just saved himself a trip to the ocean by jumping into a tree. Then the big bus was swept away and had not yet been found.

Some film-making friends were doing well. I had spent a powerful time in their circles the year before. It had then been an atmosphere of liquid protein, powder for the nose—though not for mine—and immensely open personal contacts. This time, we cleared some hours for a trip to Disneyland. Americans are great entertainers, and the moving holograms especially caught me. They are "form and emptiness," the way Buddhas should be seen in meditation.

In San Luis Obispo, some hours north, we had relatives. They had enjoyed my parents' visit some years before, and wanted to hear about

With the Americans

others who had stayed in Europe. Most of all, they asked about Uncle
Edward, whose name I hadn't heard. "You must know him," they said,
"he was a famous pirate." Gradually I understood: our sorely tried parents
had told my brother Bjørn and me so much about the well-behaved part
of our ancestry that we—ingrained troublemakers always—had begun
to wonder whether we had been switched in the hospital at birth. Now
things fit better. Not all genes in our family were those of angels!

San Francisco would have continuous programs when Karmapa
came, though often set up by the oddest people. In Santa Cruz, my friends
were supposed to work together with Trungpa Tulku's disciples. We had
the people, they the house, and Karmapa wanted the contact. It was no
success. For them, organization was a goal in itself, something fundamen-
tally good. To us it is something limiting, the function of which is only
to facilitate new levels of spontaneity, a commodity to be kept to a
minimum. Satisfied with the arrangements from South to North, we took
the Greyhound back east to Colorado, where Karmapa was just about to
arrive. We would meet him on summer solstice.

Dharmadhatu's headquarters in Boulder were deserted. People only
knew that everyone had gone to a celebration some miles outside the city.

We hitchhiked, were quickly picked up, and the driver dropped us
off at a large meadow with some strange goings-on. Attendants walked

Dharmadhatu headquarters

around in English khaki with short pants, and Trungpa Tulku was dressed in a beige uniform, a cap and black riding boots. He looked like a general from some warm country. Karmapa, Jamgon Kongtrul Rinpoche, and several monks had fallen gently asleep on the podium. Hardly anyone watched the presentation. It was something Japanese with drawn-out vowels, sudden dramatic gestures, and very strange mimics. The guests stood around, chatting in groups. We met friends from several parts of the world, but felt none of the usual centeredness and devotion. It seemed like many didn't know what a Karmapa is.

Back at the main house, Karmapa called us. The organizers were not too pleased with this. We passed a dozen guards standing stiffly wherever it was possible to put them. As we entered his room, Karmapa immediately began to speak. There were some things he very much wanted to say. First, he told us about his four "children," the lineage-holders. They had now grown up and were ready to leave the nest to carry out his activity. He said we must promise to protect them and help them in every way. Listening to his words, for the first time I sensed that something was deeply wrong, and blurted out: "But this doesn't mean that you should stop your work!" While he told us which people we'd be better off avoiding, tears flowed from his left eye. It had started that morning and a doctor came to look at it. Then Karmapa left the room for a moment and came in again. It was clear that he didn't want us to go. When there was really nothing left to say, we asked, as always, when to visit him again. He said: "Come to New York if you can or otherwise, . . ." And here he looked at us in a way we had never seen before—as if he knew that we would be very sad. ". . . You should come to Rumtek next year, on the first day of the eleventh month." Reading my mind, which was already creating the picture of a third pilgrimage, he added: "And you can bring your friends." Hannah made sure that the date was according to the Western calendar, not the Tibetan, while I—suddenly deeply troubled—jumped to my feet and said, "You have to promise that you'll be all right then." Looking out the window to his left, he answered: "Everything will be for the best. I promise you that." Halfway down the stairs, with our heads already full of plans, he called us back. "It would be beneficial for the future if you could meet Trungpa Tulku in my presence." Since Trungpa Tulku was supposed to be back by six p.m., we

Taking leave of Karmapa

promised to wait for him. When he had still not appeared by eight, we left. It was time to catch the bus.

It was good to be just Hannah and me for a change, and on the ride to New York, we nearly exploded with ideas. There we bought clothes for friends, which had become quite a tradition in the lineage. Karmapa had started it. The funniest was when he gave Hannah Tibetan dresses, which were always too short, or fitted me out in karate shirts.

In Central and Eastern Europe, things grew quickly. Since my students became anything but impotent or boring, now also their friends came. The perfectly liberating view made it all possible: that the true nature of mind is fearlessness, spontaneous joy, and active love. It gives immense confidence and richness to people's lives. Wherever a group talked well about their teachers, the number of interested people grew from one lecture to the next. If I were to list the many women and men who do excellent work there, the next chapters would look like a telephone directory. Instead, I suggest you visit our centers and meet them yourselves. They all speak English and have a lot to give.

On my next tour to America, in the winter of 1981, the basis had broadened. Again I worked for Barry and taught in the New York centers, also upstate. I spoke on the radio with Lex and stayed in Toronto with Cynthia, for another good program. On the TV tower there—at that time the highest building in the world—something very unusual happened. In this giant concrete needle, pregnant with a bulge of chrome and glass near the top, I found a "modern" Terma, a "treasure" carrying a Buddhist energy. While my logical mind watched in growing amazement, I tore out paper from between a cabinet and the glass wall of the rotating sphere. Usually, I keep my hands far away from smelly objects like food. Giving many blessings, that is the least one can do, and here they could easily have ended up holding a smeared hot dog paper or something similarly unappetizing. Continuing to dig, however, suddenly there was a triangular plastic dagger with a round shaft. It had the form of a Phurba, one of the ancient protectors of Tibet. In March 1989, as I wrote this passage in German in our Spanish retreat center, my brother Bjørn brought a copper Phurba into the room, and writing this English version in Italy in April 1991, my friend Adrian spontaneously asked who "Diamond Dagger" was, the translation of this protector's name. Who said that Buddhas are something abstract, somewhere else?

After some lectures upstate, Hecate showed me decadent New York, the better part of the East Side. Here the "old money" lives and everyone has a psychiatrist. Next came the opposite extreme. On the Greyhound across country I saw more poor people than ever before. There were no Swedish or Danish conditions here. People did not have to hide from their social worker or psychologist if they wanted to be down and out. Reagan's time was yet to come. The mentally ill were not yet designated healthy in the name of individual freedom and a better budget, but already then there were many. Most were black, and they seemed to live in and around the bus stations. Some outer influence on their lives would not have hurt. Not many had a weekly bath. The long stretches were great for manuscripts and writing, as also today, but then it was possible to do more of the latter. Though slow and not very readable, my letters at that time both held the personal contacts and conveyed information. This is what my great organizers, Sys and Tomek, today manage perfectly with telephone and fax.

The Southern Californians were again wonderful. First, Robin from Fallbrook whisked me away. Afterwards Yoshiko arrived from Mexico, and then many new contacts were built up. In San Francisco, one could most clearly feel how deeply Karmapa had touched people. Although

With my ministers for the interior—Sys—and the exterior—Tomek

most had experienced him as seriously ill, which usually embarrasses Americans, it had moved them profoundly that he worked for them anyway, that he gave them his very best. It had awakened real confidence in many. They had seen a true Bodhisattva at work.

Looking back, it was amazing that Hannah and I were not more disturbed by his physical condition. I think three reasons came together for this. First, my Viking mind has difficulty seeing people I respect as weak. Secondly, our connection is on the timeless levels of joy and truth. After all, I saw him as an ocean of golden light during every Crown Ceremony. The third reason was that a Karmapa always shows people what helps them most. To people who can see his radiant joy-nature, he manifests that; if they cannot, he uses other methods to create a karmic connection.

These bonds grow during future lifetimes until he has brought beings to a direct experience of their mind. If people could best make the connection through compassion, from knowing pain and suffering themselves, that was what they saw. Even when people came in with a half-dozen cameras, he had skillful ways. He played with their equipment until they relaxed for a moment. Then he gave them 100,000 volts of real blessing and they left in an altered state.

What disturbed me greatly in America was the lack of consistent growth. This had several causes. Wanting to make people independent, we were hesitant to "commit" them to anything, promise results, or make them cogs in an organization. It just doesn't fit Kagyu yogis. For this reason, it was easy for Tibetan teachers of other lineages to fish in Karmapa's waters and build up their own groups in his wake. This was especially easy

. . . till for a moment they relaxed

when they claimed to be close members of his family. For Westerners dreaming of an ideal world, this was enough to bypass the usual mechanisms of discrimination. They happily signed up for whatever was offered, forgetting the source of their original blessing.

When Californians changed to more streamlined schools, this was of course okay. When they stopped practicing, however, which is sad, we have to examine our part in that. There is no doubt that the traditional lamas sent were too narrow and hierarchical in their thinking. They lacked trust in Westerners, actually their benefactors. Being insecure about our skills, they did not welcome the lamas and gain from what was offered. There was too little respect for the maturity a rounded life brings, and no attempt to make the highest ideals more accessible. Though Karmapa often said that a half-good teacher was better than none, and that one would learn while teaching as long as one kept the bond to him: the sacred cow which blocks the acceptance of many a gifted teacher, even today, was Kalu Rinpoche's insistence on a three-year group retreat with strict celibacy. This rarely attracts the people we need: strong and outgoing types who can inspire others with their joy. If this retreat had been offered as one possibility among other retreats and naturally having something to offer, things could have been much easier. Then cooperation would have been possible between charismatic lay teachers and those with the traditional education, benefiting all.

In the spring of 1981, the senior lineage-holder, Kunzig Shamarpa, made his first visit to Europe. Karmapa had sent him as his representative. He gave his first teachings at "Samye Ling" and quickly increased his knowledge of English. Then Hannah organized the rest of his travels. Having no fear of speaking his mind, he frequently forced people to check their convictions. In Copenhagen, our friends had to learn about politics and the press. A sour intellectual newspaper had published an interview which made angry communists and homosexuals disturb his lecture. I heard it was quite an unusual experience for him. The rest of his tour through Europe went very well.

During 1981, Karmapa wrote us more often than ever before, but other news from the East did not make much sense. Suddenly, the rumor spread that he was seriously ill, that only his promise to work for all beings kept him going. Then, others had been present at non-stop initiations

Kunzig Shamarpa

for several days and said that he looked fantastic. We didn't worry too much about this. He knew what he was doing and had given the exact date for our next meeting over a year ago. Every day brought us closer to seeing him again. Niels sent invitations through Europe, and on the first of October, we flew off with 108 friends.

India lived up to every expectation and in Tsok Pema, most had the runs. The rock caves in the mountains were very inspiring and again the reed islands moved toward us. The blessing was strong and we were glad to contribute to the good vibrations: we cut the leads to the loudspeakers which sent Hindu noise across the otherwise silent and holy lake. I

Sarnath, Buddha taught Theravada here

seriously wondered when the Buddhists of the East would develop
enough courage to do things like that themselves. A few days in Tourist
Camp—the best location in Delhi—allowed people to recover. Here, we
heard that Karmapa was in a Hong Kong hospital but had joked and
appeared healthy and strong when leaving Rumtek. Taj Mahal in moonlight was a specialty of Niels, our tour guide. Then we saw Sarnath, where
Buddha taught the Four Noble Truths; Rajgir, where he activated his
students' compassion and wisdom; and the ruins of Nalanda, the largest
Buddhist university. As the guards would not open the gates when we
came, we became the first to storm the site for a thousand years.

Reaching Bodhgaya on full moon, it was just the time to practice
Phowa under the tree of Buddha's enlightenment. They now had a fence
around the Stupa, which we climbed. Enlightenment had apparently
turned bureaucratic in the meantime, however. As we were already half
in the Pure Realms, a monk from some southern school came running
and wanted to see our permission for sitting there. He was very insistent
and called other monks, so we stopped earlier than planned. Though I
was not surprised at such behavior from those "holy by profession," Niels
stayed angry for a long time.

Stupa of Rajgir, Buddha taught Mahayana here

Part of Nalanda University

The tree of enlightenment

The next day, the good folk of Bodhgaya watched an unusual event. We dug the water canal to Beru Khyentse Rinpoche's new monastery. In four to five hours our European friends did the work which would have taken the same number of Indians a similar amount of days or weeks, depending on the strictness of the supervision. Most of all, the pick axes were fun. They were nearly as heavy as back home and had nice long handles. Our women quickly got into their role in the warm countries and carried away the earth.

In the middle of a swing, my sandal suddenly broke, something in my back hurt, and Hannah came out of Khyentse Rinpoche's tent, crying. She said that Karmapa would surely die. I don't think anybody's eyes were dry, and though our students were young and didn't own much, they spontaneously collected money for Hannah and me to go to Hong Kong. While still deliberating if we could accept this, the next message came: Karmapa had been flown on to America.

He was now in a hospital somewhere. It was obvious that we should not follow him. Hannah still has moments of regretting that we did not see him again, but I know why: it would have harmed my work. The Karmapa I remember and transmit today is the golden Buddha of limitless power. This is more useful than the image of an ill saint.

The eastern Himalayan foothills were our next stop. We waited at Lhawang's Bellevue Hotel for the Sikkim visas which had been promised so dearly at Home Office in Delhi. After years of obstruction, we had simply walked our whole group into their cramped offices. Once again, they were either unwilling or unable to do anything, but we had the right means for dealing with that: everyone had brought a bottle of duty-free spirits from the plane. After we had kept the Darjeeling officials in an elevated state for a week, they issued what they had absolutely no permission to give: visas for Sikkim.

During this time, the Dalai Lama came down from the hills. He had blessed people in Rumtek and elsewhere. Asking him to charge my mala during the interview, he said, "This one's smaller than the one I blessed in Copenhagen in 1973." What awareness! He must have held thousands of malas since then. Deeply impressed, I answered, "The big one is with my mother and looks after her." The next day, he spoke to our group in a Darjeeling garden. This time, everyone had dressed up as best they could.

In the middle of a stroke

We arrived in Rumtek on November first, 1981, the very day Karmapa had wished. Many pujas were going on, mostly in the upper temple. They had placed a life-size statue there, dressed in his robes. It stood with its hands at heart-level in front of the relics of the lineage. One open palm had a yellow, the other a green disk, apparently to collect and transfer energy. Everyone behaved as normally as possible. People

With the Dalai Lama in Darjeeling

tried to avoid anything which could be interpreted as a bad sign, but then these came up in dreams instead. Hannah received a telephone call from the Dakinis, her sisters. From very far away, they told her that Karmapa had finished his work in this life. The same night, I received the attributes of a world monarch. I have described the dream in detail in the "Mandala" chapter of my book, *Ngondro,* about the preliminary Tibetan Buddhist practices.

While attending a Crown Ceremony given by Gyaltsab Rinpoche the next morning, young Ponlop Rinpoche entered and whispered something in his ear. In one moment the feeling in the room totally changed, and we all knew what had happened. Shortly afterwards, an uneven gang of young monks tried to carry Karmapa's statue down the road on its wooden platform. Finally, here was something for strong Europeans to do. Holding it high on our shoulders, we walked the eleven kilometers down to the river. This was the most direct way we could express our love and thanks to him.

Walking across the bridge, some energy left the statue. The face began to crack, fingers broke off, and I would have dropped it into the water, then and there. Now, only an empty form was left. The Tibetans thought differently, however, so we passed it on to them. Afterwards, we learned that they had had problems with both Indians and truck. They had been forced to throw the statue into the stream some miles further down, anyway.

Returning, the monastery was awakening, but in a different way than one might have imagined. Instead of cries and laments, there were invocations—pujas—with loud instruments everywhere. The job now was to call Karmapa back from his timeless state of clear light. By awakening the enlightened power circles, which are the joy-nature of his mind, one would bring about his re-birth for the benefit of all beings. They were at it day and night, often with a group in each of the four directions and one in the middle.

On November 9, a helicopter landed at the military airport on the other side of the large Sikkim valley. Then one saw a line of cars leaving, and about an hour later he arrived on a Mercedes truck. All four lineage

Rumtek, looking toward Tibet

Showing the Red Crown

holders sat next to the driver on its narrow front seat, and big Erik from Schwarzenberg and some other strong men were in back. They had lifted the coffin onto the truck's platform. Apparently, Karmapa had only invited Hannah and me for his death. Outside our group there were no Westerners in Rumtek. Being his first Western disciples, I was asked to help carry his coffin into the monastery.

We had to halt in the yard for several minutes. Some hundred soldiers, not in the best of style, wanted to blow trumpets and shoot their rifles into the air. Having carried the coffin into the building, we put it down in the main temple. Only then did the pieces come together. It became possible to reconstruct his last days, step-by-step and from different sources. They were indeed worthy of a Buddha.

As death approached, he had taken a half-dozen deadly diseases upon himself. Using his yogic powers, he had removed much of their harmfulness, at least for those in his powerfield. Near Chicago, home to the largest slaughter houses in the world, he had shown a timeless example. He had also allowed the physicians to test their medicines on him. Among their findings were several amazing ones: even the highest doses of sedatives had absolutely no effect. During all that happened, his interest was completely with others. He cared for their well-being and never talked about himself.

On the way to the river

On the evening of November 5, 1981, the day of Liberatrice, the doctors had routinely entered his room. Seeing that his machines had apparently turned themselves off, all had the same thought, "He's playing a joke on us." At that very moment, they started up again, worked for five minutes and then stopped completely. The next morning, when the staff wanted to remove his body from the bed, the lineage holders asked if all signs of death were present. They were not. Karmapa's body was still warm and supple, and especially his heart center was so hot that one could feel it at a good distance. This is how he stayed. On this morning in Sikkim, he was still warm and without any signs of death-stiffness. I found this out when taking my leave of him. I did this by laying my head against his leg.

Karmapa's body was put into a concentric structure—a mandala—in the hall upstairs. In this way, all could meditate in his presence. He was surrounded by butter lamps, pujas were done around the clock, and people came and went. Since nothing special was planned for the next weeks, and our visas had run out, we took the group to Nepal.

Karmapa's body arrives

Carrying Karmapa's body into the yard

Here, we wanted to receive the blessing of Lopon Chechoo, our first lama from 1968, and Ayang Tulku would be kind enough to give a phowa course.

Before the cremation, which took place one and a half months later, for once the Indians were generous: they opened the border to Sikkim. Along with some people from Taiwan—we smuggled them across the Indian border—we were back in Rumtek on December 17.

This time, we were not the only white faces. Hundreds of friends had arrived. We were especially impressed to see so many Americans from the West Coast, often quite elderly ones. The Indian military had done a good job, putting up tents with blankets and camp beds. Hannah translated and every moment was well used. It was great to tell so many what we had seen of the Karmapa's greatness over the years. He had frequently said that his seventeenth incarnation would be better, and we had replied, "It will suffice if he is as good as you."

Karmapa's seat during forty-nine days

In a free moment, Barbara Pettee took me aside and asked, "Have you seen the paper the general secretary wants some center-leaders to sign?" I had not, and gradually a remarkable story took form: during our time in Kathmandu, Trungpa Tulku had arrived with some of his closest students. Giving the general secretary, who understood no English, $10,000 in cash, they had asked him to sign a document. It stated that Boulder in Colorado, not Rumtek, should be the Kagyu headquarters until the new Karmapa was found. On top of that, they had cut the signatures of the four lineage holders from some other letters, gluing them underneath the paper to make it official. This was serious. Although they had obviously been drunk, which had shocked many at Rumtek, there was no excuse. We had to keep the lineage clean. I ran straight to the general secretary and demanded to see the paper. The otherwise dignified king from Eastern Tibet was not used to this kind of treatment. Wisely keeping it out of my reach, he rapidly slid it back into a drawer. The Scotch tape between the signatures had been clearly visible: it was a real falsification. "If you ever distribute this," I said, "you can forget about Europe! Our headquarters is Rumtek and we do not wish any contact with Boulder." He did not publicize it and must later have discovered how he had been fooled. Barbara Pettee, mother of Buddhism on the West Coast, was more important than ever that day. She really protected our Kagyu lineage.

On December 19, most stayed up all night, attending the pujas. Karmapa's body was now between the mandala and the relics in the upper room. Instead of falling apart during the forty-five days, he had shrunk and was now sitting in a two-foot high box. There was a window so one could see inside, but nobody wanted the opportunity. Knowing that I would someday tell the story, I took a good look. It was strange. A thin veil covered his face, which was a deep grey hue and somewhat shrunken. The rest of this formerly powerful man was the size of a small child. After the "Diamond Songs of the Kagyu Masters" and a meditation on the eighth Karmapa, the box was carried outside. It was inserted into a recently built clay stupa on the monastery's roof terrace. Overlooking the valley between the hill of Rumtek's protectors to the south and the snow-covered mountains miles away which are the border to Tibet, a grander view was hardly imaginable. Then a monk was called who had

Karmapa's heartsons

never had any contact with this Karmapa. Only someone like him could light the masses of dry sandalwood underneath the stupa.

Thousands held their breath as the flames exploded through the structure and stayed several feet high.

Suddenly, in the middle of it all, we saw a giant rainbow. Surrounding the sun in the otherwise clear and dry winter sky, it was something very unusual there.

A girl from Hamburg photographed it, and on the pictures many recognize the outline of Karmapa's face inside the circle of light. While still struck by this, something even more amazing happened on the side of the stupa facing Tibet. Kurt saw it at closest range: slowly, a blue-black ball appeared in the flames at the northern opening; it rolled halfway down the side of the structure and then lay still. No one knew what it was. The lineage holders called Kalu Rinpoche—the oldest present—and he again called an old Khampa warrior. The latter knew the insides of people well, having fought scores of Chinese soldiers with his sword. He wasn't able to identify the ball either, and, as it seemed to be shrinking,

The procession before Karmapa's hearse

Getting ready for the cremation

Situ Rinpoche had it laid on a metal plate, covered and then carried inside. It was the heart of the sixteenth Karmapa.

Meanwhile, a giant eagle circled the sky. He flew twelve large rounds and then headed southwest. We Westerners liked this a lot. It was grand and heroic, but it did not fit traditional Tibetan ideas. To them, the vulture is the most noble bird. In the next Rumtek newspaper, the event was therefore described as follows: "A vulture, looking like an eagle, circled above the fire the whole

I see the rainbow

time." Some traditional teachings say that vultures are Bodhisattvas, and it is at least psychologically wise to think well of those who will probably

The rainbow around the sun

The cremation

end up eating one's body. Wise Catholics should develop a fondness for worms.

The stupa was sealed, and two days later we could enter the room where Karmapa's heart was kept. It stood on a shelf at a height of about seven feet and one picked up the energy-field by touching the crown of one's head to its middle. Distance made no difference. It was unbelievably strong. Hannah found a place to meditate at once and was gone for hours.

Karmapa's heart comes forth

For once in my life, I wanted to be alone. Having made myself a piece of public property, however, that was not possible. Stunned, I passed groups of friends all wanting to ask me this or that. Saying "Yes" and "No," probably in the wrong places, finally there was nobody, and I could pour a gallon of water through each eye. What hit me hardest was that he was now so small. Here, I understood the depth of our first lama, Lopon Chechoo. His eyes had been wet since he arrived. He knew what a Karmapa is.

After this, our lineage made a political mistake that haunted us for a few years. A general Kagyu meeting was announced but only Karma Kagyu teachers were invited. This was understandable in the shock of just having lost Karmapa, but also bad style towards the representatives of other schools there. Jerome, now in Phoenix, gave the first gold towards a container for Karmapa's heart, and many spoke. My topic was the importance of holding onto Karmapa's direct blessing through the Three Lights Meditation. It brings instant access to his timeless essence whether there is an incarnate body or not. Now was the time to work hard and with maturity, to put a much larger thing into his hands when he returned. This has in fact happened wherever people have practiced the Karmapa meditation and kept their bonds. Groups which became stiff or sowed doubts, those who thought they knew better than their teachers, disappeared over the following years, or they remain as hollow shells, defined more by their dislikes than by their likes. Year by year, my compassion grows for the poor lamas who gather proud students.

On December 27, 1981, the sealed stupa was opened. It was full of relics. First, his eyes and tongue were found. They held the blessing of his body and speech and just like his heart, they hadn't burned. There were pieces of bone with Tibetan mantras on them, pearls and little balls of silver and gold. Most amazing of all: his seat had survived the ocean of flames. It was the powerfield of "Greatest Joy," printed on fine cloth. Only its corners were singed and there was the imprint of a child's foot in the middle. Some very unusual things had happened in that fire. As a parting gift, Shamarpa gave every one present a bit of the ashes, from which I collected the small golden balls, white pearls and pieces of bone. When I looked at the ashes back in Europe, they were again full of relics. Buddhist powerfields travel along and blessings are not lost.

Back in Europe, it was now time to invite Gyaltsab Rinpoche. He is the youngest of the four lineage holders. Of all, Karmapa's death had hit him hardest. Jamgon Rinpoche had asked Hannah to translate for him. They would use Copenhagen as base and move north and south from there. In fact, all were still dazed by Karmapa's death. For several months, many things happened mainly by reflex. Only gradually did the joy over the even greater responsibility push its way through the numb feeling of loss. "Karmapa" to us now meant fulfilling every wish he had made, while trusting the blessing and one's inner wisdom. During the cremation, I again had an intense vision of a map, this time not of Europe, but of the world. I was certain that its many points of light showed strong karmic connections. Here were the people and places where Karmapa's work would grow.

In the West, the task was now to instill confidence. Our friends should understand that they could count as fully on Karmapa as before. His levels of truth, joy, and protection could be accessed as effectively, and the four lineage-holders, many Rumtek Rinpoches, and we would continue his work. Practice would bring the results it always did.

In early spring, Gyaltsab Rinpoche came. He is an immensely powerful teacher and we had some instructive weeks driving him and his

Goshir Gyaltsab Rinpoche

two cheerful bear-like lamas through the Scandinavian snows. Although we got stuck north of Stockholm, the honor of carrying Rinpoche must have done our old car good—it still runs today. Hannah then took Rinpoche to Germany, while Gabi and Tina travelled with me. When she is busy elsewhere, my travelling companions are very important to my work. Having so little time, it is vital to have friends to share everything with, and after a time of intuitively picking up what is really going on, these talented women become the inspiration of the centers they then settle in. Only rarely is the shared closeness lost, and they are the life of Buddhism in so many places.

When Rinpoche had gone on to Dordogne, Central Europe once again became involved with an unpleasant aspect of Tibetan politics.

What probably disturbs us most of all is when lamas mooch: when they visit each other's centers as friends and then try to win their students for themselves. During Ayang Tulku's last stay in Europe—as Karmapa's guest—he had begun to manifest this characteristic, and in East Asia, among the enormously wealthy Chinese, the tendency had apparently gone too far. Instead of building up an organization based on his very effective Phowa, which would have benefited everyone, he here tried to win Karmapa's supporters for himself.

Traditional Chinese seldom practice. They have a well-developed tradition of sponsorship instead. Generally exploiting their workers on an unbelievable scale, they get their good karma by supporting monasteries. They were shocked that a teacher who came with Karmapa's recommendation so obviously worked for himself. The rumors first appeared in the Philippines and had followed him around the world. Ayang Tulku arrived in summer 1982 at a German Institute where Shamarpa was staying, literally seething with anger. He thought we had caused his problems and hinted political connections that could unseat Karmapa from his function as the general Kagyu head. This was deadly serious. Unwilling to try my hand at Tibetan politics, which are much too subtle for Westerners anyway, I had taken him to Shamarpa and hoped they would talk it out together. Shamarpa's regal, slightly ironical atmosphere would surely bring reason to it all. What I didn't know at that time is that the highest lamas prefer to starve out problems. They are much too gentlemanly to dig into the private affairs of others. In this case, as would later become clear, they had not gone beyond the usual niceties.

One day Kim came back from Tibet. He had taken his mother on an expensive guided tour. The Chinese had just started allowing them; Tibet was the place in their domain Westerners would pay the most to see. Before he left, I had asked him to bring me a Gau, a traveling altar. I knew it would contain something important. Finally holding it in my hands, I couldn't wait to open the palm-size silver box with the deep-red coral on it. It contained a prize beyond anything I could have hoped for: as my first direct connection to Tibet in this lifetime, a statue of our protector fell into my hand, along with a pill for long life. "Bearer of the Black Coat," as this powerful energy is called, was actually a rare form in

Tibet. He only works for our lineage and is the expression of Karmapa's activity. Karmapa used his name on me. Only now, when many Buddhists in the West are Karma Kagyu, has this form become the most well-known protector. I was beside myself with joy. A Khampa warrior whom Kim had met on a street in Lhasa was the physical source. Claude from Witten later cast copies of the statue which are now in all our centers. The original stands at beautiful Schwarzenberg in Germany.

At the University of Gdansk in Poland, there was a job to do. Two thousand professors and students wouldn't stop applauding, thankful for what was happening. It was the first public meeting after the crackdown on Solidarity, and Tomek and his sister showed real courage. The secret police had come to say that they would be held responsible for any political hints that I might make. In a setting of water-cannon and riot-police in full gear, it was a joy to lecture on the fallacy of materialism and the freedom of the mind. Contacts were also close in that town. The flat I stayed in was across from Solidarity headquarters, and there were constant messages to bring to and from the country.

With Tomek translating—Rinchen and Marek

CHAPTER TWELVE

Work Becomes Worldwide

*T*HE NEXT TOUR TO AMERICA, August through September 1982, was with Hannah and my mother. Gabi and Friedel from Wuppertal in Germany came along. We stayed with Barry in the Village and drove to Woodstock, where Shamarpa was teaching. Then my mother stayed with friends. Again we had nine days to reach the West Coast in a drive-away. In Lexington, Kentucky, we met Bob and Melanie, an American-English couple. They quickly became our close friends. As always, the West Coast was sheer joy. I taught in San Diego, where I was now nearly the resident lama. Our film friends had left Los Angeles, but there are always lots of exciting people in that town. At the home of a psychologist, our neutral-friendly attitude toward Bhagwan Shree Rajneesh suffered badly. While we were packing warm second-hand clothes for Tibetan refugees, the guru appeared on TV in a long white robe and talked deep emotional nonsense. His main thesis was that all religions are the same. One only needs reading skills to know that this is simply not the case. I had always thought that as a former professor, he would be at least philosophically sound. Also we had heard that he helped people lose their inhibitions. But here, his behavior was completely artificial. It was hard to imagine a stronger contrast to a Rinpoche's plain and natural style. I was sorry to see that. We need more good teachers, not less, and he influenced thousands of people.

Dharma Cakra Cantre,
Rumtek GANGTOK
Sikkim, INDIA TEL: 363

H. E. SHAMARPA RINPOCHE

Date: 14. 6. 1982

I hereby request Ole Nydahl of Copenhagen,
Denmark, the first western disciple of H.H.the Karmapa
and the Co-founder and organizer of most European
KARMA-KAGYÜ-Centres to do a first lecture-tour of
our S.E.Asian, African and American Centres to teach
meditation, bring new people to the DHARMA and share
his experience of Buddhisme in our daily lives.

I would be grateful if you would help him
on his way and organize teachings at universities,
with groups of interested people and at our centres.

Shamarpa.

H.E.Shamarpa Rinpoche

Bokar Rinpoche

After a visit with Dudley and my family in San Luis Obispo, we followed the scenic coast road to Santa Cruz. Tom and Rita lent us two enormous old cars for the rest of our tour. They are close friends and great and tireless supporters of Buddhism.

Here we heard that Bokar Tulku was on his way to Denmark. He is a perfect yogi and now leads three retreat centers in the eastern Himalayas: Rumtek, Sonada, and Mirek. Kim had invited him to the West for the first time. Hannah was to translate and flew back to Denmark while I drove on to Portland where Nancy had organized things. Then, for the first time, I looked farther west—to Japan and the free Chinese.

Cesar and Yoshiko were waiting at the Tokyo airport, touching as always. Cesar was now second man—"minister" as they called it—in the Mexican embassy. They lived with Yoshiko's family in the heart of the city. Driving the embassy's car back required some mental work: the Japanese drive on the left side and have lots of regulations about all things. Also their cars have built-in spies which make loud noises if the speed goes above 100 kph, the national limit. The country looked like a well-tended mini-garden, and people were disciplined and exact. There were no wide movements nor loud laughter; everyone existed through their place in the system. Here I would finally translate *Entering the Diamond Way* into Danish. I also expected to teach in Japan, though all experts said: no chance, their Buddhism was already completely political and secular. Either the Japanese visit their temples to obtain money and power, or they meet in small, extremist groups. These usually insist that Buddha had only intended to teach a single Sutra—theirs—and that the others were either wrong or without meaning. Putting on special robes, they then walk in a procession around the block—their "spiritual practice of the week." Shortly before, a wealthy Frenchman had invited Kalu Rinpoche to Japan. The visit had been well-announced and many Buddhist teachers had responded, thanking Rinpoche. In the next sentence, however, they wrote that unfortunately they had no time to meet him. After three weeks, when no one had come, Kalu Rinpoche flew back to India.

Lecturing at Tokyo University required a stamp of approval from the local Tibetan committee. This again would have taken months: it first had to be okayed by Dharamsala in India. Instead, I gave Refuge to the Mexican embassy. They were amazed and happy to find a religion which is not revealed but can be directly experienced.

Teaching in three to four temples, a dozen Westerners took Refuge. Among the Japanese, only two women were open, but they were a joy. A mixture of nationalism and materialism drives people in Tokyo. They live under enormous self-created pressures and have neither time nor power for spiritual development. In Nagoya, further south, things were different. There the members of a mortician's institute wanted to learn, though I had to promise not to put them into states of trance and meditation. They were actually touching, showed me a Shinto park—something very

Teaching in Nagaya

different—and gave me my first radar detector. Akemi became my friend there. Her family was the most Japanese home I had ever seen.

Returning to Tokyo, a gigantic shock was waiting: my brother Bjørn had been hit by a drunk driver near Philadelphia. He was in bad shape. I was on my way back across the Pacific when four divinations in a row told me that he would definitely survive. It would be most useful to pray for his quick recovery in many temples.

Japan was a true cultural experience, especially the towns of Kyoto and Nara. Their architecture was quite similar to that of Bhutan. Cesar and Akemi organized the public events, and when I had finished the book, Yoshiko showed me the streets of Tokyo. The country's smooth exterior was nearly perfect. Only once, behind a wall, did I see about a hundred tramps, sitting in a row. They were in bad shape. Whoever goes outside the norms in this society falls very deep.

From there, I flew to Taiwan. In 1981, we had smuggled a group of Taiwanese people to Karmapa's burning. They were not allowed to enter India at all. Most of all, sweet Show Loong (Little Dragon) had become a close friend. She was the right hand of a daughter of the last Chinese empress, the former female general and Kung Fu master, Kunga

Ani. This stately woman, now over eighty, had built an impressive temple in the capital of Taipei. Each brick carried half the mantra of the red form of "Loving Eyes"—in Tibetan letters.

Although geographically close, Taiwan is very different from Japan. While Japan is "dry" regarding humor, nutrition, love, and landscape, in Taiwan everything has an "oily" quality. I stayed and taught in Kunga Ani's temple. During the day people came for blessings, and in the

My brother Bjørn

evenings they would have preferred just doing the same. They all wanted a long life, good business, sons, and for their children to pass their exams. When they realized that the wishes I made for them were rapidly fulfilled, though I was hardly the type of holy renunciate they were used to, they came in droves. I always said that whatever power I had was Karmapa's blessing, but they kept talking of my "Chi." It is a kind of basic force which makes things happen. Like Taoists, they hardly distinguished between secular and liberating powers. If an energy was tangible and helped for a short while, they were satisfied. The highest liberating view was not popular. When I advised transcending expectation and aversion and learning about mind from every experience, they probably doubted my sanity. Few could see pleasant experiences as blessing and unpleasant ones as purification. When my wishes for them brought quick results, they reached their peaks of confidence.

My translators were university people, and the audience was attentive. Historically, it is quite a tale how the Diamond Way came to China. Though we often hear how the Karmapas taught the Chinese emperors from the twelfth to the eighteenth centuries and received great gifts from them, actually the number of people involved was limited. The holders of power didn't dare make the methods accessible to their subjects. Knowing their great power, they preferred to keep them to themselves. Instead, they permitted the Small and the Great Ways. The first time the Diamond Way reached ordinary Chinese was at the beginning of this century. When the empire fell apart, Kongka Rinpoche, a disciple of the fifteenth Karmapa, visited the country. Here, clear heads like Guru Han, Kunga Ani, and others became his students. In 1949, when the Communists finished conquering China, they fled to Taiwan with Chiang Kai-shek and founded centers there. Unfortunately, instead of cooperating, they now frequently competed for status.

The Chinese national day in October—Ten Ten, as they call it (the date is 10.10.)—was not a pleasant experience. My generation in western Europe had been spared that kind of exhibition. It was worse than the close-minded millions in Tokyo. For most of a day a completely mobilized nation marched. In the main square of Taipei, in front of a podium with the son of Chiang Kai-Shek, densely packed units paraded by. Everyone was there, from firefighters to bakers. About five feet tall, all had the same expression on their faces. The monotony was broken by Kung Fu adepts bending water-pipes on each other or splintering wooden boards, and then everybody marched again. For a humanistic western European, it was nothing but awful—that total contempt of humanity we had first seen in Moslem countries years before. The Chinese, though, seemed to be proud of it. Even Show Loong probably didn't understand why I reacted so strongly.

There were invitations from several towns, but my ten days on the island only left time for Taipei itself. Thanks to Show Loong's feminine wisdom, I saw something anyway. She told everyone I would leave a day earlier. Then she smuggled me on a bus to the south of the island where we visited her family and friends. She was a special woman and a good balance for the frequently bone-dry Buddhists there.

Hong Kong also got ten days, which was too much. I stayed in style with Brian and Patty, students of Situ Rinpoche. Their apartment offered an amazing view over Kowloon and the ferry to the continent. Several skyscrapers nearby had toppled during severe rain some years before. Stamps were amazingly cheap and unlike so many warm countries, they were not removed and sold again. This was the place for me to write kilos of mail to America and Europe.

A few dozen young Chinese came to my teachings in the center. They were glad to learn something practical for their lives. There was constant opposition from a block of moralistic sponsors, however. They thought only people who sleep alone would have something to teach. These traditionalists are the main reason the center has never been really useful. Instead of benefitting, at least outwardly, modern Hong Kong, it is now used by traveling teachers as a stopover. The lamas who were sent there rapidly moved on.

In Bangkok, I blessed a monastery full of ancient Chinese women. They were disciples of Kunga Ani and she had called them from Taiwan. I gave them permission for Phowa, which was just in time. The monastery had an unbelievable old-Chinese atmosphere and was situated near the amusement area of Bangkok, which I had marvelled at the night before. I would have liked to give them mind-teachings also, but for the first time in my work as lama, it was totally impossible to find a translator. The place obviously did not have the karma, and I regretted that.

Hannah had been busy with Bokar Tulku and his helper, Khenpo Donyo, in Scandinavia and North Germany. We met in Heidelberg. From there, we traveled east through Germany in Kim's twelve-cylinder Jaguar. Our next stop was Munich's Olympia Park where we stayed with wonderful Sys, a close friend of Kurt. Today, she organizes the European part of my year from Schwarzenberg, our unique center at the foot of the Alps. Here, part of my heart constantly lives. It is a jewel of the Kagyu lineage where I have the honor of being resident lama. The place is a magnificent example of what confidence, friendship, and idealism can do for the world.

A Swiss friend asked that I make a stop in the Italian Alps. There was something he absolutely wanted to show me: a deserted village built from grey natural stone in the beautiful valley of Antrona. We ascended through a forest in increasingly soggy tennis shoes, but what lay there in the snow was worth it. My divinations clearly said that we should take this place. With Swiss efficiency, he quickly set up a co-operative system for buying into the village. Later, Tenga Rinpoche built a stupa there, which one can see gleaming from the valley. The center's name is Bordo, and it is especially popular among people with children.

Meanwhile, it was again time for a journey to the Himalayas. Karmapa's stupa in Sikkim was to be inaugurated. Niels brought the

Bokar Rinpoche with Kim and the Khenpo in Munich

The stupa with most of Karmapa's relics

Danes from Copenhagen, and we the Germans from Frankfurt. This fourth pilgrimage was only to last for a month, and we arrived in Sikkim with seventy-five friends on December 20, the anniversary of Karmapa's cremation. Rumtek was fantastic as always. The heart-stupa now stood among the holiest objects of the lineage, and the new large stupa in the yellow school building was filled with other relics that had appeared during Karmapa's cremation. Almost all had strong dreams there.

Dilgo Khyentse Rinpoche's farewell to Karmapa belonged to another dimension. Here, two giants of the mind met. For what seemed to be endless time, he sat in a chair in front of the stupa, and when he laid his forehead against it to say goodbye, everything froze. As his two servants helped him down the stairs, he seemed unaware of where he was.

Dilgo Khyentse Rinpoche

Jamgon Kongtrul Rinpoche showed us an article from *Time* magazine. It stated that scientists had just publicized completely new "molecular" methods for treating cancer. This had taken place in the town of Zion, Illinois, where Karmapa had died, and exactly on the anniversary of his death. "This is how the highest Bodhisattvas work," he said. "Very few with a bond to Karmapa will die of cancer or one of the other diseases he took upon himself."

From Darjeeling we took the bus overland to Kathmandu. Here Lopon Chechoo initiated us into an important, four-headed form of "Liberatrice." Tenga Rinpoche guided an exciting pilgrimage to the holy Buddhist places of the Kathmandu valley and explained their meaning from a thick book. It was painful to discover that most had been taken by the Hindus. They were now guarded by armed soldiers who only let brown people enter.

It was pleasant to stay only a short time in the warm countries. We had gradually become tired of the dirt and lack of compassion among their inhabitants, whose behavior usually guaranteed them a future incarnation under similar circumstances. Watching people's actions is all one needs to understand why the population goes down in countries where the quality of life improves, and increases when the standards

Lopön Chechoo Rinpoche

With Tenga Rinpoche on pilgrimage in the Kathmandu Valley

decline: only few create the causes for a good re-birth. A country can choose quality or quantity, but not both.

Back in Europe, a special treat was waiting. In the middle of the cold Swedish winter, Kalu Rinpoche had planned an initiation into "Wheel of Time." He had already given a less satisfactory one some years earlier in Paris where the sound system fell out. Only the Germans were able to follow because I yelled so loud.

People from many parts of Europe took a rented bus to Stockholm. Here, he gave the deepest teachings ever on the inner and secret aspects of this tantra. It was unique and also a fantastic opportunity to learn:

when Rinpoche stopped in the evening, there were some hours for answering questions and explaining to people which energies they had now received. Here one must know what one is talking about.

Spring of 1983 was spent in Central Europe. Groups grew everywhere, and Helmut and Sabine from the Hamburg Center brought tall, red-haired Edita. She soon helped me on the road, learning very well. Vienna and North Italy showed important growth, and I was twice on Cyprus with Maria Aliferi, then the most famous of Greek actresses. She did three very popular TV shows a week and was thus excellent publicity. While many came to listen—and see her—it will probably take long before Buddhism grows on Cyprus. As became apparent later on Malta, people from small islands dominated by an intolerant religion are not spiritually very courageous. When the audience finally understood that I wasn't teaching some kind of Christianity, everybody suddenly said "Makarios" many times and disappeared. Makarios was the former Archbishop and the divided island's main political power. Since even Maria,

*Kalu Rinpoche giving
the Empowerment of
Wheel of Time*

who was adored by everyone, could not hold them, he must have had a bad secret police.

On some level, the island was still in shock. Dozens of women dressed in black came to ask if their sons might not have survived in some Turkish prison camp. During that period, I made my divinations with dice and each time the answer was "No." They had been killed during the assault in 1974. The Turkish army had then occupied forty percent of the island.

As our activity widened, the financial situation also improved. The generosity of Swiss and other friends truly boosted our work. It was the time for greatly solidifying Central Europe. Meanwhile, we received ever more greetings from Kalu Rinpoche. He reminded us to come soon for the great Rinchen Terdzö initiations he planned to give in Sonada that summer. A friend from France also brought an oral invitation, and when we received a telegram from Gyaltsen, his secretary, shortly after, there was no way out: dreary and unhygienic India called us once again. For the sake of spiritual growth, we would now have to sit through six months of monsoon rain in the East Himalayas.

Actually, it was a great honor. During this time Rinpoche would activate approximately two thousand aspects of enlightened awareness in those present. They had first been transmitted by Guru Rinpoche over twelve hundred years ago and are one of the greatest treasures of Tibetan Buddhism.

Kalu Rinpoche gave us the best possible room for our needs. Situated a few meters above the temple where everything would take place, it saved us a lot of time. The houses of the four lineage holders were right above and it was an extension of his own newly built monastery. The initiations started the day after our arrival, and everything was set up inspiringly. As usual, the disturbing factor was too many people.

The program started at seven a.m., seven days a week, with Tenga Rinpoche chanting the "loongs." These are the traditional readings of texts which transmit the inner experience of the practices; at the same time they give formal permission for doing the meditations. While this took place in one half of the vast temple hall, Kalu Rinpoche prepared his work for the afternoon behind a curtain in the other. From one to six or seven p.m., the great initiations themselves happened. Mantras were

Prominent students

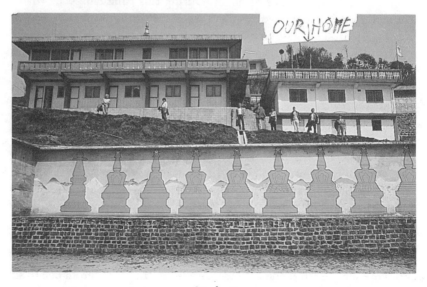

Our home

Squeezing to get in

repeated, and everyone was touched by the charged objects. In this way, Kalu Rinpoche passed on the powerfields of many Buddhas. Every day, six hundred to a thousand members of the different Himalayan races piled up in the room. It was usually after a period of pushing and shoving in the rain, which one's poor nose could not avoid picking up. Our most important collective task was to keep three central rows for the Westerners. There had to be a place for those who wanted to meditate during the initiations. Most of the natives apparently only came for the blessings. They chattered freely and let their children cry no matter what was happening on stage. Worst was the smell when people suddenly stood up. Those who thought the Himalayas were populated by hermits meditating in solitude learned something else during these months. The real yogis who also came, however, were deeply impressive. An enormous blessing pervaded everything, and we Westerners learned to appreciate our good education and become a well-functioning team. Five of us received the full transmission, and at every blessing I held six pounds of pictures in my hands: many European and American friends had wanted to take part.

Halfway through the stay, there was a three-week break. We used it for a visit to Taiwan. Everything worked exactly to the day and a sponsor paid for our tickets. We picked up our Taiwan visas in Hong Kong, where I taught two private groups. We stayed in comfort at the center where the responsible people were wondering why yet another lama had fled. In Taiwan, we again landed at the giant empty airport where my translator, Huang Houng, was waiting. As I brought Hannah this time, we were invited to stay with Guru Han and his sweet wife. They lived in a government villa near the city center.

During my last visit, I had been very pleased with Guru Han. He avoided politics and was unusually mature and balanced. Most of all, it was fine how he supported his wife's development. Chinese culture has far too many talented women who turn strange, due to the lack of real contact with their men. Both sexes fulfill the expectations set by society

With Guru Han's wife

and traditional role patterns, but never really meet. Men need less emotional contact and can let off steam in business life, but in the traditional marriages many women gradually go crazy. Where a little shared intimacy would have worked miracles, they are measured by the cleanness of their houses and how well their children, above all the boys, pass their examinations. It hurt to see this. As always, I opposed this tendency as openly as local culture allowed. I connected with the women and gave them my power and acceptance.

Since the last visit the power of my blessings had become famous, and many came. We were able to work efficiently because our contacts had not yet made themselves gurus. This normally happens very quickly among the Chinese and it thoroughly destroys the work. When a group of ten splits into five groups of two who constantly argue, there is little left. As Karmapa's representatives, this time we had to follow the invitations to the whole island. I had arrived with the idea of going deeper at fewer places. It would have been the right time to give recognition and confidence to some charismatic laymen with strong karmic connections to the lineage. At this time, people with the ability to inspire others would have been enormously useful—the kind who learn by teaching. There exists nothing more precious than these natural talents. On every level of growth, people with life experience have a much deeper impact than institutionally educated Buddhist teachers. Such people are our sources of power in Europe and America today. It would probably have required a youth revolution to bring forth a sizeable number of them in Taiwan, however, and even more time to get them on their way. People on the island preferred the rare and exotic and wanted ceremonies and incense. There was little appetite for the quickest way of all: cooperation with teachers and friends on the inner and secret levels.

Instead of being talent scouts, we functioned as official representatives. This was not boring. On one of the first days, I had the honor of inaugurating Taiwan's first Vajrayana stupa. It was a large structure overlooking the ocean from the north rim of the island. Sun I, our closest confidante, really touched my heart with his devotion, so I contributed some of Karmapa's relics for the stupa. It simply felt right. As the last prefabricated piece of concrete was placed on top with a crane, there was a moment when we all knew that something historical had happened.

After teaching in the center of the island, we were driven around the picturesque Sun and Moon Lake. There Buddha relics are displayed in a temple. They look exactly like our black Karmapa pills.

We returned to Taipei at European speed. This time, I drove. I had had enough of sloppy Asian driving. People's confidence in the lama helped them overcome their fears when the speedometer showed numbers they had considered only ornamental till then. Their trust displayed an unexpected strength in their culture and at once elevated my opinion of anything Chinese.

During the last days, we stayed with some movie stars. They fluttered around us like little fairies. We also changed our money. The Chinese historically only pay monks, but still the little red envelopes had piled up in front of me. Though they have hardly any yogis, also their tradition states that teachers who have women develop special powers. Their generosity was touching, actually paying for our whole journey from Europe to India and the months spent there. This fact quickly became known, and today when the Tibetan government no longer frowns upon visits to Taiwan, a growing number of Rinpoches finance their work to preserve Tibetan culture on that island.

Completing the stupa

At the Sun and Moon Lake

Teaching in Taipei

Back at the empowerment

We arrived in Sonada just as everything started up again. But the mood had darkened. Hannah, translating texts with Jamgon Kongtrul Rinpoche nearly every day, saw that something was disturbing him. Gradually we learned what. Our taking Ayang Tulku to Shamarpa a year earlier had not solved anything. They had only discussed niceties, and now some old Tibetan schisms had re-opened. A growing number of influential people wanted Karmapa's seat as the general representative of Kagyu Buddhism. I had always kept our work as far away from Tibetan politics as possible. They learned their strategies centuries ago from the Chinese, and a Westerner easily runs into a dozen traps he cannot even see. Also in Tibetan culture, it is the joyless people who thrived on organizations and outer power. This problem, however, directly concerned our area of responsibility: Central and Eastern Europe. I had started the centers there, and Hannah had translated for Ayang Tulku for months. It was a most unpleasant situation. In the midst of such powerful initiations one should really avoid breaking any bonds.

There was already enough distraction. Running things from Sonada was difficult. The main medium was letters to Edita in Hamburg. She was then my right hand and communications expert. Also, the initiations grew ever more absorbing and the "payment" for them, 100,000 of the hundred-syllable purification mantras, took a significant chunk of time. We wanted to complete them right there in Sonada. In the middle of so much diligence and virtue, now this unpleasant affair arose.

Our opponents worked quickly and globally. Without even mentioning that he worked for another lineage, Ayang Tulku's representative in Europe had himself invited to Karmapa's centers. Giving several protector initiations with serious commitments there, he made inexperienced people promise to do hour-long pujas from a different lineage every day. As people only have a certain amount of time, this effectively blocked the practices we taught, and people were already becoming confused. It was a challenge for me. Living up to the title of Dharma-General which Karmapa had frequently bestowed, I outlined our preliminary steps. Then I looked forward to being back in Europe soon, to take things fully into my hands.

When the initiations were nearly finished, we had the greatest experience of the whole six months: time with Karmapa's heart. So far, Kalu Rinpoche had only allowed one free day a month, that of "Liberatrice," but here we got three. This was time enough to go to Rumtek. I brought our bags of friends' pictures and the protection strings which had been blessed at every initiation. They should spend a night in front of the holiest energy we knew.

Karmapa's heart is now positioned in a foot-high stupa of gold and silver. It is surrounded by the relics of our lineage and stands next to the Black Crown. Despite the energy of the site, I could hardly stay awake. During our few hours in this holiest of holies, I frequently had to pinch myself not to fall asleep. But still, the blessing came through. Leaving with the Gyaltsab and Jamgon Kongtrul Rinpoches in a jeep, the stupa with Karmapa's heart was still there in our space. However inspiring the initiations of the next weeks were, it never left. The blessing of the teacher's heart is the ultimate Kagyu transmission. Beyond words, concepts, and imagination, it is the basis for all growth.

Our lineage holders considered an official title for me. There had never even been talk of this before now, where I would have to hold Central Europe together. In the non-snobbish 70s, it was sufficient that

Karmapa's heart stupa

I had started our scores of centers between Oslo and Athens, except for an impossible German institute. We were all friends, so who needed an addition to one's name? Together we invited Rinpoches to our centers and Hannah translated for them. A title would be useful for more than politics, however. As we grew, sometimes stiff-minded people wanted to join our happy yogi groups. Possessing narrow and church-like minds, they frequently had difficulties with my joy. My driving style, fascinating female helpers, and lack of "human" weakness disconcerted them. A high-sounding title would be an effective antidote to any sour gossip and save our Rinpoches much time listening to complaints.

It would have been simplest to call me lama in accordance with my work. This is what Karmapa did. This was not possible then, however, because of Kalu Rinpoche. Many of his lamas at that time were half out of their robes, and he needed a stick to keep them in line. Lamas, to him, had to live in at least official celibacy. The problem was that there existed no Tibetan term for my activity. Tibetan Buddhism had hardly moved from the country for a thousand years, and many things we had developed were new: the guided meditations in Western languages, and empowering selected friends to give the first teachings while also relying on feedback from the group process. Never before had there been such a grass roots movement, based not on hierarchy, but on friendship and deep devotion to Karmapa. Shamarpa first tried the title, "Kyorpon," traveling teacher, but that only covered the preserving aspect of the work. Not until one late evening, sitting with the Bhutanese Queen mother in her residence in Darjeeling, did he find a title which both expressed responsibility and left room for untraditional activity. With a big smile he said: "You will be our Buddhist Master."

This had immense importance for the future. With one stroke, it enormously increased the power and breadth of our lineage. Suddenly, our strong and devoted students were "inside." Our lay and yogic work founded on Western premises was now officially accepted. Most of all, my recognition as a Mahamudra teacher blessed our common level of practice. It was an historical moment some days later when I held the document in my hand. Blessed with Kunzig Shamarpa's signature and Jamgon Kongtrul Rinpoche's seal, it tied us together closer than ever.

On one of the last days in Sonada, a misunderstanding laid the seeds for our later tours to Tibet. During most lunch breaks, Jamgon Kongtrul Rinpoche and Hannah translated some prophecies by the fifth Karmapa, Deshin Shegpa (1385-1415). As I entered one day, the text became contemporary and very exciting. First, it gave the name of the Tibetan who, sick with fear, blew up the giant Buddha of Tsurphu. Five stories tall and cast from molten copper, it stood in the main residence of the Karmapas in Tibet. The statue had been built by his second incarnation, the famous Karma Pakshi (1206-1283) from presents by the Chinese emperor. It had lasted till Mao's cultural revolution in 1966.

Jamgon Kongtrul Rinpoche had explained earlier how it had been destroyed: former dynamite charges had exploded into the air without doing the statue any harm. As the communist Chinese threatened punishment, this man had devised the method of placing the dynamite under the statue. Beneath it they put thangkas and other blessed objects. With an enormous bang, the statue had been spread over much of the valley. The heart of the first Karmapa, Dusum Kyempa, rolled from its center, and the Tibetans hid it immediately. There is now a tiny bit of it in my relic-container. The prophecy went on like this: between the sixteenth and seventeenth Karmapa, the Kagyus in Tibet would be like powerless bees in autumn; the machines of the hostile barbarians to the East would control the skies. Here a protector and his retinue would come from the West. Of powerful expression, and with moles, he would help rebuild Tsurphu. Thinking that moles were freckles and not hearing that he would also be dark-skinned and small, I thought it might be us. From then on, it was only a question of time until scores of our Western friends carried stones and wood in Tibet.

After the initiations, one week of offering pujas was planned. Kalu Rinpoche wished us to take part in them. He also wanted us to organize a pilgrimage for his disciples afterwards. But I could not wait another moment. Europe was burning and I had to get events back under control. Now was the time to secure Karmapa's area of influence and protect his centers and students. We thanked Rinpoche with all our hearts and he let us go. Saying farewell to our lineage holders, they deplored not being able to take a political stand. Though we explained that the coming shake-out would cost both friends and confidence, all they could do officially was to write a bland statement. It said that people in Germany should listen to us.

When we landed in Frankfurt, Central Europe had already been through the wringer. We saw it in the faces of the friends who welcomed us at the airport. We explained the Tibetan side of the story to them and shared what had happened in the Himalayas during the last six months. Then Hannah and I went to the German institute for the first major show-down in our history, confronting the then leaders of our organization for not doing as we said. Rumtek fired them a few months later, but it was not the last time we had problems with that place. It seemed to attract box-headed people.

All in all, we got off cheaply. In America, where they shunned the conflict, the problem still reappears from time to time.

So there was ample reason to spend the autumn of 1983 in Europe. Many things had to be redirected into the right channels. Though several people left—not the best of friends anyway, often it was more a relief than a loss when they went—we managed to protect the lineage, and most grew through the turmoil. Our friends learned to take a stand and trust their observations, instead of expecting people from other continents to tell them what was happening right under their noses. Bringing the critical discrimination of the West to the blessing and timeless wisdom of the Diamond Way benefited both.

In the winter of '84, there was again time for other parts of the world. While Hannah translated in Europe, I landed in New York with a group of friends. Where can one be closer to one's students than on the long slow stretches across the vast American continent? Close connections across the Atlantic are only beneficial. Organized groups in America easily become stiff and need periodic injections of free yogi spirit, while Europeans need American skills in communication. Since our cultures are so similar, many things can be shared directly. This is also my aim today.

Having driveaways to southern California, we stopped at the centers along the route. Staying with Bob and Melanie in Kentucky, Edita and I were awakened by bone-chilling screams. Melanie stood there holding her six-week-old baby. It had died during the night. Although the body was completely cold, I transferred its mind—and everyone watched a very unusual sign: a two-foot strand of hard foam came out of the baby's nose.

Detroit "quality" and some old karmic connections decided the next phase of our tour. Near Santa Rosa, New Mexico, the crankshaft of one of the cars broke. They had probably added too much lead to the alloy and overdone the planned obsolescence. We just managed to roll into a solitary garage standing in radiant sunlight on a high mesa. While admiring the casual way they had left a big-caliber loaded revolver in the tool box, I happened to remember that we also had some meditation

groups in this part of the country. Both Karmapa and Kalu Rinpoche had
been here. My address book was once again a reliable friend, and soon
after, Lama Dorje was on the phone. He invited me to teach in Santa Fe
and also told us of a Karmapa group in Albuquerque, started by Khenpo
Karthar from Woodstock. This was where the car would be towed to
anyway.

The red mountains were breathtaking, scarred by wind and
weather, and the bright blue sky was overhead. In Santa Fe, most were of
mixed spirituality and already knew everything, but in Taos it was a real
joy to stay with Norbert, a friend from the very first days in North
Germany. His company, Southwest Spiral Designs, carved the traditional
wooden columns of the area, and he lived on a high mesa in a fantastic
domed house. The weather became completely erratic when we arrived,
and his main window jumped out of its frame. There were definitely
energies to work with in the area.

We skidded rather than drove through masses of powdery snow.
Retrieving the car in Albuquerque, it immediately broke down again.
As several programs were waiting, I flew on to San Diego while the group
had it fixed once more. Robin and her kids were at the airport and also
Crystal, who organized for me during the first important years. It was a
joy to strengthen old bonds and share that snob-free humor which is
Denmark's gift to the universe. It was a useful antidote to yet another
batch of rumors about a lama further north in California. When the
morally outraged women had seen the situation from the outside and had
their first good laugh, more interesting matters quickly got their attention—like catching me.

Up the coast, our friends in Encinitas, Santa Barbara, and Santa
Cruz were doing well. Deeply and steadily, Karmapa's blessing was
becoming part of their lives.

San Francisco hosted a few exotic cases, as usual, headed this time
by the Army Street Group, comprised of about thirty families and couples
in a large loft. All lived side by side with no separation and were thus
automatically privy to each other's joys and sufferings, day and night. A
strong, charismatic man had put them on this trip on Hawaii some years
earlier and then died. Nourished by the devotion of good people but
having no timeless dimension, their structure disintegrated as the mem-

ory of his power faded. It was a good teaching not to make a cult of one's charisma or to pass on one's own limited understanding. Lasting benefit only comes from one activity: giving people methods and freedom to experience their timeless Buddha qualities themselves.

Mount Shasta is a dormant ash-volcano in northern California. Here a Russian yogi had collected extraordinary jewels of Tibetan art in his Mongolian felt tent. Among them was a special thangka from Dolpo in the Himalayas. It shows Karmapa in his blissful state, united with the

Thangka manifesting the joystate of the Karmapas

Diamond Dakini. It is a great rarity, and copies of the photo he gave now grace our shrines everywhere.

Back in Berkeley, some old karma ripened, and I stirred up a wasps' nest. A minor initial cause quickly produced a lot of effects. Wendy, a sweet and natural girl of Danish extraction, wanted to organize an evening for me. She worked at the house of the Dharmadhatu in Berkeley and held the position which they so meaningfully call "Ambassador."

She didn't call headquarters in Boulder first, where they apparently have to ask permission for everything. Instead, following the recommendations of Karmapa and Shamarpa and her own common sense, she gathered the students she could reach. The scene touched my heart. There in front of me, flanked by beer-bellied bodyguards with ties and red noses, sat a hundred people of unusual devotion. For years, they had somehow put up with the whole show. The spiritual sustenance of many had been some not too sober teachings, morale-boosting songs, processions by the organization's "Army," "Navy," and "Air Force," or some Japanese bush

Trungpa Tulku on horseback

cutting. Without much instruction, their main practice consisted of sitting down, and these hours were counted. Only after a certain number could they go on to the next artificially created step.

My years of Tibetan training were useful, and I quickly said all the flattering things I could find about the organization. After that, I gave the teachings on relative and absolute truth which everyone needs. During the next few hours, I really opened up to them. We finished with questions, a Karmapa meditation and blessings which people thirstily absorbed. On our way home, Wendy and I were happy. We had fulfilled a part of Karmapa's wish.

During the following teachings in the San Francisco Zen guest house and elsewhere, I kept to the good style. Whenever members of Dharmadhatu—easily recognizable by their tamed behavior—asked whether they should follow me, I advised them to stay with what they already knew. In reply to the questions of many, I represented the sexual and alcoholic weaknesses of the organization in the best possible light. Still, there were signs of future trouble. Boulder was getting the news of my popularity, and Wendy's friend, one of the top members of their hierarchy, heartily disliked our cooperation. During a last celebration before taking leave of America, it was clear that something was fermenting.

In Europe, Hannah was translating for Beru Khyentse Rinpoche. It was great to have her near again. While still in Copenhagen in March, Siwaldi came. He was the red-haired giant I had doubled up during Karmapa's Crown Ceremony in 1974. He said, "Ole, I have just inherited some money from my mother. Before I die from drinking, I want to do at least one useful thing in my life. Please come to Iceland with me for a week and bring the dharma there. I'll pay your ticket."

Edita managed to cut five days out of my super-tight schedule, and these were extraordinary. There was a stop in Scotland, and when we arrived in Iceland, the weather went wild. This was nothing new. It often happens when I introduce the powerfield of Karmapa and "Black Coat" to a new place. Every quarter hour, there was a new combination of rain, snow, wind, sun, and hail. The Nordic gods reacted to the new and ultimate level of consciousness, although Odin, their leader, had certainly met Buddhas before. He had given an eye as the price for timeless wisdom at Mimer's well, and his ravens, Hugin and Mugin, showed him the world. Not knowing anybody on Iceland, we stayed in the cheapest hotel, the Sailor's Home, and got used to a diet of dried, salted fish. Everything else was just unbelievably expensive. The next days I could only teach a few people at the university, and I had to put up the posters for the teachings myself—a strange experience. I gave interviews to newspapers and to anyone who showed even the slightest interest, but there were not many. The spiritual thirst up there was not unquenchable.

Nature made up for all that, however; some local people showed us their island. It started with an icy mountain pass in raging winds. One could barely stand, and the ice crystals cut into our faces. At the end of the majestic plateau were volcanic sulfur springs and a stream of ice water. Made to run together, they were perfect for bathing. Snow swept luxuriously over us, and the rock face above looked exactly like Karmapa's face. It was breathtaking. Another experience of nature came through a lady Viking in a local disco. She had decided to take me home. She already had me over her shoulder, but since she was so drunk that she wouldn't have recognized me the next morning, I decided to make myself scarce. Not until the last of the five nights, at the Theosophical Center, was there some real benefit for Iceland. Their questions didn't stop until 2 a.m., which was totally unprecedented. Going from them straight to the airport, we had the good feeling of having at least done something.

Spring of 1984 was filled with the best I know: time with our countless friends. Germany had digested the recent troubles well, except for the leaders of the Munich group. They now wanted to demonstrate independence. Practice based on dislike, however, doesn't work too well. This can be seen from the culturally memorable parting words of a lama they had invited but not cared for: "You are proud like swans. Everyone tries to hold his neck higher than the others. You are like horse droppings, smooth on the outside but rotten inside. The group is like a dead cow: one only looks once to see that it is dead." Since 1986, a new center started by Ulla and Detlev represents us marvelously in that important town.

Work in Poland knew no bounds. The commercial gurus stayed away till Polish money became convertible in 1989. This meant that for fifteen years Buddhism was almost the only spiritual offering. It permitted us to avoid much confusion. Also, Poles are receptive on many levels.

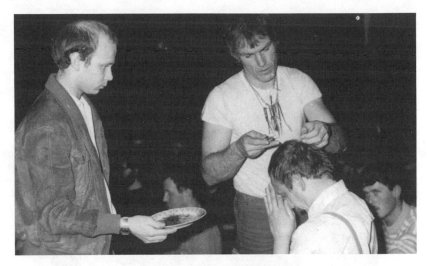

Giving Refuge in Poland

Beru Khyentse Rinpoche in Poland

At the Mayor's office in Poland

They know how to take what is useful and filter out what is not. On any of my usual ten-day visits, about five hundred people take Refuge, an openness not surpassed till my 1991 tour through the Ukraine and Russia. There we frequently made the same impact with two lectures. For years my teachings in Poland didn't finish until seven or eight in the morning. At that hour I regularly fell asleep on the people I was blessing, and everyone was back again by eleven, eager to learn more. Few people give so much of their lives as Poles, and this tendency is not lost when they move to the West. It quickly brings them a central function in many centers.

When travelling across the country, a hundred friends often come along. They board the train when I start the car, and we meet again for the next lecture. Even after a week of frequently hearing the same introduction, they find new dimensions in what I teach.

Unfortunately, there was less and less time for Northern Scandinavia. We had invited two fine traditional lamas there for that reason, and excused ourselves by saying that we didn't want to disturb their teaching methods. In truth, distances were too large, and there simply weren't many people. Though Hannah and I will probably look for our next rebirths in their gene pool, our work karma pulled us steadily south.

On a beautiful day that spring, Alex called from Vienna. He had been my close friend and student since starting in Athens in 1976. His father was the Austrian Attaché of Commerce there. In Vienna then, most Buddhist groups had rooms in a vast house in the medieval center of town. Everyone therefore knew what the others were doing, and Alex nearly exploded as he told his story: Dharmadhatu in Boulder had sent a "wanted" poster of me to their groups. It was accompanied by an—actually quite flattering—photo and instructions that it be hung everywhere and not removed. What their "Regent" wrote here was no trifle.

Alex and Tina from Vienna

Comparing me to Rudra, for example, he must have known that this is the closest Buddhism comes to something absolutely evil. Also, the claim that I was without humor, and destroyed and perverted the teachings of both the Buddhas and Karmapas, was a bit off. Naturally the Dharmadhatu had reason to be angry. Danes cannot keep a straight face or hold back jokes when we meet with false or self-important spirituality. But I had not been hostile. The times they had bounced off me, I had been correct, though not to their advantage. For example, they had tried to slip a representative of Trungpa Tulku into Europe as an already accepted teacher without even contacting us. When my friends called and asked what to do about their organization's introductory letter with all the fine stamps on it, I could only answer: "I do not know this man." This sufficed, and their organization never really took root.

My friends were sour. Hundreds of powerful Central Europeans who could each eat a dozen Vajra guards before breakfast felt that their lama had been attacked. They were ready to take the first plane and tear Boulder apart. Edita, though, had a better idea: to publish my Berkeley lecture, the official reason for their strong reaction. In this way, people could judge for themselves. This was what we did, and my Berkeley lecture is today the booklet, *Basic Dharma.* It can be found in our centers everywhere and has been trans-lated into nearly a dozen lan-guages. From that time on, I shunned any further contact with their organization. Such an overreaction from Trungpa Tulku's "Regent" was too evi-dent a sign of weakness. Small dogs bark, big dogs don't need to, and after my four years of boxing, I had a good feeling for people's endurance and limits. Thus Ole became a good Bud-dhist, who doesn't take revenge.

For some years, the Sufis had demonstrated the effective-

A good Buddhist

ness of longer courses. They bring people together, highlight teachers, and produce money. Now, some members of the old Munich group, students of Lama Chime in England, wanted to do something similar in South Germany. Only Hannah and I could make Tenga Rinpoche leave Nepal for this. However precious he was to us all, he didn't have the time; he had also promised to do a course in Denmark first. Hannah saved the day for the organizers, who had also announced Shamarpa as the main attraction without even having talked to him. Of course, he did not attend. I made a quick stop there, but didn't like the many New Age and Yoga programs. They made everything Bhagwan-like and unclear.

Instead, Edita, Sys, and I drove my first used Audi, a "100," to the southern coast of Spain. There, we had been promised a meeting with some wealthy people who might sponsor our centers. Unfortunately once again, the species proved elusive, but we met the leader of the local Gelugpa center, a fine idealist. Here lived the parents of a child who later went through the world press. He is said to be the incarnation of Lama Yeshe, who had died in California some years earlier. Conditions in the area were first-class for retreats, and I made strong wishes for a Karmapa place. In fact, this is where Pedro and Dorrit Gomez gave our lineage the center, "Karma Gon," some years later. During my lecture on space and joy inseparable—Mahamudra—you could have heard a pin drop. This was new also to the learned Geshe there. The Gelugpas mainly study the philosophy of the "Middle Way," a somewhat less ecstatic matter.

Autumn 1984 again brought the conditions for a tour around the world. We had planned to meet Niels and a hundred friends in Calcutta in January. Six of us flew to America first, and this time Hannah came along. I wanted to teach where I had missed last winter, in New York and Albany. Up there, an artist friend gave me a bear's tooth and introduced us to Native American rituals at their holy places in the woods. It was sheer nature mysticism, positive but not liberating: many experiences but little about the experiencer.

This time I didn't work for Barry. I could earn what was needed through my lectures, and my task was actually to give people access to Karmapa. Again, we drove two cars through the snow westward, visiting the centers from the year before. For the first time we saw the beautiful Sedona valley south of Flagstaff and met the Phoenix-Tempe group. We

VAJRADHATU

An Association of Buddhist Meditation Centers

11 April 1984

Dear Sangha Members:

       At the request of the Vajracarya, I am
writing to inform you of a situation that recently
took place in the San Francisco and Berkeley
Dharmadhatus. It seems that a certain Mr. Ole
Nhydahl presented himself at the Dharmadhatus with
a letter from H. E. Shamar, Rinpoche, introducing
him as an authentic dharma teacher authorized by
His Holiness the XVI Karmapa to teach and perform
refuge and bodhisattva vows. He randomly teaches
students vajrayana meditation techniques, such as
a visualization of His Holiness Karmapa, and so on.
In addition, he blesses people with a reliquary
amulet which he claims holds a single hair from
each of the sixteen Karmapas, along with other relics.

       According to reports from the Ambassador
to San Francisco and other senior students in the
Bay Area, Mr. Nhydahl managed to provoke considerable
confusion among our students there, and in general
to violate the atmosphere of sacredness. According
to all reports, his teaching style, more than the
content, runs contrary to everything we have been
taught and have come to recognize as genuine. Our
students' basic perception of his approach is one
of self-aggrandizement accompanied by a so-called
"spiritual zap" which he seemingly transfers to
other people. He talks of "having wonderful powerful experiences that are good for all sentient
beings," and he also speaks extensively about his
own personal experiences of being benefitted by
various yidams. All in all, his presentation of
the dharma has been described as a hard-sell approach
with little or no humor and a marked absence of
ordinariness.

Letter from Dharmadhatu

11 April 1984
Page 2

        The Vajracarya has instructed me to tell you that Mr. Nhydahl is not welcome at any of our centers in the role of a teacher. The Vajracarya feels very strongly that there is some real perversion of the buddhadharma taking place by Mr. Nhydahl, and a definite perversion of His Holiness Karmapa's intentions and wishes. As we know, because of the power of the vajrayana teachings, there are many warnings concerning the breaking of samaya and the possibilities of Rudrahood. There have been instances in the past where students, out of confusion, have misused these precious teachings to create a personal fortress of charlatanism and egohood. This appears to be the case with Mr. Nhydahl.

        Therefore, you should be extremely cautious and refuse outright any attempts on his part to teach or otherwise act as a spokesman of our lineage.

        The Vajracarya has requested that this letter be posted at your center, along with the enclosed photograph of Mr. Nhydahl.

        The Vajracarya sends his blessings for your continued health, prosperity, and success on the path.

        Yours in the dharma,

        The Vajra Regent Ösel Tendzin

VROT/dbh
Enclosure

became close at once, and Erma, their teacher, has fine inspirational qualities. We stayed with Randy, and several in the group had the necessary space for the Diamond Way. They took us to the holy sites of the Native Americans in the desert of Arizona, and we meditated under age-old giant cactuses. They asked me to come as often as possible. I have been doing that on a yearly basis ever since.

In Del Mar, north of San Diego, a deep friendship was growing with Carolyn and Van Hudson. Their generosity made much of my work between Mexico and Vancouver possible. They offered us a home no matter when we came, or with how many people, or how totally exhausted we were. Year after year, we have been driving the thousands of miles up and down the west coast in their cars. From there, we traveled north on a schedule which Crystal had organized.

In San Francisco, I taught the Theosophists, again an intellectual joy. Their leader was Joe Miller, a classic power-genius with a white goatee. From time to time, he suddenly chanted unknown mantras at great volume. On Sundays, he led many spiritually interested people through a local park, and everyone loved him. Here, I also noticed Carol

On one of Joe Miller's Sunday walks in San Francisco

Carol

Aronoff for the first time. She had attended one of my former programs, but this was the first time we met. She had exactly the qualities to strengthen Karmapa's work there. Her background included the London of the sixties. She was a humanistic professor and taught Holistic Health: Eastern Perspectives, at San Francisco State University. With her idealism and skill, she was an influence that would keep things pure. Together we drove west via Los Altos to Nevada City, where we decided to publish my books in English; Paul Clemens of Blue Dolphin Publishing would print them at his Press. As the books filled our European centers with exciting people daily, we thought they must also be useful in America. Carol started by editing *Entering the Diamond Way* and did not let me go until the work was done.

After Mount Shasta, we drove down through California and returned the cars to Van and Carolyn. There was just time for a quick visit to my film-making friends in L.A. Then we flew to Hawaii.

Our tall group in Japan

The first teachings were on Kauai, the oldest and lushest of the islands. Rodger and Janet had gathered a group there. Then came Maui with Lama Tensing, where Hannah and I both dreamt intensely of Karmapa. Maybe this was the place he had especially wanted to send us ten years earlier. In Honolulu, we stayed with Nancy, my friend from Portland. Here, I stopped using snuff. Although it was a direct transmission from Karmapa, this renunciation gradually became necessary. The Americans often wondered if my persistent happiness was due to the brown powder or the blessing of our lineage. If anyone doubts that nicotine brings physical addiction, they only need to watch the video of my following lecture: for two hours I twist like a snake, and my hands move constantly from my shirt-pocket, now empty, to my face, which is expecting a new hit. The clarity of the lecture was not affected, however.

Our next stop was Japan. Here, our group was clearly too big for the country's bourgeois style. Already at Tokyo Airport, we goofed. As there was little room for our luggage in the noble Toyota flagship, I jumped on the trunk as one does with European cars. This one was Japanese, however, and immediately showed a big dent. My attempts to push it out again only made things worse. Next, a ladies' man from our group was seen getting too quickly acquainted with a local lady of good repute, and somebody else didn't want to see the "Old Emperor's Castle," a national treasure. He went shopping instead. Fortunately I found time to prepare Yoshiko's very gifted mother for her death. Now that Cesar and she are in Mexico again, which allows for more latitude of expression, our friendship is again unhindered.

Korea was fresh and exciting, a real relief. Apart from people there, our brave East Tibetans, and some small central Asian tribes, I have met no Mongolian nationalities who are direct. Among nonwestern-educated Chinese and Japanese, one rarely knows what goes on beneath the smooth surface, and also Central and Western Tibetans play a lot of games, in private as well as nationally. On this peninsula, however, people looked into our eyes and showed what they felt. They reacted spontaneously, which felt good, although not everything happened on the highest level of poetry.

We didn't want to become absorbed by the capital, Seoul, before having visited some of the country's historical places. Also, the hotels seemed quite expensive, so we took the first night train south along the coast to Pusan and on. Here we spent two days at their Buddhist national monuments. They are much more national than Buddhist, by the way. Disliking the fact that their culture had its roots here, the Japanese had been burning their castles for centuries and banning their language. The Koreans had always rebuilt them immediately, and today they are impressive monuments to the country's toughness. The beautiful halls were empty of meditators, however.

The country shows how supply and demand also function on the spiritual level. Having abandoned the worst sufferings and achieved the most important freedoms, we in the West will naturally look within and for teachings which make sense. In unfree countries with much suffering, however, people search outside and for emotional examples. They want others to suffer for them, gods and prophets who tell them what to do.

When mentioning that we were enjoying their country on a Buddhist pilgrimage, frequently the answer was an unexpected: "But we are Christians." There were improvised churches and crosses everywhere. Apparently their local brand of Buddhism had managed to become so ritualistic and foreign to life, so ossified and monastic, that people with something to give couldn't work within its frame. Now, they were searching elsewhere. As in Japan, where Christian communities are also springing up, their Buddhism has simply grown too hard, demanding, and elitist, too masculine. Their Christianity, on the other hand, permits the repressed feminine aspect, allows people to be weak, their condition most of the time, anyway, and grants forgiveness so one can make a new start with little psychological ballast. Our inherent Buddha nature is surely less obvious if one works twenty hours a day, feeds fifteen children, is without education, and oppressed.

We bought the country's cheap but sturdy products, mostly shoulder bags for friends. One could pick the designer label oneself, and we chose "Hang Ten." We also got some thick and very cheap leather jackets, still in use today. The hotels were exciting: the heating was through air channels in the floor. It was the part of the body facing down which stayed warm. The food was generally coarse, but breakfast, soy soup sold on the streets, was an experience. Here we met the main actors in the nocturnal hotel dramas: people who nearly broke down the doors and didn't stop screaming.

Jamgon Kongtrul Rinpoche was on Taiwan. It was wonderful to walk directly into one of his initiations. Coordinating developments afterwards, he also said how glad Rumtek was that we had tackled the recent political problems head on. My meetings with the local Chinese were not so cordial, however. Several tried to run away. People who had emphatically promised to work together and provide a real opportunity for others had started playing gurus themselves. This had badly split up the groups. Superstitious, badly educated, and taking things way too personally due to insecurity, they now did more harm than good to their followers. They really didn't like seeing me again. Only the oldest had kept their style. Guru Han lay in the hospital with a broken thigh bone and let himself be shaved with the calmness of a Chinese mummy. He also had a few things to digest: half his students had left him after his accident. They now wanted to follow a teacher with more "chi."

All in all, Taiwan was embarrassing and I decided to do less there in the future. Without compassion and devotion there is no Diamond Way, and broken bonds destroy everything at once. Having so little time, it should be used on those who learn in order to help others.

Also in Hong Kong, the essential thing was helping people work together. Interviews were more important than teachings, not a good sign. When invited for a meal, several times we had to change restaurants. The beautiful aquariums with live fish were not ornamental; one was

Guru Han

expected to choose a specimen which then became one's meal. It was not as bad as the dogs and rats later on, in continental China, but it was too much for us. Fortunately, there was always a place with tofu or beef nearby, and our hosts followed us without complaint.

Bangkok, our last stop before India, was flooded and bustling. We visited the most important temples and noticed with amazement how peoples' voices took on the tone of deepest religiosity when explaining the amount of gold and precious stones in the statues. The country certainly benefited from Buddha's teachings, but we missed the deep devotion of our Tibetans. It seemed much more like the "something-for something" system we knew from so many other places.

We landed in Calcutta on January 1, 1985, and met Beru Khyentse Rinpoche in the airport restaurant. Hannah had translated for him in

Tenga Rinpoche together with Hannah and Niels, our organizer

Bokar Rinpoche in the Bellevue Hotel

Beru Khyentse Rinpoche teaches on Bodhisattvas

autumn and they had much to talk about. Then our hundred friends arrived with Niels, Bjørn, and Edita. After some hours in the chaos of an Indian airport, we flew on to the Eastern Himalayas. Darjeeling was cold and damp. Once again the authorities blocked our entry to Sikkim, and we decided to pay them back. We would now smuggle seventeen Poles without any papers. While we made arrangements, precious Bokar Rinpoche came and taught in Lhawang's Bellevue Hotel. Arriving in Rumtek, again without official permission, we attended teachings by the lineage holders several times a day. It was a great experience. Even the newest of our students quickly knew this: Rumtek is home. Then followed the classic evil bus trip to Kathmandu. Here Beru Khyentse daily taught the old Mahayana text, "Bodhisattva Behavior," in the Vajra Hotel. Finishing the course with an especially heavy warning against the bad influence of women on one's practice, Hannah and I had difficulty keeping our faces straight. We knew he was getting married the next day.

On this tour, teachings were more important than holy sites. Our friends should learn as much as possible. Because of the close connections along the European north-south axis, information would spread everywhere, even then.

It was great to return to Europe; North Italy solidified that spring. Though only a few showed real consistency, and there was too much white powder on the scene, the friendships started then have continued to grow. Our main contact is Bibi and I am "resident lama" to the group in Brescia.

Buddhism in Switzerland developed like everything in that country, steadily and with roots. Already years earlier, we had started a center in the historical heart of Bern, their capital. Today, we also have a house in Zurich given by a close friend, Annemarie, and most of a mansion outside Basel. All work closely together with the German groups. Being at the top of any lama's wish list, the country would have no difficulty attracting visiting teachers. What we had to make sure, however, was that they also taught. Several have been content to just have a luxurious time.

The first two weeks in June, I taught the preliminary practices at my first course ever. Though it took place at the Danish retreat center, most who came were German or Polish. As all seemed pleased, similar arrangements would soon fill the summer months of every year. Carol

Our Brescia group in 1991

Center in Basel, Switzerland

arrived with her hopeful son and started working on my rough draft of *Entering the Diamond Way*.

Later during this stifling summer, the Dalai Lama gave the great "Wheel of Time" empowerment. It happened near the Rikon Institute in Switzerland. Though most had already received this initiation from the Tenga or Kalu Rinpoches, we had still asked our friends to attend. It would strengthen the Tibetan cause. First the Dalai Lama gave a "Guru Rinpoche" initiation which was very powerful. It was preceded by many long explanations to the audience of mainly Gelugpa-oriented people, students of the "Path of Virtue." They frown upon this great hero because he had so many women.

It was impossible for most to follow the "Wheel of Time" initiation. The translator overdid it. Even Carol, a professor, could hardly understand his English terminology.

Right after the initiation, we drove to Paris and received Kunzig Shamarpa at the airport. The next stop was "Vajradhara Ling," a retreat center of Kalu Rinpoche in Normandy. One can still recognize the Viking architecture in the buildings there. Shamarpa gave the Bodhisattva Vow, and I changed my alcohol vow from "absolutely no alcohol," which I had kept since 1971, to "not getting drunk." I hoped to widen my social range in this way, but it was a mistake. With the joy I constantly experience, alcohol is only interesting on the level of taste, anyway. The chemical effects are rather unpleasant and a waste of time. This is the reason I again drink no alcohol today.

From northwest France, we followed the beautiful coast road south. Hannah got off in Dordogne, where she translated for Shamarpa, and I took a car full of friends to the Bavarian Alps. Here, Tenga Rinpoche had asked me to give the evening teachings at the summer camp. He himself taught in the mornings and Lama Chime during the afternoon. It is a great inspiration to work for Tenga Rinpoche, a true master. I cannot claim, however, that the rest of us excelled in flexibility or tolerance over the next weeks. Lama Chime's students—Bhagwanese and flower-children—and my former troublemakers and hard cases, developed an ever worse relationship. They were simply too different. Even Tenga Rinpoche's endless love could not bring us together. I thought that his lightweight style belonged in England, that it diluted Karmapa's work, and he said that I was fanatical and sectarian. As an added spice, the camp was organized by the old group from Munich, the people who kept inviting Ayang Tulku's representative. Things being like that, German Buddhism lived through some healthy purifications during those years. People came off their rosy spiritual clouds very quickly. Very early, they had to decide where to place their trust.

After the course, I drove our old BMW via Basel to the Dordogne, probably in record time. Being alone, I didn't have to think of safety. Hannah was still translating for Shamarpa. Whenever she is with our Rinpoches, their close bond and deep confidence fill the room. With her as the mild and virtuous part of the family, my night life and activity as "Dharma General" were well-balanced. This was one function Karmapa expected from me and a title he had regularly used. Who else would bash the egos which got in the way? Then we drove on to Amsterdam. Hannah was already expected in Malaysia, to organize Gyaltsab Rinpoche's schedule. I was just getting into the car when her plane flew above the parking lot. At low height, heavy, and with immense noise, it moved slowly over my head. I knew she was in good hands. "Black Coat" traveled with her.

A close bond

During the next years, when a new and fatal disease struck, Maia became an important bodyguard. Her parents had been in the first group when Hannah and I brought Tibetan Buddhism to Central Europe. Together we had protected friends from the police in the sixties. Even before we went east, they and their two beautiful daughters had often visited our house in South Sweden. On the stretch from Germany to Copenhagen, their farm was a convenient stop, and Maia was often alone when I came. Thus, she had come to represent idyllic Denmark to me, while I was the wide world to her. Once when I put a statue of "Black Coat" into her hands, we both felt it move. She had now grown up, had a fine son, and a strong mind. Through her, I would relive a rough period of my life in a mild form—without fist fights every night.

In north Germany, the influence of our centers in Hamburg and Wuppertal grew steadily. At the same time, and inspired by Schwarzenberg, a net of free-flowing friendships and shared joys made the south of the country into a net exporter of good vibrations. Here life and practice enriched one another in ways that today inspire our centers around the world. Every day spent there was a gift on all levels.

With Maia at the retreat center in Poland

Upper left: Schwarzenberg seen from the air

Also the map had shrunk. My students now provided me with German used cars in the two hundred horsepower range—European drivers stay to the right so one can pass—and Sys organized my schedules so every moment was used to the maximum. Never had the basics for growth been as good as this December, when we went to America again.

It was Maia's first visit there. With the carefree confidence of people in socialized countries, she had simply gone to the nearest bank and borrowed the money for the ticket. Maxi from Austria and Deborah from Hamburg also came along; Wolfgang and Burkhard were there; and Gabi and Ulla would join us later. New York brought the joy of meeting Roland, a close friend of Maxi's from Austria. Somehow, his bright face remained etched on my mind. Building up the "Rolo" boutiques of

*My close friend
Roland*

trendy quality clothing in San Francisco over the next years, he became an example that the American dream is very alive. Though we have many fine spontaneous donors, nobody found ways to integrate their skills and resources into the Dharma in such a pervasive and natural way. Writing this in summer of 1991, I still haven't met anybody who faults this man. We stayed in the center on Manhattan's west side, where I taught for the last time till today. Every visit got worse: I nearly stood on my head to bring some good vibrations to the group, but they insisted on being heavy as lead. Though individually good people, collectively they were under a deadening influence, some said from the Dharmadhatu. This time I was to commit a true sacrilege on their premises.

Looking for a place from where I could see everybody, I innocently seated myself on a pillow that was also used by Khenpo Karthar Rinpoche. In Europe I teach from thrones, and there was no sign saying that this pillow had become an object of veneration. Today, I cannot recall the trepidations that must have struck the true believers. I do remember, however, that I had to work even harder than usual to send people home in a halfway acceptable state of mind. It was not easy for them to come, and I really wished them happiness from the depth of my heart—women rarely dare take the subway at night in New York, and one often needs half an hour just to find a parking place, usually in the prohibited or tow-away zones.

Once again, AAA Driveaway Company on Times Square had the right vehicle: with our mountains of luggage we would plow through the snow drifts and cross the country in a giant Jeep, a Bronco.

The high Taos plateau had never manifested as beautifully as in the deep snow. Wanting the closest possible bond to America—also physical—Maxi and I each gave Norbert $100 to buy a plot of land. It lay near yet another very holy native American mountain, and with a later addition, we today own two plots of the mesa. It has a breathtaking view, but the nearest water is miles away and eight hundred feet down. It is great to have a physical presence in the U.S., and one day we will build retreat cabins for Karmapa's students there. Returning to Albuquerque, my heart filled with joy. Paul and Nancy Clemens from Blue Dolphin Publishing had sent the first box of *Entering the Diamond Way,* the predecessor to this book. It was beautifully made, and we had to hide one

Our few square yards in the U.S.

or two copies to show in the following centers; all the others disappeared at once.

We delivered the driveaway, and Van and Carolyn again lent us their sturdy VW bus and diesel Rabbit. This time we would stay longer in San Francisco. The Bay Area now had people who would hold the energy, always the most difficult thing to find in America. Everybody moved into Carol's idyllic house in Marin, north of the Golden Gate Bridge, and soon we were joined by exciting Gabi and Ulla. They were able to stay for the last fine weeks. As this was America, the focus of our work changed from one visit to the next. This time, giving confidence and structure to "guru"-damaged people was very high on the list.

Carol had arranged impressive P.R. As my book had just been published, she had been able to set up several TV and radio interviews. She and the Marin group were willing to become a steady presence in North America. Teaching such a wide humanistic subject, Carol could use meditation to deepen her students' understanding, and I asked her to share her rich experience by guiding meditations and teaching Dharma on weekends up and down the coast. Having taken Refuge with Karmapa, she was open to his energy field and we keep a good contact.

Maia flew home before we traveled on. She missed her son, and sharing me with so many was too much for her. During the last ten days, we first thanked Paul Clemens in Nevada City for publishing *Entering the Diamond Way*. The color inserts, his own idea, made the book really high quality. Though we were never good at advertizing ourselves, it sold briskly by word of mouth. Then we took time for Mount Shasta, another holy mountain of another Indian tribe. It is strange how often sacred mountains—like Kailash in Tibet—do not consist of exciting rock walls which can be climbed, but of land left standing after the surroundings erode away. Mount Shasta itself is a heap of volcanic ash. Here, the spiritual and the heroic don't quite meet.

December 23, we arrived in Seattle. Brave Ann Robben, who so honored our connection after the Dharmadhatu letter, had organized two evenings in the local Sakya center. It was a former church which the Tibetan community had bought. There was a good turnout and people were fortunately not driven away by a moralizing Tibetan lady. To our amazement they gave initiations at $50 apiece, but though people were generous—maybe due to the time of year—no one wanted to take responsibility for a group. So we left them with some addresses of centers farther south and a list of books.

Our audience with Dabshan Rinpoche, also in Seattle, was a great experience. Solid, powerful, and in Western clothes, he leads the Sakya School of Tibetan Buddhism in tandem with Sakya Trinzin. His blessing struck from an unknown angle and stayed with us for a long time.

Christmas Eve happened at a "Denny's" fast food place. Gabi, Deborah, and Ulla entertained everybody. Then we drove on south. There were checks along the way to ensure that cars had snow chains for the passes, but we avoided them. As Europeans, we felt above that. After an exciting descent into ever denser California, we slept some hours at Carol's and then took the main road south to San Diego.

A thick fog had forced me to drive mainly by instinct. It disappeared near L.A. With the white hills illuminated by unearthly moonlight, I spontaneously started to talk about my mother. I told how she still called me "little Ole" and how wonderful she was. Already in bed at Van and Carolyn's, I was called to the phone. Maia was on the other end of the line and said, "At 9:30 this morning, your mother was hit by a

truck in Lyngby. The police have just been here. They say she is dead."
She also told of a rainbow around the sun when it happened and other
unusual signs.

It was both a shock and a relief. A great loss for us but great luck
for her. My mother had become eighty-three years old without ever being
sick and had an excellent bond to Karmapa. Her greatest wish had been
not to become a burden for others, and since death had been instanta-
neous, she had not suffered.

I called Hannah in Taiwan. She had just scared an armed robber
from the house by scolding him in Danish. She really kept her style.
When she heard that my mother had died, she wanted to go home at
once. This would have blocked Rinpoche's program and wasn't necessary.
She is always with me, anyway. Van and Carolyn booked my flight back
and I honored my mother's memory by giving the evening lecture in her
name. Though my voice got somewhat thick from time to time—I love
her deeply—everything went well.

In Copenhagen, Bjørn had prepared the cremation. Early in the
morning, about sixty-eight hours after her death, I woke up in our
basement room. What I experienced was no dream: my mother was with
me, clear in every detail and on my right side. In front of us was Karmapa,
as big as a house. He was transparent, golden brown, and sat on a chair.
Smiling, he threw the large black "Mother" pills on us which changed
into rainbows when they struck. One of the last hit my left foot with
great power. In the meanwhile, like a diver letting go of ballast, my
mother moved ever faster upwards and then disappeared. Never had I
been more grateful. Everything fit. After three days of unconsciousness,
her mind had suddenly awakened without a body and come to me.
Meeting Karmapa's powerfield, she had been guided directly into his
Pure Realm. The same had happened to my father, who had died of a
brain stroke in 1976. Among his contributions to Buddhism was a full
translation into Danish of Marpa's life-story in the mid-seventies. The
last thing he ever swallowed had been one of Karmapa's "Mother" pills.
They were then still obtainable. A highly cultured neighbor was mirac-
ulously cured of an evil cancer on that occasion. In 1945, and dressed only
in a nightshirt, he had come running into our apartment in Lyngby, north
of Copenhagen, to say that the war was over. Whenever my father

My wonderful parents

appeared in my meditations afterwards, there was only a pillar of light, and on our next visit to Rumtek, Karmapa had suddenly asked: "Where is your father now?" Without any hesitation, I answered: "In the Pure Realm of highest joy." Looking up for a moment, Karmapa answered: "That's right," filling me with intense gratitude.

The funeral was Christian-Buddhist. A priest who was my father's student-friend led the ceremony. Bjørn and I thanked our mother from the depth of our hearts and decided to simply spend more of our busy moments together. Nothing would gladden her more than that.

Maia had set up some events in Copenhagen. New Year was in Hamburg, and after Vienna and Graz, I was back in San Diego. Gabi, Ulla, and Deborah had held the fort, and Carol and Wolfgang came down from San Francisco. They said the lecture that night was like 10,000 volts. Meanwhile, our first tour to Tibet had been planned and I flew east via Hawaii, where lovely Kiffer was waiting. She thoroughly opened me to nature there. Sunrise at Haleakala, the world's largest crater, was an explosion of incredible colors and shapes. It can easily hold both Manhattan and its skyscrapers. She had also set up a lecture on the Big Island, where I met a dozen close friends from the sixties. The volcano here is several kilometers wide and about three hundred meters deep. Its masses of molten lava erupt periodically, flow into the ocean, and thus enlarge the island. The ground was pitch black and somehow smelled age-old. I offered the crater's power to our protector "Black Coat" and can still feel its energy today.

On the last afternoon, of course, I had to bodysurf the biggest wave. "Sliding down," as they say locally, my neck produced some unusual noises as I dug my head into the sand. With a flight leaving the next morning, I could either visit a hospital or take leave of Kiffer. So I simply had to hope that nothing was broken. I thank both the Buddhist Protectors and my Viking forefathers that everything was okay.

Lovely Kiffer

CHAPTER THIRTEEN

Secret Journey to Tibet

*H*ANNAH AND KURT WERE ALREADY IN HONG KONG. We stayed in luxury with a German couple, and I taught both their friends and a Chinese group. Pedro and Ilse arrived soon after, while Jatzek had to fly on to Communist China. He had a Polish passport and they didn't want any Communists they could avoid on the island.

Pedro's vast mind became obvious when shopping for the journey. He moved easily with that illusory and empty material called money. Bringing a fine video camera down to a price which made the dealers wince, he enabled us to film forty priceless hours in Tibet. On the same occasion, he got an excellent pair of East German binoculars for only $100. Also Kurt was an expert. He had brought Alpine clothes which can keep one warm at nearly any temperature. Fortunately Hannah's and my economic habits did not decide the equipment. We were well prepared on our first trip to Tibet, though as a matter of fact, I wore my old Army gear as always. Wanting to protect the expensive outfit, I kept it in the bottom of my sack the whole way.

Pedro left first. He wanted to find Jatzek and help him. The rest of us took a noisy speedboat up from Hong Kong. It went as far northwest into China as possible. Going up the river, all our antennas were out. We wanted to sense the vibrations of the country that had conquered our beloved Tibet. It was important to know how they were.

The shoddy factories, the piles of junk, the run-down houses—the best general description was "loveless." There was no warmth or joy. Things were depressing, and nothing seemed to fit. The contrast to Hong Kong was striking: here people sat or plodded around; there they walked briskly or ran. Nearly all wore the standardized blue or green uniforms, and we soon again called them "twins." In 1968, in Nepal, this name had been our first reaction to the phenomenon. Knowing that about a billion people had this ant's karma was not easy to bear.

The boat stopped at Guanchu, a city built to English specifications. We were brought to a hotel at once, and the waiters tried to keep all foreigners inside. They had little success with us, and an evening at the market in the city center was very instructive. People gaped at us and no one knew how to make contact. In school, they are still taught that we are "White Devils." Everything was poor, grey, narrow, and unfree. The great Socialist brotherhood had obviously failed, and the alienation we are supposed to suffer from in Capitalism had definitely not been removed.

The bus to Guilin takes one through amazing nature which looks like the props for a special school of Chinese art: the so-called "dragon teeth landscapes." It consists of tall, thin mountains which jut abruptly into the sky from an otherwise flat landscape. Even the gnarled trees looked exactly like the old paintings. As far as we understood, the formations appeared when lava was forced up through a former ocean floor and then hardened in the water. When the pressure of India against the Eurasian continent caused the whole area to rise—also bringing about the Himalayas—the dragon's teeth appeared.

The city of Guilin was active. It was situated in a "semi-liberated" economic area, and people were allowed to exploit each other to a certain degree. This kept them in good shape. Fewer wore uniforms and several smiled. One or two were nearly sexy and many wanted to exchange dollars. This always came first. With such currency, they could buy the better products in the tourist shops.

After a day on the people's own buses, we reached the next major city. People were unbelievably unpleasant here, as was the cold desert they lived in. This was the China most tourists remember, the reason so few want to return. For a while I pushed people around to see if their

The proletariat at play

embittered faces could get even more sour, but then it was time to move on. This was not easy, however. Communist China has holidays only once a year. They take five days off during Chinese New Year, which falls in January or February. Everyone who can get the necessary permission therefore travels at this time.

An official lady who seemed to take a liking to the white devil's blue eyes arranged standing space in the aisle on a train to Chendu. This is a city of five million people, lying only a few hundred miles from the mountains of East Tibet. Literally every square inch along the way was cultivated, which was really overdoing it. The effect was strange. It was also painful to see the caged dogs and rats in front of the restaurants, waiting to become somebody's dinner. We often wished for a good pair of pliers to open their cages.

Chendu was vast, grey, and dreary. Its air made Mexico City and Athens seem like health resorts. Millions of ineffective coal fireplaces made it nearly impossible to breathe, and half the population wore gauze masks in the street. In addition, the town was damp, unfriendly, and extremely cold. It was really no place to hang out.

Entering the biggest tourist hotel, Pedro and Jatzek came down the stairs. It was a giant yellow box surrounded by a garden where hundreds were killed during the revolt in 1989. It felt good to see them again. They had taken a more travelled route and had already made photos of a well-preserved Buddha down the river. They also knew the best exchange rates and some places where one could eat without getting sick. At $9 a night, the hotel was more than we would spend, and on the way to a cheaper place we went via an underground coffee house. To our amazement, it contained real people, modern types. After only three days in Red China, we already gazed in amazement when meeting somebody awake.

A few hundred yards down the street, we found a cheaper hotel. There was only one room, which was like a steam bath: the main water pipe of the building had burst. The night there, a dubious meal on the train, or the many Chinese soldiers I had disposed of during my last life—something was too much. In the morning, Hannah and I had high fevers. Stumbling back to the fine hotel for our dry clothes, Pedro and Jatzek gave us their beds. They would sleep on the floor until we were

In the train through China

well again. I told Kurt, Ilse, and Burkhard to fly ahead to Lhasa. They caught the last plane before everything shut down for Tibetan New Year. Up there, they could arrange for us all.

Turning the experience into bliss and the free play of the mind took some doing. We were sicker than ever before, perspired constantly, and had splitting headaches. During the ten days in bed, we saw little but the hotel's Kung-Fu films from Hong Kong and the amazing dreams high fevers produce. Outside, the Chinese enthusiastically increased pollution with tons of noisy fireworks. They simply didn't stop.

Deciding we would rather die in Tibet than in China, it was now our turn to fly to the roof of the world. The day before, I had been on a short walk. Some of my strength had returned.

The mountains of East Tibet do a gigantic north-south loop, and Pedro took some good forbidden footage, the beginning of our video of the tour. The landing strip was a brown stone desert, and the first Tibetans we saw looked gnarled and small, but were warmly dressed. They carried triangular red and green flags which they were apparently allowed to fasten to their houses. Waiting for the bus driver to do the hundred meters to where the passengers were standing, we once again sensed how dead and meaningless the world was to a red Chinese. He didn't start up till we directly threatened him.

The Tibetan Himalayas

The Potala

The road followed a winding river and we stopped to pee at a place which stank. I wondered what people ate to produce such an odor, and a few days later, I found a probable cause: some evil-smelling green onions from a valley further north.

Lhasa comes suddenly and is much smaller than one thinks. After a few administration buildings and a broad street with some intersections and traffic lights, you are there. Leaving one of the low buses with windows that prevent you from looking up, you find yourself right at the foot of the giant, shiny Potala, the palace of the Dalai Lamas. Though destroyed and terribly poor, Tibet is an oasis after China. We quickly got well while Pedro and Jatzek could enjoy everything right from the start.

Kurt and the others had rooms in the "Bernakshol" hotel on Happiness Road. It is one of the few Tibetan places where tourists were then permitted to stay. They were always overfilled, while the Chinese hotels stay empty. Not knowing the local languages, Westerners could only vote on the political issues with their feet. Every day, one heard somebody say: "Tibet for sure, but China never again." Somehow the red Chinese there were incapable of treating other people nicely. Their emotional range covered the area between insult and jealousy with occasional orgies of gloating. Reminding ourselves regularly of our Chinese Dharma-family in the free World, we hopefully avoided getting too racist.

During our first circumambulation of Johkang, Lhasa's most important temple, something unusual happened. It was worth forty precious minutes of video to Pedro. At the main entrance of the circular building containing the Jowo, Tibet's national shrine, I was attracting a crowd. They were East Tibetan Khampas, powerful men from the tribe of long-faced warriors who had been the only ones to really fight the Chinese. Self-assured and with red New Year threads woven into their braids, they were an impressive sight.

Deeply absorbed by the timeless familiarity of the scene, by the strong light, and the people moving about in slow motion, I now realized that something was happening much closer. I was being thoroughly checked. It wasn't my passport or money they were after. The vibes were completely different.

Suddenly, a strong-faced man in front nearly bumped his head into my stomach and without thinking, I blessed him. Then, everything exploded. Still only on half power, during the next hours I was shoved around the Johkang by thousands of people who all wanted a blessing. As in the West, I used my small round container to transfer the energy. Karmapa himself had filled it with relics for this purpose. At every later stop through Tibet, the same thing happened—people all wanted a

In front of the Jokhang

The reconstructed Jowo—
the main Buddha

blessing—and the eyes of the Chinese officials nearly popped out of their heads. A Tibetan Rinpoche doing this would have had his case examined. But what could they do with a tourist?

The full moon night in February 1986, two weeks after New Year's, would be a historical date. Already in the afternoon, the city hummed with frustrated energies while the Chinese cordoned off its center with buses and jeeps. It was obvious that only special guests were expected for the evening's ceremony. So we skirted the problem by inviting ourselves. It would be the first "Monlam Chenmo," meaning "Big Prayer" in twenty-six years. Jumping over some jeeps and passing some soldiers who weren't able to stop us, we fooled the police by scattering over the open area behind the Johkang. Then we disappeared among the few hundred select people who stood in front of the building. In glaring spotlight, maybe two hundred monks from the three largest Gelugpa monasteries were chanting, while lay people fastened big boards with multicolored, traditional butter decorations to a high scaffolding. These are offerings to the Buddhas. The scene was both touching and embarrassing. Though there was little open expression under the Chinese cameras, they had at least won back some freedom. In former days, there had been twenty thousand monks, but even so, they seemed like a crowd. The Panchen Lama was there, but though we saw him from a short distance, we weren't able to form an opinion of him. He closely resembled Karmapa, but I sensed no real powerfield. This may have been due to the heavy tortures he had endured.

The Tibetans we talked with were intensely unhappy about him. They disliked the fact that he cooperated so closely with the forces occupying their country. Above all, they suffered when he officially praised the Chinese. More than any other factor, however, it was surely his activity from the center of power—he was one of China's thirteen vice presidents—that had increased their religious freedom over the last years. Among the oppressed peoples of the world, tragic heroes are much more popular than the tacticians who make their lives at least bearable.

H.H. the Panchen Lama in Jytte and Peter's house, Sydney, Australia

It will be interesting to see which opinion becomes standard during the years to come. In January 1989, on the day before his death, the Panchen Lama probably expressed what he really felt. From Shigatze in southern Tibet, his home base, he thoroughly criticized the Chinese. He said they had destroyed both his land and his people.

As soon as his car had left, the Chinese opened the blockades. Now there was real action: thousands of Tibetans came out from under the buses, many with their clothes torn or oiled. Pushing each other against the walls, the vast square quickly filled up. They just wanted to get in. Some had travelled for months to take part in this "Great Prayer," the first since their freedom had been stolen. People fell left and right when no longer held up by the bodies around them, and several surely died. Some sirens howled, but no one could get to the squashed people who were now hopefully on their way to a Pure Realm.

One knows Lhasa after a few days. The place we really wanted to visit was Tsurphu: Karmapa's main seat. It lies seventy kilometers northwest of the city, but getting there became a real trip. When at long last our impossible driver managed to start the truck—several hours late—his next ingenious act was to pick up a man with masses of wood right in front of a Chinese checkpoint. Westerners are not allowed to travel outside the organized tours so they wanted us out of the truck. We photographed the officials and threatened to complain about them till they gave up on punishing the driver and handed him back his papers. The next forty kilometers on the asphalt road going north, we were

Tsurphu before the destruction

Tsurphu in '86, seen from the meditation caves

stopped twice by the military and had to walk some miles to avoid a checkpoint. At an especially jagged mountain, we turned left down thirty kilometers of rocky valley road. At its end lay Tsurphu.

Some kilometers before the monastery, the driver simply gave up. He had not improved his weak style from the morning, and now he also thought it was too icy. So we had to shoulder our luggage while the wood would be loaded on yak oxen later. We were at an altitude of over four kilometers and in the bright light of the full moon. Including a change of tires, he had driven the seventy kilometers in a record twelve hours.

The area was magical. Stumbling along under heavy loads, we followed the path walked by our lineage holders since 1150. After a final rise, we stood among majestic ruins. They instantly reminded me of bombed-out Hamburg after the war.

The entrance to a reconstructed building was lit by a single gas lamp. Inside were a dozen older lamas with many questions. After much tsampa and tea, they led me upstairs to their best room, where so far only Jamgon Kongtrul Rinpoche had stayed. Seeing me gesture for Hannah to come along, their eyes grew wide, and they looked miserable when discovering that our sleeping bags were zipped together. After all, they were monks. In order to preserve their peace of mind, we separated both sleeping bags and mattresses, and they left relieved.

This famous relief of Loving Eyes appeared spontaneously
on a rock near Tsurphu. During the destruction
of the monastery its lower half disappeared,
but after the rebuilding started, it returned once again.

It was difficult to sleep in the thin air, and the energy of the place was intense. I glided in and out of dreams, which must have covered several lifetimes. At dawn, tossing myself to face the valley, I received an extraordinary and special blessing: I looked right into the black-blue dog's face of Shing Kyong, the local protector. He is very important to Shamarpa and Tenga Rinpoche. Apart from what Pedro's video of our

Where we lived

In front of the main building in Tsurphu

The Tsurphu retreat place

visit shows, we didn't see much. We offered lots of pictures of Karmapa, our highest Lamas, and Black Coat, then took the truck back to Lhasa. We now wanted to plan a trip no Westerner had managed before: a month to the holiest sites in forbidden East Tibet.

Under a moon which was still nearly full, we climbed onto an open truck. It already held a dozen Khampas and other Tibetans. As we had to bypass several Chinese checkpoints in the dark, there was no stop until the next morning. Halting in a river bed where one couldn't easily be seen, people prepared tsampa and tea. We habitually improved this mixture with some protein powder and vitamins. I wondered why the Khampas on the truck didn't fully accept us, but gradually the reason became clear. During New Year's celebrations in Lhasa they had repeatedly invited Burkard, who is about two meters tall and very strong, to bouts of arm wrestling. Pushing down the polite giant's arm before he had even understood what was going on, their estimation of the white race had suffered. This must never happen. People judge all members of a group from their first contact. As before in foreign lands, it was again up to me to save our honor. This took some doing, however; being a lama, I couldn't simply invite the strongest man for a match. A few days later, the appropriate situation came up. While they were testing their strength at a table, I said: "Oh, this looks just like our games when I was a child. Can I try?" Quickly putting the strongest man's hand down three times, I continued: "It really is the same. How funny!" Afterwards, there was no more pushing for space on the truck. We were now accepted on a level everyone understood.

The first real stop was in Bowo or Bomi, as the town is called. It lies north of Bhutan on the border between the northeastern Himalayas and the high ancient plateau of Central Tibet. Here the formations of the Jura age meet the youngest and highest mountains of the world. One travels for weeks along a clearly visible line through the landscape.

Rock painting of Black Coat
at the entrance of Tsurphu

The lineage in Tsurphu

Our driver simulated an engine repair. He wanted a few days with his family and invited us to stay at his farm in the village. It was great to again sleep under the open roof of a barn. We had a view across the valley and were surrounded by silently falling snow. While we usually flee Tibetan and Sherpa houses because of their darkness and the acrid smoke from the open fireplaces, a neighbor was a joy to visit. He had the only stove we saw in Tibet.

The region was already in bad shape. The Chinese had taken down countless old conifers without planting anything. Often, the trunks rotting on the ground were so thick that one couldn't look over them. Having no machines to move the thickest parts, the workers just left them there. We had ample time for both meditating and seeing the area. People only came for blessings in the evening.

The constant shaking and bumping on the road had been the worst part of the tour so far. Now cold took over. East of Bhutan where the Himalayas make a curve from north to south, there was no way anymore to avoid the high passes. Everyone kept a stiff upper lip, and we piled our warm stuff on Hannah and Ilse. People often died from exposure on that stretch. On the last pass before Chamdo, a town which the Chinese had now made the capital of Eastern Tibet, Kurt kept the totally exhausted driver going. We just had to avoid being caught in the constantly falling snow.

The trucks are actually the unsung heroes of the poor countries now trying to industrialize. The way India would totally break down if the "Tata" diesel trucks—built on Mercedes' license—were to vanish, China is supplied by an antique construction: a four-cylinder, side-ventilated gasoline engine first built in the early thirties by Opel. Produced unchanged by the Russians after the war, this example of fine German engineering was the only thing in China which didn't break down. The trucks carry the people allowed to travel by day, the illegal ones by night, and are always full. Their main use here was freighting the stolen wood out of Tibet. We only saw one bus the whole time, which apparently was chartered. People weren't supposed to visit each other and compare their grievances and there were no private cars at all. Only the uppermost party-members were allowed to have them and they didn't seem to like the hills.

People came from everywhere for blessings

A stop on the track

Another flat tire

Two local beauties

Sawing logs

We just made it

After a cold night

East Tibetan countryside

In the winter of 1951, the Chinese had annexed most of Kham, the eastern and most exciting part of Tibet. They had then made Chamdo the new capital. Arriving there at five in the morning, we first disappeared behind our luggage to hide from possible police. As soon as dawn broke, we saw the scars of heavy bombardments in the town. From here we would arrange the tour to Karma Gon, the second most important site of our lineage. The first Karmapa, Dusum Khyenpa (1110-1193) had founded it around 1160—before Tsurphu—and no white man had been there before.

While asking around for a truck going in the right direction, the police appeared. They wanted us out of the town as quickly as possible. For our destination, we gave them the city we had just come from: the Chinese always send you back to the last stop. Staying firm but friendly, we gained a day. Their leader spoke Tibetan and actually seemed okay beneath his well-creased uniform.

The next morning, we scrambled on a truck with all our luggage. Sitting high on bales of tea, we drove north through an idyllic valley. The road followed a river and the driver sometimes stopped to push a stake into the ground. He wanted to check that the road could bear the truck's weight. It was a few hundred meters down, and the road was worse than anything further west. Already there, half the trucks fall down in summer, but with Karmapa's protection and the frozen ground, all went well.

Nature was a sheer joy. Up till then, Kurt had been the enthusiastic one with the many mountains reminding him of his Alps at home. Now he was drowned out by Pedro, who recognized countless flowers from his childhood near Salamanca in Spain. In the villages along the way, I distributed the last blessing cords of the "Chig She Kun Drol," an important series of initiations by the ninth Karmapa. The previous autumn Tenga Rinpoche had given them in Germany.

Late in the afternoon, the road ended. We again spent a night in a barn on top of a house. The next morning, the people had promised horses for traveling on. It took amazingly long to get them together, and when they brought mine around, even I could see that it had no stirrups: the lama was to be led and not bring the animal pain by goading it on himself. This condition lasted exactly till they could no longer see us. Then, the boy walking with the reins got a blessing and I rode on as well as possible without footholds. Apart from my behind aching, it was okay. In the

Kurt testing a horse

Karma Gön

afternoon, Hannah, Kurt, Pedro, and I reached Karma Chu, galloping. It is Karmapa's interim station on the way to Karma Gon. The others preferred a more stately speed.

The place was excellent. Real Karmapa disciples: independent, capable men had built what looked like a wild-west fort in an enormous, triangular river-bed. Working inventively with the rough materials available, they had done a fine job. We talked till late and their level of information was amazing.

They actually knew where in the vast world several of our teachers were and the general direction of their work. Hearing of our fascination with speed, they gave Kurt and me some very fast horses. When these had run themselves tired, we followed a river through picturesque landscapes. It was a strange but deeply familiar feeling to bless people from horseback along the way. In the early afternoon, after pulling the horses across the ice of a river, we had arrived. Ahead and to our right loomed Karma Gon's vast and only partially destroyed buildings.

People were lined up in front, waiting. They already knew we were coming, although we wondered how. Dismounting at the monastery's main entrance, we bowed down and entered. It was wonderful to see the

Arriving at Karma Gön

many old thangkas and smaller statues they had been able to save. They had created a fitting new environment for them and had just restored the temple's main Buddha. Their efficiency was even more enjoyable as this was Karmapa's second most important center.

While a single man had instigated the rebuilding of Tsurphu—we called him "Beaver" because of his front teeth—work here rested on the shoulders of three strong men. During the few hours here, we were taken to many special sites. Situated near a half-moon rock prophesied by Gampopa, Milarepa's main student, every part of the area had enlightening significance. Much was also practical. A partially destroyed stupa built over a tooth of the second Karmapa was very popular with the locals: they touch their heads against it when suffering from toothaches. I gave blessings and we left nearly all the remaining gifts. The laminated photos from Schwarzenberg were especially popular. East of Lhasa today, there are some thousand pictures of Karmapa, the lineage holders, "Diamond Pig Girl" and "Black Coat" on the local altars. In return, our hosts gave us some very special relics: pieces of the hat, shirt, and shoes of the first three Karmapas. At the inauguration of the new main Buddha-statue two days later, these strongly charged objects would be put into its heart.

The Beaver

For the way back, we had decided on a romantic ride. Everything worked well while there was light, but at Karma Chu our friends advised us to stay. We would have benefited from their better insight. An hour later, everything was suddenly pitch dark and our romantic notion that animals can see at night proved false. Hannah followed Kurt down a wrong path and when he called for her to go back, there was no room to turn. Getting off to make the process easier, her means of transportation unceremoniously ran away. Kurt's horse went wild. It galloped ever faster down a gorge. The guide sitting behind him had wisely jumped off, but that was not Kurt's style. As the animal crashed, it landed only inches away from him. My wishes at Karma Gon that work would never be boring had apparently been heard, and during the whole drama, all felt the power of our protectors. Everybody had the good feeling that nothing serious could happen.

A few minutes from there, people waited in front of their houses. They must have had a good laugh at the whole circus, but now they

wanted blessings and trade. While explaining the "Three Lights Meditation" in Tibetan around an open fire, both the lost horses and backpacks
reappeared. Only the local acquisitions remained in the night: a frying-
pan made from part of an old oil drum and the dried leg of a yak-ox which
Pedro had frequently transformed into excellent cutlets.

The next evening, the tea truck didn't show up. What was worse:
also Kurt didn't appear. He had gone ahead on the fastest horse to have
some fun and should have been there before us. People grew nervous, but
just when my Mo said he was okay and would arrive soon, in he came on
his sweat-dripping horse. He had lost his way in a neighboring valley.

Though the Tibetans loved it when I held my beads to do a
divination—they call it a "Mo"—most didn't know how they work.
Many considered it a technique for changing things. This is not the case.
Doing a Mo, your intense wish to benefit others awakens the mind's
timeless wisdom-nature. Going beyond the limitations of time and place,
one simply "knows" in one's bones what tendencies will be active when.
Like everything else in the "Diamond Way," this ability is transmitted
by one's teacher.

Stupas in Karma Gön

Karmapa's tooth's stupa

The truck's delay gave us that rarest of commodities: time for meditating and writing letters. We were also invited by an aging yogi couple. They had decided to spend the rest of their lives together in retreat. It was moving: they had gone in with only the barest of instructions. We had to nearly fight not to leave the room with half their possessions, things they would sorely need themselves. Finally, a truck arrived. The road we had come on had fallen down right after and they had now improvised a zig-zag route on the other side of the river. Crossing the only bridge, an ancient wooden construction, the driver insisted that we walk ahead first. Then he drove across at full speed. Doing less than that, the truck would have simply fallen through the planks.

During several weeks, we stayed in regions where people had never seen a white face before. Aside from coming for blessings, it was a relief that nobody stared at us. Also in this respect, the Tibetans had more style than most of the third world. On the other side of the river, it was actually we who became the beady-eyed ones: the shapes and sizes of the buildings were so perfect and in harmony with the landscape that the village felt like a living organism.

A very old altar

The inserts for the Buddha

To our amazement, there was a bus between Chamdo and Derge. They were not allowed to sell tickets to foreigners, but risked it for the treasured tourist money. We were always amazed how bourgeois the communist Chinese were, what length they would go to for some slightly better products. It was sheer luxury to travel the washboard road in a sitting position and with a roof above our heads, not half-lying in snow on open trucks. The girl at my side was the shame of her family. She had fallen in love with a Chinese, which almost never happens. In front of her sat a Mongoloid child with an inventive mind. Every few minutes he made erotically educational signs to the girls in the bus. Being noisy and obstructing our view of the fantastic mountains, I pushed him into the seat a few times. He only became quiet, however, when a powerful Khampa lady suddenly said, "Let us see what he is offering," and went for his private parts. The nomads and their tents were fascinating. They still had the shepherd-sized red-brown dogs. In central Tibet the species had ended up in the Chinese cooking pots. Only at Karmapa's destroyed summer residence had we seen—and especially heard—a single, neurotic member of this breed. Though impressive-looking, their lives were miserable. They fed on the same stuff as their Nepalese neighbors.

The Tibetans tell the story of a great lover, who brought joy to many a nomad girl. Whenever the guardian dogs of some camp became aggressive, he sat down as if wanting to empty his bowels. While the mutts were looking for their expected meal, he would then jump into the next beauty's tent. The free, unconcerned style in the round felt tents was even more pervasive than among the settled Khampas. They really didn't have to care what their neighbors thought.

The soldiers guarding the bridge to Derge slept. Jumping off the bus with our army sacks, we hid between some logs until the first lights

Wall paintings

Doing a Mo

were switched on. This happened in a restaurant owned by a "Tibetan-ized" Chinese. He proved to be pleasant and even had a world map on his wall. Here, China covered much of Russia as well as the whole Himalayan region. When we told him that the rest of the world knew nothing of these borders, he shrugged and seriously didn't care.

Derge, too, had scars from the occupation. The valley was a dream-target for fighter-bombers and had been hit hard in the winter of 1950-51. Among the many explanations for the Chinese attack on Tibet, I today give most credit to a simple one: some dissatisfied generals were closer to Beijing than Mao liked. Before they could become unpleasant, he had sent them to Tibet. They had invaded the eastern area and kept the region up to the river we had just crossed, costing Tibet the best third

Faces

Nomads

Architecture at Derge

of the country with the strongest and freest women and men. Only one important cultural monument of the city had been spared. It was even still operable, but must have been heavily controlled. People panicked when we wanted to see it from the inside. It was the "Bakhang," Derge's famous woodblock press.

Our hotel manager was evidently a spy. His behavior was servile and the Chinese don't grant a good position to a Tibetan for efficiency. They do it when he is so compromised that they can count on him. Though he affirmed his national attitude constantly and lamented about the occupiers, all our visitors fell silent when he appeared. A year later when Pedro came to Derge again, the manager was like a wall. "Operation Openness towards Westerners" had obviously run out.

Hundreds were expected for an Easter course in Wuppertal, Germany, so we had to move on. This meant crossing the 5,6 km. ridge before Kantze, the next town east. Four travelers had just died there from cold. Arriving on top, we hardly felt the altitude and celebrated the fantastic view, and our adjusted lungs, by jumping around. From then on, two impressions etched themselves on our minds: the mineral wealth of the mountains, and the groups of Chinese gold diggers standing in the river, obviously finding something. The earth was so light that the masses of dust thrown up by the truck's front wheels immediately covered everything. It stayed above the road as far back as we could see. We were lying on the back of the truck, covering Pedro's video-camera and other technical assets against the dust when Hannah and I suddenly jumped to our feet: we had seen a fortification through the clouds which we simply knew. Asking about it in Kantze, the next major town, we learned that it was part of Atub Tsang on the Gold River. This is where Karmapa had taken his sixteenth rebirth in 1923. Jumping off the truck in Kantze, we nearly landed on some old lamas from a local monastery, run from exile by Kalu Rinpoche. They were happy to have news about the highest Rinpoches and we enjoyed having some last pictures to give them.

We found seats in one of the typical and unpleasant eating places, a proud accomplishment of the new order in Tibet. Like everywhere from Lhasa and on, their doors had to be constantly open, causing a bad draught. This was to prevent people from just sitting around, happily and unproductively. While I was blessing people on the main road to the higher-lying ruins in the Tibetan part of town, a highly decorated officer in a dapper uniform stopped his motorcycle in our path. He drove an imported Honda, a sure sign that he was way up in the hierarchy.

He spoke excellent Tibetan and demanded that we appear at the police station at once. There they might grant us permission to see the monastic ruins later. With joy I saw some dozen Tibetans drawing closer. It was a situation I had been itching for, a chance to publicly break a lance for them. Loudly and jovially, I repeatedly slapped the officer's back in a school-masterly fashion and said: "You know, that is something we won't do. We are much more interested in the old temples than in your police station. When we have seen everything, you can visit us down at the buses. That is where we stay." The Tibetans gasped and the officer spun up dust with his rear wheel, speeding away. We neither met him again nor did we see his colleagues.

Also in Kantze, only one major cultural building had been spared. It was a fine old Sakya temple and contained the statues of many protectors. Here, I could finally express my devotion to Guru Rinpoche. Anything from him is much more exciting than the statues and murals

The policeman just left

which had been re-erected in many parts of the country. Though representing highly virtuous rinpoches and monks and often well executed by members of the Gelugpa school, they just didn't have that zap. What had hurt me most in Tibet was probably the near-total lack of outward signs of Guru Rinpoche's influence. Hardly any stupas or pictures of him remain, although he is unique among the world's cultural heroes and brought the "old" school of Buddha's teachings to Tibet, back around 750 A.D. Doing similar work for Karmapa in the West today, I often feel him very close. While Pedro, Kurt, and I carried two-foot clay statues of him through the night, my eyes filled with tears of joy. Taken out in biscuit tins, they support our practice in Copenhagen, Schwarzenberg, and Frankfurt today.

Continuing east, we passed Tibet's oldest suspension bridge. Its chains were invented six hundred years earlier by the great yogi, Tangtong Gyalpo. His inspired mind also fathered the invocation to "Loving Eyes," used in our centers everywhere. It is one of the practices always chanted in Tibetan. After passing a giant stupa of "Wheel of Time," a single cloud hung in the sky for hours. It was blood-red and the complete likeness of a dorje. Pedro filmed some secret Chinese installations and

Guru Rinpoche, unique among the cultural heroes of the world

A stupa of
Wheel of Time

soon one only saw groups of men along the road. They worked hard with pickaxes and shovels, while Chinese soldiers pointed their guns at them. The region must have been a prisoners' camp, and the last Tibetan town we stopped in only had male inhabitants. The video of our journey, *Secret Journey through Eastern Tibet,* ends with the blessings I gave the people there. On the pass leading down to the river and China, all in the bus threw handfuls of small square papers into the air. They bore the imprint of horses with jewels on their backs and were an offering to protect Tibet. Not until here did we leave the country; everybody could feel that.

The cheapest flight was from Chendu to Canton. Here we took buses south. In the newest economic zones bordering Hong Kong, people could now do just about anything. Child-labor and similar time-honored practices were already attracting Hong Kong's capitalists. Here, one was back to timeless Asian standards and people were judged by what they owned. Old man Mao must have rotated in his grave. At the border, the X-ray machines fortunately didn't pick up the pieces of iron mail I was carrying. They were from armor worn by the Tibetan national hero, Ling Gesar, and I had collected them in the ruins of Tsurphu. Ling Gesar had conquered the Muslim invaders, keeping Tibet free, and had many magic powers. The small iron plates carry his energy-field and now protect our centers everywhere.

With Tenga Rinpoche

Hong Kong was sheer luxury, and after a few days with our German and Chinese friends, Hannah left for Nepal. During the next months, the lineage holders and she would attend initiations there. Urgyen Tulku, a great yogi, would pass on a series of important initiations he had received from the fifteenth Karmapa. The rest of us couldn't wait to get back to Europe.

It was great to be back on the fast roads, and the public halls grew fuller with each lecture. Keeping a list of addresses was more difficult though. From north to south, our centers followed the old nomadic tradition: they moved—to ever larger houses.

May 1986, I was in California. Here, Carol had been polishing a few of my manuscripts. Then followed a wonderful summer course with Tenga Rinpoche. Hannah translated and I taught in the evenings. Niels came to the Danish retreat center and we organized our next tour to Tibet.

After Denmark, Hannah translated for Shamarpa in the Dordorgne, France, while I taught during the evenings for Tenga Rinpoche at a German institute. It was the time for some collective growing up. Here, many Central European Buddhists finally developed the necessary sensitivity to broken bonds. They are in fact the deadliest of poisons on the Diamond Way. While deep trust permits a quick absorption of enlightened qualities, nothing is more destructive than negative rumors. In my teachings, I had only rarely covered this point. Considering the subject distasteful, I had always hoped that it wouldn't be necessary. So far it had been possible to solve our few cases one by one and without all the high-sounding words. Due to some outside assistance, however, events behind the brown walls of the institute suddenly made the old teachings very relevant. The administrators of the institute and a jealous English translator tried a wide range of tricks to disturb the cooperation between Tenga Rinpoche and myself. He also pestered Shamarpa, who telephoned me and called the translator a "bad man." Finally Rinpoche chose Carol from Marin to publicly state that he was completely behind me.

Kuchary at the purchase in '85

In the atmosphere of openness and confidence, the whole process was painful to many, and I did nothing to speed it up. I wanted it to be long and embarrassing. This was the time to learn the anti-gossip lesson. If people wouldn't trust their own experience and take a stand, my fifteen years of work had been wasted, anyway. They would! Shaking off the sweet illusion of a spirituality where one doesn't have to choose and think, the German Giant awoke.

Before the course ended, we piled into a VW bus. It was time for a trip to Poland with Friedel and Claude. In Krakow, five hundred people were waiting in a big tent. Situ Rinpoche had just left and they were now waiting for the wide open nights, where we always mix our minds. In Warsaw, we were awakened by loud voices. Our friends had just discovered they were broke. The money for renovating our large country center in Kuchary, which I had bought for only $400 the year before, had been spent on the visit of the Rinpoches.

They had tried to pay with the red wool-cloth used for monks' robes—a product then available in the state shops—but that had not worked out. The Scottish organizer apparently hadn't realized how difficult it was to get hard currency in Poland. He had accepted the cloth and then asked for the dollars on top.

There were hundreds of people everywhere, as always, and the usual five hundred took Refuge. It was great to present Friedel and Claude, my students and fine teachers and healers in their own right. They still go there to work today.

Attentive faces

With Claude and Friedel in Poland

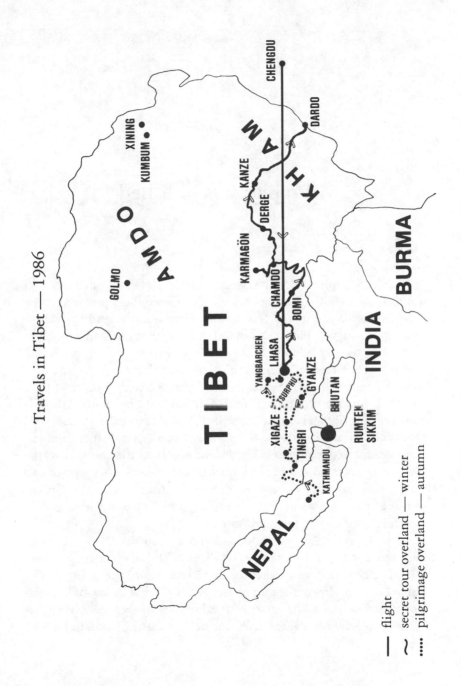

Travels in Tibet — 1986

CHAPTER FOURTEEN

A Prophecy Is Fulfilled

ALTHOUGH I FELT EVER LESS LIKE LEAVING THE WEST, autumn 1986 was the time to fulfill the prophecy which we thought concerned us: the "freckled protector from the West and his friends" must now help rebuild Tsurphu. Though by now the Chinese tried to extract much money, Niels kept total expenses below $2000 each. Forty friends packed spades and working-gloves for a hard stint behind the Himalayas.

We started in early September and planned to stay in Tibet for a month. It became educational. Both Chinese and Nepalese excelled in lousy organization and even worse will. The road before the Nepalese-Tibetan border had fallen down. This brought us an afternoon of climbing narrow paths between bearers, cattle, and goats. At the checkpoint, the Chinese hardly cared and we spent the first night there. They gave us two tin barracks, probably to keep our decadent influence from the Tibetan working class. The world enjoys being seduced, however, and soon they were full of locals who even meditated with us.

In the morning, we exchanged money and discovered that our mini-buses and oxygen masks weren't there. Niels had ordered them from Europe. They had been rented to American tourists at a high price instead. This could save us a lot of money. As my divination said that all would survive the altitudes without additional oxygen, we took a Tibetan-chauffeured bus instead. Fortunately, it was just standing there.

We fixed the price to Lhasa at $20 a person. Once again, Hannah's tenacity and perfect Tibetan made things work.

One is always advised to see Tibet overland. There was ample time for that during the next days. On some hills the bus hardly surpassed walking speed. Already the first afternoon we crawled upwards for hours through a narrow gulch. While the plants changed from subtropic to those of an arctic desert, we approached Milarepa's city of Nyelam.

The dark hotel had neither fleas nor lice, but our friends woke with splitting headaches caused by the altitude. Eight kilometers further on lay Milarepa's main cave. The Gelugpas from a small neighboring monastery obviously hadn't delegated their most talented monk there. He kept getting in the way, apparently unable to grasp what the site meant to Karmapa's students. Finally, I put him in a corner so we could meditate above the expanse of the valley. Here, a thousand years earlier, Milarepa had watched fads and people come and go. There had been few visible changes since then.

Our next stop was on the northern route between Nyelam and Shigatse. People let us sleep inside an L-shaped barracks, the keys of

Tibet overland

In the Milarepa cave

which had been lost. They looked politely the other way while I tore off
the locks with my German army-dagger.

Shigatse was exciting. The center of town was still Tibetan. We
stayed in a hotel at the main market and there was no doubt about the
hosts' loyalty. They didn't even object when hundreds of Tibetans
crowded in to receive my blessing.

Our group was disgusted by the public brain-washing. In Chinese-
ruled cities, everyone is awakened by giant loudspeakers at six a.m. Until
eight in the evening, they douse the population with moral and boring
propaganda and tuneless socialist songs. The three causes of the local noise
were clearly visible on the mountain beyond, just below a ruined castle.
I wondered how long Westerners would have put up with them. So many
accidents can happen to such devices!

Everybody had a chance to get tough. As most suffered the headaches or palpitations of altitude-sickness, we wanted to move on as

quickly as possible. After emptying a restaurant where—possibly by mistake—they had displayed their products in a nearly appetizing fashion, we piled into the bus again. The journey became ever more a test of courage and our friends passed it. Travelling over vast expanses for days, always at altitudes above four kilometers, the only way to get thicker air was digging a hole in the ground. On an interminable 5,3 kilometer pass in a snow-blizzard, a sixty-year-old woman lost consciousness. She was a friend of Niel's and the only one traveling as a tourist. Due to a bout of TB as a child, her lungs were less flexible. The others kept me informed about her condition and I guided her through her conscious and unconscious states, like one does with the dying. This did not only bring benefit on the pass. It freed so much energy that she fell directly in love with a kindly Dutch doctor in Lhasa.

The Chinese tourist organization specialized in disinformation and prohibitions, but our unofficial Tibetan contacts had worked. In then

The tour guides

overcrowded Lhasa, we were expected at the Bernakschol Hotel on
Happiness Road. Sonam and other friends from our first trip had held
rooms for forty people at no extra charge. We spent the next days in Lhasa.
As guides for our group, we visited places we had found no time for
during our last trip. Johkang from the inside was very impressive, and in
its powerfield, I made strong wishes that Aids and other viral infections
would rapidly be overcome, that a vaccine might be found which even
poor countries could afford. Our Tibetan friends have amazing stories to
tell: without the factor of "blessing," it is inexplicable how so many of
them can still be alive today. For example, several of the higher-positioned
Khampa women who had not been killed or starved had had to live in
pigsties for years. Though they had been fed the same stuff as the animals,
many had survived and had not lost their style.

Within a few days, we had arranged two trucks for going to
Tsurphu. Starting before dawn, we could pass the checkpoints before the
Chinese had manned them. The people of Tsurphu had done much during
the last eight months. It was amazing how much they had built. Even
before we rolled out our sleeping bags we were already busy. This was no
job for sissies. Working physically above four kilometers was exhausting
and nobody enjoyed the near-constant headaches.

Reconstruction goes on

At the bottom of the work pyramid

The Tibetans used neither levels nor several other devices we had always thought essential. It was fascinating what a handful of elderly and somewhat alcoholized gentlemen could construct, apparently straight from memory. Though we had some architects in our group, there was no reason to confuse the locals with unknown methods. Instead we took our places right at the bottom of the workers' pyramid. For a month we carried the stones and wood which became the building's walls.

During the first days, where frequent pauses were necessary, we nearly got into a third-world system. One man pulls at a rope attached to a shovel which somebody else sticks into the ground. It looks ridiculous to a Westerner, however, so we took turns instead, or used the smaller military spades we had brought from Poland and the U.S.

In Lhasa we met Yongdu Ward Holmes from Hawaii. Tall, lanky, and sincere, he had been a friend since 1971. He was in town to exchange a lot of money for a Rinpoche in Nepal. Twice, Karmapa had taken him as his chauffeur in America. Our talk there became the start of the Tsurphu Foundation which is instrumental in reconstructing Karmapa's seat in Tibet. It's a place where even a few dollars does great good.

Coolies of the world unite

After two weeks we went to Lhasa to organize the return of part of the group. Down Happiness Road, we saw the outlines of figures who could only be Bokar Tulku and his rotund assistant, Khenpo Donyo. I always call him "The Smile." Bokar Rinpoche is heir to Kalu Rinpoche's work and one of the finest examples of yogihood in Tibetan Buddhism. They had just taught their nomad tribes in North Tibet. Rinpoche's mother and a truckload of their students had come along to Lhasa. We could now go to Tsurphu together.

Politely we declined seats in the front of the truck. We thought that the mother and other older people should sit there. It was more gallant than intelligent, however, and assured us of a terrible trip. We were the only ones with thin clothing and had no protection against hours of rain and snow.

In Tsurphu, Bokar Tulku donated all the money he had received from the nomads, about twenty thousand dollars. He also gave an initiation into the second Karmapa and on this occasion he praised Hannah and me until we were thoroughly embarrassed. After all, he was a yogi and no politician.

This ended my relaxed career as an anonymous bearer of stones and wood. People now came at all hours, especially to get pictures of Karmapa and "Black Coat." They also wanted blessings and "Mos." In return, they gratefully placed little packages of the famous "Rigsels" in front of me. They are small grey-white pearls which have appeared there since the early eighties when a banner representing victory over negativity was erected. "Rigsels" are high on the list of relics. They are the condensed

With Bokar Rinpoche

People come for our posters

loving-energy of Enlightened beings. Just as precious were the pieces of copper which people brought. They were parts of the largest cast statue in Tibet. Karma Pakshi, the second Karmapa, had poured it around 1270 and it was the one mentioned in the prophecy. It had been blown up in 1966 and there are hardly any remnants today. If one puts even the smallest piece of it into a statue, it is immediately blessed. It has been an immense joy to spread both pills and fragments around the world since then.

Looking down from the steep mountain behind the monastery, it was amazing how much people had built. At that time, about a third of the houses already had roofs again. Especially an old nun marvelled at it all. Though half-blind, she was the best at finding the small pearls. Hiding in the mountains during the destruction, she had also witnessed that.

Here is a rough summary of what she said:

In the beginning of 1966, some Chinese officials had come to count the statues. Three weeks later, trucks arrived to take whatever precious metals could be found to China. Then the destruction started: during

The witness

eighteen months, every weekend the proletariat of Lhasa was brought out there. With Chinese guns at their backs, they were forced to tear down the buildings. Being no braver than most people, this is what they did. After that, farmers and nomads were forbidden to live in this part of the valley.

There were also inside reasons for the thorough destruction. The Chinese were especially angry with Karmapa. Most of his disciples were Khampas, born warriors. Protected by his powerfield, they had caused much damage to their army. With swords and muzzle-loading guns, the

Khampas had brought them heavy losses. What the Chinese liked least of all was a principle of keeping "face." Among all the great lamas who had fled, only Karmapa had taken his full entourage and all relics with him. In a dignified and well-executed manner, he had left the country in the middle of their attacks. Some years earlier, he had produced a popular song containing his exact predictions about Tibet's destruction and including information on the best direction to flee. It had given many a chance to escape.

In Lhasa, we bought some of the funny trifles which socialism produces, quaint gifts for our friends back home. The best were some silk prints for long life which had been blessed by the Panchen Lama himself. It was always fun to trade with the government-employed Chinese. They follow an established pattern: as one approaches their domain, they hold their noses high to indicate that one is not welcome. Then they move as far away as possible from what one wants to buy. Knowing this isn't too difficult. In most cases they have only one functioning product. When the hopeful buyers have honored them long enough through constant attention, they first try to sell their damaged pieces. Finally getting at

Yangbarchen—the ruins of Kunzig Shamarpa's main seat

Blessing in Shigatse

what one wants, there is one last snag: they refuse to make change so one first has to return to the street to do that.

This is an efficient means of limiting consumption. It improves the pride of shop-assistants and works well where there are no alternatives. Since we were always in a hurry, however, I had to cut the ritual short. This is totally feasible. One simply jumps over the desk and takes what one wants. This brings service astonishingly fast. Then, if one is not pleased with the clerk's grimace or other signs of ill humor, one finishes by stretching out one's hand. Most men are dumb enough to do the same, and the grand finale is to watch them jump with amazement while one squashes their hand. This is also the part of the procedure where one should praise their kind cooperation. The ladies—often even more frustrated—are best entertained with a broad erotic grin. If one's motivation is that people in weaker positions be treated better in the future and that the holders of mercantile power be liberated of bad karma, it is even okay from a Buddhist viewpoint. One mustn't be really angry, however, or enjoy it too much!

A whisper of former grandeur

It was impossible to find a Tibetan driver for the tour back to Nepal. We had to make do with one of the ill-humored communist Chinese instead. He sat all alone and wanted no contact with the "white devils." In Shigatse, he parked at a Chinese guest house, but as we simply stayed in the bus, he had to drive on to our Tibetan hotel. There, we made sure that he was treated well. He needed it. He lived on cigarettes and bitter tea, and with all his anger he would rapidly destroy himself.

The next morning, we saw the monastery of Tashi Lhunpo, the main residence of the Panchen Lamas. Several of his institutions had been spared. Chatting with the monks, we could still sense its former greatness. Although only a handful of them are allowed to live there today, half probably Chinese spies, all the good energy had not left.

Gyantse, our next stop, had a stupa of great power. Like Tashi Lhunpo, it was under the Panchen Lama's responsibility and had been preserved. Its dozens of rooms on several levels are accessed from the outside and contain the well-crafted statues and thangkas of peaceful, protective, or united aspects. They are the exciting forms Buddha emanated out to awaken people's potential in the fastest way. It was just the place to again meet Bokar Tulku and his Khenpo. They and their truckload of students were also on their way to Nepal. Further up in the

Tashi Lhunpo

building, Hannah and some of the group must have done something wrong. Suddenly a monk locked them up and only let them out again after a while. Most had some unpleasant experience in Gyantse and the city generally vibrated with anger.

Tingri, our last stop before the border, was a broken town. Without the signs of fighting found all over East Tibet, the place felt like a museum of folklore: well preserved and very Tibetan. People had paid dearly for this with their self-respect. They had little dignity and their children often begged. This was exactly what the communist Chinese wished: exemplary Tibetan serfs for exhibit. The atmosphere was unpleasant, but at least people still spoke Tibetan, which was no longer the case in Nyelam, Milarepa's village. We hoped it would enable them to find some source of inner power later.

The Chinese border guards now wore black Mao uniforms. They were young and easy to fool. We simply carried the things around the customs station we didn't want them to see. After hiking down the eight kilometers of mountain slope, a bus was waiting with a warning from Niels: the real danger lay with the Nepalese. We should keep anything we wanted to smuggle on our bodies. The first group had been relieved of many of Bokar Tulku's valuables, which they had put back into their luggage too early. Usually one isn't checked for precious metals by the

Hannah's prison

country one enters. Fortunately Niels had managed to get back most of
the confiscated goods. The ritual objects of pure silver would gladden
many a lama.

In Kathmandu, Lopon Chechoo and Tenga Rinpoche took good care
of us. Then the twenty or so still with us headed east. For some reason,
we had received genuine Sikkim visas this time and could stay with our
lineage holders in Rumtek for a full ten days. The people living there had
left Tsurphu with Karmapa in 1959 and were overjoyed at our work to
rebuild their old home. They wouldn't take any money for our stay and
treated us even better than usual.

In the midst of so much good feeling, I decided that the "Fearless
and Joyful," as I had growing justification to call my students, were ready
for another test. They should learn more about life in different parts of
the world. The means for bringing this about was a tour to Kalimpong,
for which we had no permission, and then via Darjeeling to the Indian
lowlands. At that time, the Gurkhas' revolt for national rights was
switching into highest gear. A dozen houses were torched every day and
two or three men were killed on each side. The Indian soldiers suffered
their losses to snipers when removing trees felled across the road. They
then retaliated by shooting into the protesting masses.

The Gurkhas' complaints were easy to understand: they were always
the lowest man on the totem pole. They picked the tea which others
drank. It was hard to find a solution, however. They don't lean much
toward intellectual pursuits, and each time the state built a new college
in their region, the same thing happened: in the beginning, its students
were 80% Nepalese and 20% Bengalese, some of the brightest Indians.
But three years later, it was just the opposite. If one still found Gurkas
there some years after that, they were most likely to hold brooms in their
hands. Then they complained again. The government started another
Nepalese school or college somewhere and the whole thing began once
more.

Darjeeling was a town under siege. Hannah and Niels found that
out when they visited the district commander. While discussing the
journey onward with him, the communist Gurkhas were moving up from
the south, while the Nationalists came down the hills. "Shoot to kill!"
was his only comment as military phones informed him of their approach.

Leaving Rumtek

Our group spent two sunny days high above the scene on the roof terrace of Lhawang's hotel. It offered a clear view of Nepal, Sikkim, and Bhutan and it was very exciting. We couldn't stay for the party, however: if we didn't reach Kathmandu in two days, our tickets to Europe would be invalid. The Gurkhas had imposed a total ban on transportation, so we had to insist on being evacuated. It was all a complete circus. They beat anything we'd seen of Indian organization up until then. The bus which the military had requisitioned for foreigners suddenly filled up with the screaming relatives of the local bigwigs. Forcing themselves into the front section which was secured with iron bars, they apparently expected us to be their human shields. After our more dignified entry,

Upper bazaar with Kachenjunga

seventeen fully armed soldiers also somehow squeezed into the small thirty-seater. Since several buses had been set afire over the last weeks, I asked a few of our strongest men to come along to the roof. Armed with iron rods, bayonets, and big Maglites, no one would get at the doors or our luggage.

Everything happened in true Indian style. The bus broke down six kilometers out of Darjeeling. This cost us our only asset in getting through: the element of surprise. While it was being repaired, passing Gurkhas shouted that they were waiting for us down the road. There was a lot going on. We counted a dozen burning houses from the pass and when we reached Kalu Rinpoche's town of Sonada, the street was blocked by about two hundred drunks. First, they tried to kill the driver. He had been forced to drive by the Indians and the soldiers were supposed to protect him. During the first assault, he received a deep cut on his forehead. While the wealthy Indians in the protected part of the bus screamed with fear, brave Hannah forced the door open so that he could enter the main section where our group sat. Once inside, he hid under Pia's skirt, trembling with fear. The next attack was a hail of stones. They destroyed most of the windows and the headlamps. Meanwhile, the seventeen tall, healthy-looking and fully armed soldiers with giant moustaches put on a gallant act. They quietly disappeared with their long guns and hid on the left side of the bus which was not under attack. In my whole life, I have never seen anything as ridiculous and cowardly. I shouted to them to at least fire their weapons into the air but they seemed completely paralyzed.

I would gladly have helped with the upbringing of one of the Gurkhas. He made my fingers itch. He was the tallest, had the longest knife, and constantly shouted and pounded his chest. Concentrating all my meditative powers, I could just keep him from slashing our tires. That would have ended any hopes of reaching Kathmandu in time. Here, the main task shifted from examining one's mind in unusual situations to protecting our group and luggage. So far, no one had been injured by the stones or shards of glass, but now they called for gasoline to torch the bus. I called down to Hannah that no one must leave and promised a warm welcome to any one who tried to climb aboard. It was total chaos and all grew even more angry. Finally, a local driver had the bright idea of backing the bus out of the city, parking it in front of the stupas Kalu Rinpoche had built; they depressurized the brakes and then disappeared.

Some hours later, reinforcements arrived: several jeeps and about a hundred armed soldiers. With loaded guns, they advanced through the now-empty streets of Sonada. Halfway down to the lowlands, however, the glorious Indian army could show its mettle. Some Nepalese who didn't remove a tree stump from the road quickly enough were kicked and hit with rifle-butts till we stopped it. There was no end to the embarrassment. Both civilians and soldiers managed to make complete idiots of themselves.

In the Siliguri hotel, they had no mosquito nets and the next night we bumped along in a bus through Nepal. It was a joy to get on the plane back to Europe. We desperately looked forward to being with people who can keep their style.

That autumn, Pedro and Dorrit made an incredible gift: a mountain ridge with a deserted village east of Malaga in Spain. We postponed all busy schedules to go there together. After I gave them Refuge, they had kept unshakable confidence. It became very useful there. In the curves

Stupas in front of Kalu Rinpoche's monastery

down through Europe, I tore half the tread off our tires. On the southern slope of the Pyrenees, we slept some hours in a small and newly built hotel. The next morning, while Pedro and Dorrit offered us equal partnership in the center, we looked out the window. The outline of the mountain above was very familiar. It looked exactly like the one that had inspired Gampopa, the first Karmapa's teacher, into making his famous ritual hat. Nine hundred years before, he had modeled its impressive shape over one of Milarepa's shoes. Apparently, this was the right place for such an offer.

Much of Pedro's family now lives in Madrid. We stayed with his sister, Fe, who is also a treasure. From there we drove due south to the Lion Gate. Here the high Castillian plain falls down to the Mediterranean. A fascinating mountain area east of a historical tower was ours, and I named it "Karma Gon." It has an unbelievable view in all directions. A mansion in the Pyrenees which Karmapa had given this name to had disappeared. This was a concrete way to honor his wishes.

At that point, Karma Gon was two rows of run-down cottages. They lay on an eastern ridge about halfway between the ocean and the mountain

Pedro and his great gift

Karma Gön in 1986

pass we had just crossed. A path nearby had been traveled by anyone from Phoenicians to Vandals for thousands of years. Already by spring 1989, much had been built: 250 students lived comfortably there during a course of Phowa. Whoever thinks that idealists can make no imprint on the world today need only examine developments there. Due to the qualities of the land, Karma Gon can even satisfy the standards of Prima Vera, the producer of the purest essential oils today.

Driving west via Gibraltar, I blessed a place on the Portuguese South Coast. The country is much milder and less noisy than Spain. Some Germans there wanted a good bond to Karma Gon. The curves on the road north made our tires completely bald, and we re-entered Spain near Salamanca, where Pedro had grown up. Having experienced every possible kind of poverty in his village, he had entered the "Escorial" at the age of ten—the fortress of Spanish Catholic conservatism. During the following ten years, they taught him the ways of their monks: everything from self-flagellation to Aristotelian philosophy. Finding little blessing or growth, he wouldn't just run away. Instead he sent enough letters to the Vatican to make them let him go. It was the first time they ever released someone in this way. After the hard drill of the Spanish army, his desire for light nights and fair-skinned people fortunately led him to Denmark. After two expulsions as an illegal alien, he met beautiful Dorrit the third time, on the plane to Mallorca. Today, they have two fine sons. Their first visit to the center in Copenhagen was on one of the rare occasions that I was there. When everything became light during my blessing, they knew they had found something which works. Becoming our close family, they help everyone around them.

In January 1987, Hannah and I flew to America. Pedro and some German friends came along. At that time there was no trouble with the landlady and we could all stay with Carol in Marin. She had once again provided wide publicity, coordinating several radio and television programs. Though it was very important to some of the minority audience that Danes come from the Caucasus, at least nobody claimed that Buddha was black like later in Los Angeles. In Carol's old Volvo, which was apparently indestructible, seven of us drove with full luggage through the important southwest corner of America. To my shame, somewhere between Flagstaff and Albuquerque, I drove the Volvo into a ditch. After joking about the locals parking in the snowdrifts, I did exactly the same thing. The road was just too icy for our speed.

It became ever clearer why Karmapa had insisted that I go to America frequently. It was simply necessary. Our groups and centers across the vast country often have only one teacher visiting a year. Mostly it was the venerable Khenpo Karthar Rinpoche from Woodstock, a deep and fine teacher. Sometimes nobody comes at all. Since no other lama seemed to empower people to do their meditations in their own language and trust their own abilities, it was understandable why there was so much less growth than in Central and Eastern Europe. The goal of Buddhism is independent, grown-up people, and if one doesn't learn to rely upon oneself, nothing can ever grow.

Actually, there were several problems. The cultural differences between East and West, which people want to see as enriching, frequently disturbed the good feelings. Except for Portland and Santa Fe, I think there were problems everywhere, and in all lineages. Westerners disturb Tibetans with flakiness, bad family relationships, and by mixing up their precious transmissions with strange kinds of spirituality. Most lamas who became resident also goofed. Worst was probably the tendency to make students feel unappreciated or second-class, even those functioning as their attendants. Statements by teachers that they don't like the West and are only there because their own lamas insist, also don't warm any hearts. Usually they are defensive in nature, the result of many childhood beatings. Their aim is to show that one is still a good monk and not seduced by the soft life. But what are the supporters to think who are spending precious time and money trying to be kind? Finally, even the friendliest of observing eyes did notice a general tendency by teachers to stake out territories. Often this was not to protect the teaching or students, which would be valid, but to keep a basis for service or power, which is bad. Airing problems like these was necessary from time to time, and I know Karmapa expected that of me. It kept the valuable people from leaving, but was not the way to make friends with the establishment. Though there was only one frontal attack on me—the letter from the Dharmadhatu—whenever organizations grew, some always felt threatened by my activity. Testing spirituality on the scales of growth, humor and ordinary common sense was not popular. It increased the workload and severely limited the power-games people could play.

Kim, our Danish economic wizard and friend, invited us to the gambling town of Reno. Since 1971 in Sonada, we had always kept in close contact. He and Bo, his brother, supported our work, and he had a leading position in our Copenhagen center.

Kim wanted to show Carol and us something amazing, a show with five hundred dancing girls. Unfortunately however, they either had the day off or suffered from a collective cold. Instead, we enjoyed some really funny comedies—Americans are the world's best entertainers—and also tried gambling a bit. I won $100 at a table, but stopped when I sensed the power to influence the other players. Then we lost it to the slot machines. Before dawn, Kim left in a big-motored car. He could afford the transportation others only dream of and was never afraid to share his joy.

In April and May 1987, an old wish was fulfilled. Lopon Chechoo had found a few months for us. He became our first teacher in 1968 and is the main protector and organizer of Buddhism in Nepal. His importance in the Himalayas is so great that the Bhutanese government had marked down his age by ten years on his passport. Then they felt justified in piling even more responsibilities on his shoulders. He will probably keep his power for years: the medical examinations in Copenhagen

Lopön Chechoo in south Germany

compared his inner organs to those of a forty-year-old man, at the age of seventy. His condition for coming was that both Hannah and I accompany him, and except for Sweden, Norway, and Greece, for which there was no time, we showed him Karmapa's centers in Central Europe. It was a great joy. Countless friends already knew him from Nepal or from *Entering the Diamond Way* and met him with complete confidence. He had watched us build the Kagyu lineage from nothing in central Europe and now treated us like a loving father.

His interviews, which Hannah translated, met people's needs precisely. The teachings were mostly only an hour long, after which the time was mine. The programs now frequently stopped around one or two a.m. This was not because we were becoming bourgeois, but the sleepless nights we had shared for years were now rarely necessary. Beyond all ordinary levels of endurance, my students and I had established total trust. Our power field now functioned, and we would automatically act in unison and as Karmapa wished.

Quantity of hours and quality of teaching could now find a better balance. More rest looked good to new people, and brought depth to the work. For years, I had nearly fallen off my throne from fatigue most nights, not a sight people expect when making their first Dharma contact. Although the transmission at the lectures is so strong that people hardly notice, it was awkward to have both audios and videos circulating where I repeat meditation phrases or switch between different languages, out of exhaustion. Though I will do anything to be useful, even my Viking body can't work around the clock.

Rinpoche especially enjoyed Rodby, Wuppertal, Graz, and Brescia. He immediately understood the difficult conditions in Poland. He had experienced even stranger systems himself and knew both the Russian and Mongolian bureaucracies. The absurdities of Nepalese and Indian organization beat most things, anyway. Cruising at two hundred kilometers an hour in my old BMW, we drove a cosmopolitan lama through Europe. At the same time, he was our loving and precious teacher and friend. We left Rinpoche late in May at the Dutch border, where friends were waiting for him. After so many hectic weeks, he should now have a holiday.

In Poland

CHAPTER FIFTEEN

Mustang and Bhutan

*I*T WAS AGAIN TIME FOR A PILGRIMAGE to the Himalayas. We landed in Kathmandu with fifty friends, and my divinations, which had been exceedingly bad on Tibet this time, had only shown the tip of the iceberg. Probably due to deforestation, whole mountainsides had slid. Both on the far side of the border and where it had been necessary to climb the year before, the road was out. One or two porters fell to their death on that stretch every day, and there was no transportation from that point on. This is where four friends from the Wuppertal center had witnessed a miracle. Seeing several cubic yards of rock in free fall towards their bus, they called on Black Coat, our protector. Against all laws of nature, the giant stone suddenly changed direction and left a trail of broken trees down the mountain instead.

So Tibet was out. We didn't want the main party to be stuck for days, wasting precious time. Also, several of our friends had already been up there and mainly wanted to be with us. Secretly, I had a hope somewhere in the back of my mind, which I had only told Hannah about: there was a chance of adding a new and very special dimension to this journey. Fortunately, Tenga Rinpoche's Mos showed that a small group going to Tibet would get through, and we gave them sorely needed donations for Tsurphu. They had been a main reason for going there. Now, we would instead fulfill an old wish. With luck, we could reach Mustang between the tourists and the rainy season.

The test of strength

Renting a bus to Pokhara, we stayed in a hotel near the airfield. Next morning, we got tickets for half the group. Flying always stopped at ten when gusty winds made landing impossible and, like most places in Asia, at least twice as many people were waiting as could possibly go. In the poor countries, you never get anything in style. Here, Tomek did the pushing and shoving.

The flight from Pokhara to Mustang is unique. In the crystal clear air, the world's tallest mountains seem so close that one wants to touch them. The highlands of Mustang behind are really part of Tibet. As the

Gurkhas had conquered the area in the 18th century, the Chinese had had to leave it alone.

The pilot was good. On the second attempt, he managed to stay on the narrow air strip near the capital of Jomsum. It was like coming home. In the thin air, the colors were unbelievably clear. The houses had flat roofs, and there were mantras written on the stones. Completely out of place were the many Nepalese soldiers. They just didn't belong in this piece of central Tibet.

The next morning, we ordered pack horses for the other half of our group. We hoped they would be better than the one we got. It behaved so impossibly that we returned it even before paying. Instead, we divided the loads according to strength. The trek along the river under the burning sun was not easy. Soon, people cursed every cigarette they had ever smoked and every extra gram of fat.

Above all, it was a test of will power. A highly educated friend from southeast Germany was especially impressive. Overweight and allergic to horses, he wheezed like an old train. In a few days, however, he won everyone's respect.

After a rapid mountain stream lay the picturesque village of Kagbeni. It was as close as one was allowed to the Tibetan border and the place to sleep. Being in the area at Lopon Chechoo's invitation, we had to play by the rules. It was not the time to go farther north. The Khampas

Crossing a brook

An interminable rise

living there had often attacked the Chinese occupational forces in Tibet, and Hannah and I had even considered going to help them even in 1968.

Early in the seventies, the Khampa general, Wangchuk, had been hunted by the Gurkhas. He fled from one valley to the next until just before the Indian border. There, a high military post was already waiting for him. Khampas are very popular in that country. While the paratroopers and commandos in the Indian Army are Tibetan, the locals are not so brave. He and his group had nearly made it when they were bombed from helicopters. Many never forgave the Nepalese for this. The communist Chinese, however, must have been satisfied. They had an account which paid out money for things like that.

The next day revealed more of Kagbeni. It was exciting and sad at the same time. To the superficial eye, the city's atmosphere had been preserved. One was surrounded by stupas and colorful mantras. A closer look, however, showed both buildings and art to be in an advanced state of decay. No one took care of anything and soon there will only be ruins left. As so often before, it disturbed me how few traditional Buddhists see karma as opportunity and chance. Like most people with little imagination, they accept it as fate. Our knowledge of cause and effect obliges us to create the best possible world, but far too many use it as an excuse to remain passive and put up with what is.

Instead of retreating from a world which increasingly sees inner calm and good manners as signs of weakness, they could have recarved their deep culture in simple ways. Teaching their children their own language was an important start. It could prevent them from becoming yet another caste of rootless people somewhere in the central Himalayas.

It was Buddha's Enlightenment Day, which put the whole thing into a harsher perspective. We took five or six bearers from the local water mill with us. We offered them more than they would earn there, but it was still less than a dollar. There was no benefit in inflating the local economy. Then all walked up an endless slope. Our goal for the day was a Sakya monastery, the biggest in the area. It is the last stop before Tjume-Djasa—the Hindus call it Muktinath—the place where "earth, stone and water burn." It is one of the oldest holy places of the Himalayas.

Along the way, nature was beautiful beyond words. There was much more variety than in uniform central Tibet. Taking a shortcut up the mountain to the uniquely positioned monastery, there was a very special blessing: we climbed right into a procession of local women.

They were a fine mix of beautiful, stately and wild, and carried the wisdom texts of the Diamond Way. The leader of the monastery was obviously a good Yogi who could awaken people's potential. While the rituals were still going on, we were already sharing years of teaching the Dharma in East and West.

Sharing information

When we had just settled into the local guesthouse, our seventeen friends arrived. Having made a shortcut around Kagbeni, they came up in one day. Tomek, especially, had done terrific work. First, he had pressured the airport's officials for permission to fly and then he did the same to the pilot. Upon landing, they found the horses and bearers we had ordered for them. On this short and direct route, Tomek had been up and down the trail to help everyone, which is just the way he is. Now, they needed some strong men. Two of the women had broken down on the slope and one had the runs.

Our group gave the new arrivals the best sleeping places in the inn. Wanting to check out the local energies, Hannah and I stayed under a straw roof a few minutes away. When larger groups of pilgrims arrive, that is their place to sleep. It was neither private nor conducive to lucid dreams, however. Starting at dawn, some lovely children kept waking us with the same bright question, "Why do you still sleep, when there is light?" Explaining that white people work at night and therefore sleep in the mornings, offered no respite. Like in Tibet, they just stood there looking at us. It was a bit like a zoo. While we dressed, peed and brushed our teeth, they commented on everything, objectively and a bit precociously.

The next morning, the Yogi-lama came to be our guide; he knew the holy site very well. The path led across an open ridge with fantastic light and clouds and past an army checkpoint. Here we registered as Donald Duck, Joseph Stalin, Popeye, and other celebrities. A well-educated officer on horseback pestered us a bit. To his co-officers' joy, he confronted us and said that as inhabitants of the wealthier part of the world, we were obliged to send more money to the poor peoples. Their faces grew long when I told them to control their populations instead. As long as they produced so many children, money now would just mean more starvation later. Obviously, they had never seen the wider angle.

After the checkpoint, one sees both the high pass to the Manang region and the lush green triangle of the "burning waters." The temples are situated in a poplar grove before the ascent. A few of us, mountain-happy, had already hiked there the day before, but now we had an expert along. The lama told how Hindu officials had first forced the Buddhists to pull down the age-old Mani-Walls. They stand all over the high

Where water, sand and stone burn

Himalayas and consist of stones with mantras chiseled into them. Then, they had forbidden the renovation of buildings which fell apart. Most painful was probably a big cuckoo's egg they had laid right in the Buddhist nest: a Hindu temple in Kathmandu style which absolutely did not belong there.

  The sites where burning gases pass through stone, earth, and water were still on Buddhist lands, however. They were situated under the altar in an ancient temple dedicated to "Loving Eyes." It lay to the right of the entrance. The "Mirror of Karma," a place high up in the rocks, changes between dim and shiny, depending on the tendencies of the people who look. It welcomed us with bright radiance. There is also a place where one hears the murmurs of earth spirits. Only a temple to Guru Rinpoche was new. Some years earlier, it had fallen apart during a storm. The roof and the upper floor had collapsed symmetrically around the three main statues without touching them. This impressed even the Hindus: they

Archetypal situation

granted permission to erect a simple construction to protect the apparently so holy statues.

The next day was one of sports, for both the more and the less intelligent. The former got up early, brought equipment and rations and moved up the pass at a leisurely speed. Some other friends, Tomek and I only discovered at noon that we actually had some free time. Then we wanted to jog up the 5.6 kilometer mountain pass. It was a unique chance to see what shape we were in. Rarely was there an opportunity like that during the daytime. I taught the woman in the little teahouse on the first steep slope the Karmapa-meditation, and then we moved on. Running till we fell and continuing as soon as we could again breathe, we reached the ice walls of the mountain. Not knowing when darkness would fall, we also raced down. Our well-equipped friends, on the other hand, arrived with little sweat about a half-hour later. They also had had a wonderful time.

The next day, we returned to the capital of Mustang. Here we would stay with the family of Lopon Chechoo's foremost organizer. Though he was Buddhist, his name was Krishna, that of a Hindu god. This happens in uneducated and culturally mixed regions of the Himalayas. Arriving there in the afternoon, some unusual looking people were waiting for us. One learns to distinguish the special marks of the Buddhist schools. They are the same in East and West: Gelugpas look boarding-school. Sakyapas—especially the women—are very principled. We Kagyus—at least my students—are robust, and Nyingmapas often seem to be assembled from parts which don't quite fit. These people, however, went beyond any "Buddhist" scale. Some had big heads and small bodies, others the opposite. The leader was tall and thin and had the narrowest head I ever saw. They hadn't come to be admired, however. Lopon Chechoo had asked them to do us a great service. We immediately followed them along a narrow path between the fields. After about an hour's walk, mostly up, we reached a village under a grey-blue iceberg. A half-dozen people brought keys from different directions and then we followed them into a temple.

After the bright light outside, the room seemed dark at first. It also had a somewhat strange vibration. It took a while to recognize that we were in a Bon temple, run by shamans. While we picked up on similarities and differences to Buddhism, the men opened a solid leather box with the many keys. Now, it became exciting. Wrapped in dozens of silk scarves, here were the treasures Karmapa had taken a long detour for in 1956 on his way between Tibet and Bodhgaya. Already in 1970, he had told us to absolutely see them. They are the most precious collection of Guru Rinpoche relics in existence. Dating back to long before 746, when he went to Tibet and spread the teachings for five years, they are called Kuternga and consist of statues Guru Rinpoche had crafted himself. Also included are his shoes and the vest he wore at age thirteen, as well as some pieces of cloth on which female Buddhas have danced. We placed every piece on top of our heads, imagined them falling into our hearts, and absorbed their energy. With much luck, we reached Jomsom just as total darkness set.

The next day was the end of the flying season, and although monsoon clouds gathered on the horizon, the pilot risked two flights. Otherwise, we men would have had to walk through rain and leeches for five days. The bus was waiting in Pokhara, and Kathmandu now felt like a big city. Back in the Vajra Hotel, we planned the next weeks. There was still the option of walking to Tibet. While the professional porters

War council in Kathmandu

fell down daily, we would carry less of a load and my Mo looked good. Getting to any place in the country with culture, however, would take very long. As the road was destroyed, nobody drove.

Our real hope was for a journey into Bhutan, which was actually impossible. They only let in 2,000 visitors a year, in small groups, and each has to pay $150 a day, all things included. This was the way it had been for years. Lopon Chechoo was on our side, however. Already in Europe, he had said that he would try to get us in. Shortening his precious vacation in Holland by a week, he had flown straight to Bhutan. It was a time of both romance and organization: after bearing him some fine offspring, four of Rinpoche's nieces would now officially marry the Bhutanese king.

The necessary documents would be sent to Bhutan House in Calcutta. For going there, Niels and I each praised the concept most in accordance with our lifestyles. Niels said, "Fly to Calcutta. It only costs $70 and you have had enough hardships. Be a little kind to yourselves." And I said, "What doesn't kill you will make you strong. You should experience the overcrowded night buses to Siliguri and Calcutta. The vertical iron seats and lack of sleep will reveal new aspects of your mind. Also, you'll save $55. You can use it for shopping or give it as an offering in Bhutan."

Twenty-eight chose the hard way. The seven who flew, quickly joined us. They had been swindled at the expensive airport hotel and so came to Salvation Army on Sutter Street instead. The area offers a liberal education: people die on the nearby streets everyday. In the early seventies, most hotels were booked up, but as India grows stiffer and more bureaucratic by the year, fewer people go.

On one floor of Bhutan House they knew nothing. But on the other, my divinations were proven right. As telephones don't function in those parts of Asia, the Mos were our way of knowing what was going on. We had double luck. The invitations were there, and the plane we should have flown on was being fixed. We could hardly have afforded it. Instead, they offered to send buses to the Bagdogra airport. This way, we could both enjoy the drive up through the mountains and save money.

After hours of driving east with the Himalayan foothills to our left, we rolled through the "Gate for Honorable Guests" and into Puncholing. This town is Bhutan's window to the world. Two hotels had free rooms. When everybody was satisfied and we were just on our way to a local temple, several Tibetan friends cornered us. They all asked the same question, "When will we see him?" As so often before, we answered that it must be soon, that Karmapa's letters about his next reincarnation were clear, but that there were still reasons for keeping things secret. As usual, few trusted we'd said all we knew.

The next morning while people packed the buses, we ran to the temple. It contains an impressive standing statue of Guru Rinpoche. Then we drove past the "Resthouse" and the "Guesthouse," our places of internment and meeting with Karmapa in 1970. Winding up the mountain past the same checkpoints as last time, we made few and short stops.

Reaching Thimphu in the evening, our friends on the buses were unusually quiet. The vegetation had impressed many. Fertile and green, it was the total opposite to the arid desert in Mustang. Also quite a few were still digesting the impression of the dying people in Calcutta. We had the choice between an expensive, a half-expensive and a cheap hotel. Already that evening we discovered who else to thank that we were now in this pure realm: Topgala Rinpoche, the main secretary of Rumtek, had helped, and even the young king had been sympathetic. He had read *Entering the Diamond Way,* my first major book, and apparently liked it.

Although the minister of tourism would have liked to see some money, we were in Bhutan as fellow Kagyupas and not as a source of revenue.

During the following days, we did what we had come for. Hiking up and down the mountains, we visited many holy places. Some especially charged-up caves were now off limits. Hannah and I had meditated in them during our last visit and knew their power. After so many years we could still pick it up. It was understandable and a pity at the same time. Cigar smoke from rich tourists was probably not the Buddhas' first choice of incense, but beings need all the blessings they can get. Buddhas and Bodhisattvas, after all, are not "mighty people" with likes and dislikes. To them, everything is fantastic and they are happy about any access people can get to their state. "May I be a bed when people need rest," Tenga Rinpoche writes in a poem.

In Thimphu there were still white faces, mostly German and Swiss developers doing a good job. They were rare, however, in the region we would visit next. A few years earlier, the road to East Bhutan had been opened. It was built a lane and a half wide so one party had to stop when passing. Our goal was Karmapa's first area of residence after he'd left Tibet in 1959. It was in the holiest and hidden part of the country called Bumtang.

Our buses crawled up countless curves. After a certain altitude, the view expanded in all directions, becoming magnificent. There was also time for close-up looks: every few kilometers, people were clearing the road of landslides. The monsoon had already started, though rarely where we stayed. I couldn't take my eyes off the workers, Naga tribesmen. In a region with little physical violence, they were somewhat out of the ordinary. When the pressure of overpopulation drives the Bangladeshis into the East Himalayan foothills, the Nagas periodically kill a few thousand of them. It was strange to look into eyes which didn't react to closeness or emotion, but simply watched. I knew that they sold their turtles leg by leg while the animals were still alive and that they poisoned successful travelers, expecting to pick up their good energies in the process. Apparently the Bhutanese had become aware of the problem of their high fertility and were making plans for rotating the foreign work-force.

Building Karmapa's school in Bhutan

Löpon Chechoo's house in Bhutan

We stayed at one of Topgala's castles and in some hotels. The beautiful high plateau and cultural treasures of East Bhutan were deeply impressive. Things had changed from the first day when our friends charged into a traditionally ornamented gas station. They thought they had found a temple. It was just as amusing as when local people prostrate to Western helicopters, thinking they're gods. We had already experienced fantastic things daily on our walks. Still, there were situations nothing could prepare us for, such as entering the first temple directly under Karmapa. Though it was not as richly ornamented as the great national sanctuaries, it totally grasped our hearts. Here, no one was a "general" Buddhist, but everyone sensed the deepest connection to him. Walking through his rooms, and later when I guided a meditation at his bed, few had dry eyes. Karmapa's energy was as close as if he were here himself. We met Lopon Chechoo in Punakha, the winter capital and almost had an audience with the king. We had much to thank him for.

Je Khenpo

In front of the Bhutanese seat of government

Our group with Lopon Chechoo, Topga Rinpoche and Achi Deki

The afternoon spent with Je Khenpo, the highest Lama of Bhutan, was very special. He lived in the giant governmental palace and officially had the same power as the king, only on the spiritual level. People often waited years to meet him. Again, this was due to the influence of our fantastic friends. The near-constant motion of the fine muscles in the Khenpo's face showed his importance. Like Karmapa, he was the focal

Diamond Paunch

point for masses of spiritual energy. He taught in clear and simple words on "Loving Eyes," about confidence in the love and power of space. When the time came for pictures, he clapped his hands. Three monks entered the room. They carried a silver plate with a set of well-polished dentures. After he had smiled for the photos, they took them out again.

Our group had a last breakfast with Topga Rinpoche and his precious wife, the princess Achi Deki. She was exceedingly kind and even prepared our food herself. Then we drove west to the Paro valley, famous for its "Tiger's Nest." Here, Guru Rinpoche had appeared as "Diamond Paunch." Black-red, wrathful, and standing on a pregnant tigress, this form of deepest inspiration is embodied by Karma Pakshi, the second Karmapa. Unlike other daily walks to holy destinations, we reached this one without rain. Even when we arrived wet and cold, however, all our tours had been fully worth it.

The way to "Taktsang," as the place is called, was breathtaking, and Hannah and I found the temple even more impressive than on our last visit. Wishes made there will last into future lifetimes, and I held all friends deeply in my heart.

Back in India, we aimed straight for Nepal. A strike there kept us in the impossible border village of Kakabhita for ten hours. Only after Tomek activated the military, did we get a bus to Kathmandu. At the Vajra Hotel, we met our South Germans. They had just returned from an exhausting trip to Tibet. They had spent many days waiting for vehicles but had reached Lhasa and delivered the money for Tsurphu. This was very important. So much renovation was made possible with every penny.

Tiger's Nest

CHAPTER SIXTEEN

The World Shrinks

OUR DANISH RETREAT CENTER AT RODBY had grown. One hundred and thirty friends could now stay comfortably and Lama Tashi steered developments well. Together, we gave a two-week course on the preliminary practices of the Diamond Way. After that, a similar course was planned in California. Sys, Irmtraut, and Christiane from Europe came along; contacts across the Atlantic needed strengthening, and they deserved not always being the hosts. In San Francisco, Carol, Kiffer, and some dozen other friends were waiting at a wonderful site.

They had rented some deserted military barracks just behind the steep coastal cliffs. Permitting an extraordinary view over both San Francisco and the famous Golden Gate Bridge, the area is a sheer joy. Going straight for the practices, the European women were good examples to the more talkative Californians. For me, it was wonderful to have time for manuscripts, letters, and close friends.

During the same period, Hannah translated for Jamgon Rinpoche in Frankfurt. It was his first visit to Europe in ten years and lasted from July until December. Together, they visited the centers from north to south. Rinpoche was the first of the lineage holders to study how our groups operate. Only Lopon Chechoo and Tenga Rinpoche had done this before.

The third Ngondro course of that summer was in Poland. After three dozen Californians who would actually rather have been discussing

Blessing malas in Rödby

their experiences, here over five hundred people practiced single-mindedly and hard. The course was magical, like everything we do in the formerly communist part of the world. There is simply so much pent up devotion to work with.

One day, also the neighbors wanted a slice of the power-field. In front of the dreary rural store, tastefully positioned at the entrance to our formerly so noble center-buildings, a group of drunk farmers zeroed in on me. They had long wanted to see the lama and had also brought their wishing-list.

"If you are such a holy man," they said, "why don't you give us a few days of dry weather? It has been raining for two months and our harvest is rotting." "I will see what I can do," I answered. This is what my own teachers always say. Then I made strong wishes. Three days of sun and wind followed and on the second evening, thirty local farmers

"I'll see what I can do"

brought their families to take Refuge. Only a few miles away, and over the rest of Poland, it kept raining without interruption.

We returned to Denmark shortly before Jamgon Kongtrul and Hannah. Then came a time of loss.

Kim, our close friend and partner, committed suicide. While his brother Bo and he were building up a branch of their company in San Francisco, people with little skill had ruined its Danish base. Coming home, he had simply lacked the strength to put the pieces together again. It happened while Jamgon Kongtrul Rinpoche and I were in the country and Bokar Tulku—his main teacher—was traveling through France. During our last meeting, the feeling was in the air. Hannah gave him a handwritten meditation on Karmapa, and I blessed him longer than ever before with Karmapa's relics.

I should have spoken at the cremation, but couldn't. The first Phowa given by a Westerner was already underway. Arranged by Maxi and a handful of friends, one hundred and thirty of my students had assembled on a farm near Graz in Austria. They wanted to learn conscious dying. The day before returning to Asia, Tenga Rinpoche had given me his transmission for teaching it. The practice was hardly different from what the Phowa master Ayang Tulku had taught us in 1972, and Kunzig Shamarpa had asked me to give it to those who wanted it. Since I never have time for preparations, we just started out.

At this first course everyone had the result within seven days. It was a cause for true joy. If they kept their bonds, they would now enter the realm of highest bliss after death. The visible signs impressed all: spontaneously appearing holes or blood near the whorl on the crown of one's head. More important, though less tangible, was the inner development, and finest of all, their steadily growing trust. Here, death lost its fangs. Even somebody as critical as lovely Caty from Hamburg said that after the Phowa, there was no way back to materialism. The power of the Buddha of Limitless Light, and our devotion, had really met.

*Jamgon Kongtrul
Rinpoche*

Buddha of Limitless Light

Hannah came to Austria while Jamgon Kongtrul went back to Bhutan for his new passport. The following month, we visited the southern half of Europe and the Alpine countries. In Vienna, they knew about an old wish of mine: a parachute jump. The thirty-five seconds of free fall felt like riding an extremely fast motorcycle on the Autobahn, but the landing was not that exciting. Hannah says she had seldom seen me so enthusiastic as then. Such a jump offers the yogi a chance to check his understanding of emptiness and even a much shorter bungee-jump with my students from the Hamburg center later was like a shared initiation.

On Malta, people's interest did not take off. They didn't mind Enlightenment as a gift, but were not sure if they would work for it. One afternoon, I felt an intense desire to lie down. I never do that during the day. Dropping into a half-trance, a series of intense experiences began. Broad like a tank, I saw myself walk through Kim's house and flatten every obstacle. At one point, I held a big round mirror in my hands and I wondered what it would sound like if it splintered. Instead I put it gently aside. Next, I took Kim on a far journey to something extremely wonderful. Returning to ordinary consciousness, I had blood on the crown of my head and knew that I had left my body.

The original translation team

This very moment, Maia called from the Copenhagen center. She supplied the other half of the story. Waking up some hours earlier, she had the strong feeling that Kim had entered her room through the closed door. Knowing that his mind was looking for me, she immediately told him that I was on Malta. As we had been there together earlier, she supplied a good mental picture, and then he was gone.

The Diamond Way teaches that most spend seven weeks as awareness energy between death and their next incarnation. Since I abhor teachings which sound fundamentalist and lack a logical explanation, I usually try to "humanize" them with a little disarming psychology. Nevertheless, whenever I am able to check them out, they prove to be right. It was the forty-ninth day after Kim's death and none of us had known. Suicide disturbs the mind even more than murder, but now I felt good about him.

In early September, Hannah had to go east again. Kalu Rinpoche wanted her presence in Bodhgaya, Buddha's place of Enlightenment, in northern India. He needed her help with the translation of forty very concentrated Tibetan texts. Called "The Treasure of What One Should Know," they are one of the five main works of the first Jamgon Kongtrul Rinpoche. At that time, Kalu Rinpoche was staying in Beru Khyentse Rinpoche's new monastery, surrounded by thirty of his closest disciples. Most had done the three-year retreat twice. As no normal human can stand India for very long, however, their numbers soon shrank below ten. We hope more will get involved in the future. The translation project was Kalu Rinpoche's final wish, and they are really important texts.

In Europe, Christmas 1987 was a great party in the snows of Schwarzenberg. During the next days, we dug out the basement of our center in Wuppertal. I taught in the evenings, and every container we filled gave more space for Karmapa's activities.

After New Year, we flew straight to New York. This time, we were five, and Tomek had arranged for us to meet Jamgon Kongtrul Rinpoche at the airport. In front of the building, classic psychology found a noisy expression. The famous pecking order functioned perfectly. A policeman's anger traveled down a Hispanic family of ten to a dog, which received a hefty kick.

On our way with Rinpoche to the first class lounge, the expression of the Europeans changed from surprise to real embarrassment. I wasn't

The Enlightenment Stupa in Bodhgaya

too happy, either. It was a strange meeting with old friends. The leaders of the once so alive New York center I helped build had changed amazingly. After they'd come under the influence of the Dharmadatu, stiffness had taken the place of joy. They regretted not being able to invite

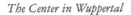

The Center in Wuppertal

me because I had given my last teachings there from the Khenpo's cushion. Rinpoche visibly enjoyed joking with us. He kept asking about developments in Europe and when we were on our way out, he called us back several times. There was no doubt he would have loved to come along.

In the evening, my Greek student, Lisa, showed us downtown Manhattan. The World Trade Center was something to see. Some of the bums crowding the bottom floor were in bad shape. On our way to the building's roof, the guards had a lot of questions. They said I looked like someone who would jump down with a parachute. A few blocks away, Maia and Lisa left a toilet looking somewhat pale. They had fought their way past two black girls, each with a needle up their arm.

Lisa's apartment was too small. We took the cheapest local offer instead, an hour-hotel with mirrors everywhere. Even without any knowledge of pornography, the loneliness and narcissism of the whole thing was evident. One always sees one's partner. The reason for so many mirrors is to see oneself.

At thirty degrees below zero centigrade, we drove the usual sixteen hours to Kentucky. Here Maia drove a car for the first time. As it was an automatic model, I quickly explained the pedals to her and then dozed off, trusting perfectly in our protectors. After Bob and Melanie had moved to Albuquerque, there were good friends but little Buddhist activity in Lexington. The trip on to St. Louis was truly exciting: we had a real snowstorm the whole way. Though there were frequent warnings to stay at home, I had a lecture there in the evening. Also, the great healer, Claude, was arriving from Witten in Germany. Andre and Nora had organized well and two dozen people took Refuge.

Some hours out of the city, a true miracle happened. It was witnessed by seven sober and well-reputed citizens in our car. Happily driving 150 kph for so long—the national maximum is 85 kph—Maia had gone speed-blind, and when we exited the freeway, she couldn't brake on the slippery road. We were headed directly towards the right iron pole supporting one of the giant green street signs, built to withstand even a midwestern tornado. Massive as railroad tracks, they are fastened to concrete foundations with four large bolts. Already bracing for the embarrassing sound of tearing metal and splintered glass, the pole swung elegantly to the left instead and we drove through. Then I found the handbrake under the luggage and we stopped.

Looking back, we saw the black lines from our tires in the snow with the iron pole standing untouched in the middle of the tracks. Just five minutes earlier we had fastened plastic-coated pictures of "White Umbrella" and "Black Coat" to the car's ceiling. My subjective experience had been of a giant hand removing the obstacle with great speed. Not knowing that learners may drive in the U.S. when accompanied by a licensed driver, I started on before any police could come. At the next gas station, there was not a scratch, though the car's metal was of that Japanese quality we had dented with only our hand before.

Big Erik from Schwarzenberg joined us in Albuquerque, New Mexico. Here Bob and Melanie were doing good work. Like in so many established centers, however, the "old" practitioners had occasional out-breaks of that most dreaded of American diseases: puritanism. We again stayed with Norbert. He had bought us yet another little piece of America, now above the planned stupa on the mesa of Taos. In Phoenix we had an exciting horse ride through the desert and mountains and back on the West coast, Van and Carolyn again lent us a car. They were doing

Teaching Bob the family smile

well. After stops up through California, Carol and I worked on *Practical Buddhism,* a new booklet. This time, Faustin and Brian recorded the evenings professionally. These and other videos and audios are available today from Sound Photosynthesis, P.O. Box 2111, Mill Valley, CA 94942, Tel. (415) 383-6712 in America. Not able to be physically everywhere all the time—though I do try—books, booklets, tapes, and videos in about a dozen languages strengthen my work immensely. Containing view, way, and goal, their aim is making every experience part of our growth. Nothing is more important today. In this book, for example, the teaching is the most direct possible: a view through the eyes of an unsentimental Danish lama. Dissolving people's stiff ideas, much neurosis will naturally disappear. If the karmic connection is there, no faster way to mental health exists.

The frequent visits to America had paid off. We had become a symbol of quality and the halls were full. Many had taken the letter from

Lama Ole Nydahl's Tour Around the World—early 1992

JANUARY

3-4	Depature from Berlin for an overland tour of Russian and Siberia.
5-24	RUSSIA: Teachings in St. Petersburg, Sverdlovsk, Omsk, Novosibirsk, Krasnojarsk, Irkutsk, Chabarowsk, Vladiwostok.
25-27	Continuing overland via Mongolia to Peking
28-30	Flying Peking-Bangkok, Calcutta-Bagdora
31	Rumtek, Sikkim. Tibetan New Year.

FEBRUARY

1-10	Rumtek, Sikkim
11-12	Flying Bagdora, Calcutta, Bangkok, Melbourne
13-26	AUSTRALIA incl Melbourne, Canberra, Wollongong, Sydney, Surfers Paradise
27-29	Wat Buddha Dharma (Sydney area) Phowa Course

MARCH

1-3	Wat Buddha Dharma (Sydney area) Phowa Course
4-7	Sydney area
8-14	NEW ZEALAND, Christchurch. Incl. Phowa Course on Banks Peninsula/South Island
15	Flying from Auckland—Honolulu—Kauai
15-17	HAWAII—Kauai—Karma Kagyu Centre Kauai
18	Honolulu
19	SAN FRANCISCO—Karma Jigme Ling
20	SONOMA, CA
21	EUREKA, CA
22	SAN FRANCISCO—Karma Jigme Ling
23	SAN LUIS OBISPO, CA
24	LOS ANGELES
25	SAN DIEGO - KTC San Diego
26	PHOENIX - KTC Phoenix
27-28	SAN FRANCISCO-MARIN-KDOL
29	ALBUQUERQUE, NM
30	TAOS, NM
31	Travelling overland

APRIL

1	Travelling overland
2	HOUSTON, TX
4	MIAMI
5-8	VENEZUELA-KTC Caracas
9-17	COLUMBIA incl. Bogota, Medellin & Phowa Course
18-23	PERU-Lima incl. Phowa Course
24-27	MEXICO-Mexico City
28	NEW YORK
29	Flying back to Frankfurt

A typical spring schedule

the Dharmadatu as proof of my purity, while others found the fresh European yogi-style suitable to their lives. Here, also, Paul from Schwarzenberg arrived. He is among my "young lions" that I have asked to teach.

In Nevada City, the meeting was in Paul and Nancy Clemens' shrine room. In Ashland, Peter Giffen had organized and thirty people took Refuge, a large number for America. Once again Mount Shasta was more private than public, but a joy to visit.

Arriving in Honolulu from Los Angeles, we slept a few hours on a bench. Then we took the first plane to Maui. Here, and on Kauai, another of the unique Hawaiian Islands, the yearly visits had brought lasting results. People had become family and meditated on Karmapa. Our fusing of minds with Sandy and Dan was a timeless joy. They basked in the direct style of Buddhism which caused so much apprehension in the more monastic Honolulu center. They have helped a lot in the funding of my recent books.

While our group returned to Europe, Tomek, Paul, and I went east. After Seoul, Hong Kong, and Bangkok came Calcutta in India. Here waited Hannah, Maia's mother, Pia, and the Findeisen family, sponsors to our large Hamburg center. I let our friends have the experience of buying tickets for an Indian train, and the next 170 kilometers north

Nancy and Paul Clemens at Guru Rinpoche shrine on their property in Nevada City.

took twenty-seven hours. In Siliguri, we had the yearly drama: no Sikkim visa. Though the highest bosses had given Hannah their personal word in Delhi several months earlier, not a scrap of paper was there. The civil war continued, which had been so educational to our group in '86. Every day people on both sides were killed. Buses were still stoned or torched, and there were burning houses on the mountain slopes. The government didn't want anybody to see their undeclared civil war, but some influential contacts at "Sikkim House" somehow got us through. As soon as their permission had arrived by phone, we were on the bus to Gangtok.

Rumtek was wonderful and we had the usual strong dreams. In the rooms where we met with the Shamar, Jamgon, and Gyaltsab eminences, the sound of gunshots was especially clear. At the bridge between Sikkim and India, the Gurkhas were just blowing up some gasoline trucks. That was the end to road transport in that part of the Himalayas, and we had to return by helicopter, which was amazingly cheap. It was a great experience—our first full view of the mountains we had lived in for years.

In Bodhgaya, we again had two days with Kalu Rinpoche. We also met Bokar Tulku there. Together with some old lamas, he had recently made a group of scientists from Stanford University hold their breath. H. H. Dalai Lama had sent them to Rumtek "to see real yogis" and now they had to explain what their instruments had registered. More difficult still was the fact that our skin keeps its temperature when inner heat arises. The warmth which melts snow and preserves life in extremely cold conditions starts an inch from the body and radiates from there. When we praised him loudly for increasing our good Kagyu name in critical places, his answer was: "I only prayed to Karmapa the whole time."

In Kathmandu, the Lopon Chechoo and Tenga Rinpoches held the powerfield. I taught mainly Westerners in the Vajra Hotel and in Thrangu Rinpoche's monastery. During those days, he gave the Kagyu Ngagdzo Initiation, the treasure of Kagyu Mantras. It was the last chance to do something like that for a while. Since Nepal had taken money from China to drive out pro-Tibetan Westerners, it would take time for so many talented people to assemble there again.

A visit to the joyful Khenpo Thsultrim Gyamtso cleared the air. He had accompanied Karmapa on his tour through Europe in 1977. For years, his students had created the worst gossip about other teachers,

Thrangu Rinpoche

probably as a kind of diversion from hard intellectual studies. The rumors
had caused some bad feelings, so it was a relief to see how far he was above
all that. After lunch, Khenpo took us to the roof of the school he rented
in Bodnath. He explained which Rinpoche was currently building what
and, seen from above, it was even more impressive than taking a walk
between the temples. A Taiwanese monk told me later that half the money
for building there came from his island, that most of it had been given
to Karmapa. Also lamas from other lineages had quickly found out how
famous he is among the Chinese. They then happily used his name when
making collections. Not long after, the Hindus held a big meeting at one
of their holiest shrines nearby, where little growth happens. Becoming
jealous of the wide Buddhist activity, they put pressure on the Nepalese
government, which is Hindu. At the same time, China made similar
demands. As a result, the government ordered a total halt to building.
Today, it is still unclear if and when the temples can be completed.

Hannah stayed in New Delhi to help the lineage holders. The
welcome given at six in the morning by over seventy friends at Frankfurt

KhenpoThsultrim Gyamtso

View over Kathmandu

Our new Freiburg center

airport blew me away. The many years on the Autobahn had not been wasted: these people were the finest of family. During the following tour through Germany, a lecture in Freiburg became the basis for my book, *Mahamudra,*also published by Blue Dolphin. In May there was a large spiritual congress in Krakow, Poland. It enabled Hannah and me to do a double program. During the daytime, the large cultural institute held a dozen spiritual teachers of different kinds. Hundreds of interested people went from hall to hall in the large building, comparing and taking notes. Then Hannah and I were driven to a park outside town, the site for teaching until six or seven in the morning. Every night, about five hundred of my students endured this, packed like sardines into a classical former garden house. The place had tradition: when the Solidarity movement was crushed in '81, we had secretly met in the cellar of the same building. I still remember their burst of emotion when receiving the Bodhisattva vow. Giving them power to fight their government without hating its ignorant members nearly pulled me out of my body. As so often, we stayed with Hannah and Krzysztof in their historical flat in the old city. Now again, the streets were full of storm troopers, the so-called Zomo. They were trying to break a university whose tradition of freedom their two fine academics represent so well all over the world. Nobody abhors the present P.C. or "politically correct" wave in American universities more deeply than those who have fought for the freedom of all to say what they think.

The Polish reaction to the phenomena of the "New Age" was interesting to watch. They were like the uncorrupted child facing the "Emperor's New Clothes." First, they checked everything politely and thoughtfully, looking for a consistent philosophical view. Then, they asked about methods. When they also couldn't find any goal, they catalogued it among the expected signs of decay afflicting late capitalism. Disillusioned but still polite, they walked away. I was proud of them. They did honor to centuries of Western thinking. In matters of philosophy, they still put the horse before the cart. They looked for real answers.

Next came southern Poland. In many places, its inspiring Tatra Mountains still hold an unbroken medieval atmosphere. Josef from Budapest picked us up from a friend's retreat house and we drove south through Czechoslovakia. In the claws of an especially unimaginative brand of communism, the country was collectively dreary and sad. Shortly after the Hungarian border lay a retreat house with a stupa. Due to Alexander Koros, a Hungarian and recognized Bodhisattva who visited Tibet a hundred years ago, we were not the first to spread living Buddhism here.

Though the Germans had fought to their last man in Budapest, hoping to win time for their scientists to invent yet another war-deciding weapon, the town now looked as if the Hapsburgian emperors had only just left. During the fifties when people could still trust communism, they had rebuilt everything according to the old plans. The Poles did the same in Warsaw and Gdansk. We spent four days at a students' organization and were thoroughly checked out. Before getting close, they wanted to be sure that we functioned on every level and really knew joy. They definitely didn't want to be stuck with a boring or inhibited teacher. Only after taking us out every night and filling us with sweet wine did they risk opening themselves. Thirty took Refuge. They were strong people and this was a promising beginning.

In Budapest

Returning to Denmark in June, things did not look good for our first trip to Russia. The visa took longer when one wanted to live in tents instead of paying the expensive hotel bills, and we knew nobody to invite us yet. We already had fixed programs in Sweden and Finland, however, so Maia, Pedro, Hannah, and I piled into my big black BMW and raced north into the breathtaking "white nights." Nothing is more fascinating than those weeks of Scandinavian summer when it never gets dark. Then followed four days in our center near Malaga, at Pedro's invitation, and late in the month, Hannah flew to East Asia. She would translate for Jamgon Kongtrul Rinpoche in Malaysia.

After two weeks of teaching the Ngondro in Rødby, my most intense course started so far: a Phowa in Kuhary, Poland for four hundred Poles and one hundred fifty western Europeans. Polite as we are, the Danes immediately occupied the front rows and got the signs very quickly. Then I distributed them throughout the tent to share the good energy and the Germans moved up. After all the elbow-Capitalists had nice holes in their heads, our well-mannered hosts sat up front.

The first Phowa in Graz had taken a week. This time, however, I had to stop after five days. Everyone was through and some were getting too many holes. Before the great party the last night, I felt the power of a long life prayer. Sabine from Hamburg had written one for me.

Over five hundred attended the first Phowa in Poland

Suddenly, everyone in the tent jumped to their feet and chanted it in Polish. It was like being under high voltage.

August 10th we landed in San Francisco. The first Phowa was planned for America and fourteen Europeans came along. Among them was the first solid group we ever managed to start in Frankfurt—a difficult town for spirituality. We would practice at the army camp where we had done the first Ngondro the year before. It was important to regularly bring a strong blessing there. I couldn't spend enough time in the area, and Carol, who held the center, was totally overworked. Everything went well and that which I wanted most of all happened: Americans and Europeans became friends.

Even the healthiest teacher must include the factor of impermanence in his planning, especially if he prefers driving at above two hundred kilometers per hour. I was very aware that the courage and independence which my students develop are worth little if they don't also become friends and work together. In spite of some American complaints that after being totally accessible for years, I was now so closely surrounded by Europeans: it was not enough that I came alone . . . if people didn't get to know each other, masses of dynamic power would never arise. Democracy and freedom have gained through cooperation across the Atlantic: Buddhism would do the same.

Our group flew back to Europe, while Tomek and I went on to Manila. Seventeen hours, seventeen beers, four movies and more than a hundred letters and cards later, we landed in the Philippines. Lovely Hannah was waiting with a chauffeured Mercedes. After a drive to an incredible mansion, they had kept seats next to Jamgon Kongtrul Rinpoche. We were the lucky guests of Ms. Dee, an impressive Chinese businesswoman and great supporter of our lineage. Sitting in a tropical garden with the evening free, there was lots of news to exchange. Among the lineage holders, Jamgon Kongtrul Rinpoche had traveled longest with Karmapa and knew his wishes very well. As usual, our activities were exactly parallel, although we so rarely had time to talk. Karmapa's transmission works like that, and not only on the level of planning: the topics Hannah translates for her Rinpoches regularly come up in my

At Point Bonita, with my brother Bjørn (sitting), Ulrik and Tomek

lectures on their own. Whether we are aware of it or not, his powerfield operates everywhere.

During our ten days in the Philippines, we were lovingly taken care of. Among the Chinese communities in non-communist Asia, the group in Manila was among the most "modern" we met. I taught in a youth-prison, to the narcotics police, and at some other official places. Like in so many of the warm Asian countries, only the Chinese elite seems to feel a need for a structured view of the world. If the average population isn't Moslem and fanatical, everything is good and comes from some god. They can swallow any philosophical or religious camel sideways which drives the Christians especially into despair. They would like to make them believe at least a few dogmas.

A day's drive through the country and a visit to a museum were very instructive. Catholicism had evidently contributed the principles of sin and suffering to the national culture. Hundreds of pictures and statues of tortured saints provided a light and joyful atmosphere while the Japanese had simply slaughtered them. America's enrichment of their lives had consisted of a democracy they didn't understand and Coca Cola. An afternoon on Subic Bay, America's largest overseas base, was impressive. Here we taught Rinpoche how to swim. It didn't take long. He only needs to hear things once.

Tomek and I spent twenty-four hours in Amman, marvelling at the countless ways Arabs put each other down. Then we landed in Vienna. It was now early in September and many were going with us to Graz for another Ngondro course.

Not long after, our connection to Russia was reawakened. It happened thanks to Michael from Kiel, a genius at keeping contact behind the then "Iron Curtain." He had prepared everything and once again Hannah and I crossed Sweden and Finland in our fast BMW. We had exactly nine days before the Dalai Lama and half his government were expected in Copenhagen. They would stay in our center for four days.

Finland was beautiful, cold, and non-spiritual—as always—but Russia was a completely different world.

The uniformed officials at the border—the secret ones are of a different caliber—were all young, tired, and shy. One felt no holy flame of socialism there. Driving through the country's security zone was a trip.

It consists of seventy kilometers of depopulated woods on the way to Wiborg, an old Finish-Swedish town. Here, we had a chance to adjust to the vibrations of this vast block of countries; we had only seen the airports since 1968. What I felt most was a profound state of shock. It was more intense than in China, where people have never had idealistic European expectations regarding human nature. Another point was the extreme sloppiness in handling the outer world. Strongest of all was their deep and longing search for something beyond the material; it was a striving most hardly dared admit to themselves. We were stopped by people giving a then incredible rate for dollars and before Leningrad, we slept in the car for some hours. We didn't know that we had stopped right in front of the only tourist hotel. When it became so light that we could read the official signs asking us to register, we drove on into town at once. We wanted to make our contacts before the officials might start tailing us. Among the cities we have visited, the streets of Leningrad are probably the worst kept. They could drive even an eastern Turk up the wall. People with a hard karma had frequently taken their birth here. More than a million had starved during the Second World War and Stalin's secret police had killed even more, frequently the most intelligent.

We called our contacts and left the car near the famous Winter Palace. This is where the Russian Revolution started in 1917. Though millions of paintings and books have portrayed the healthy proletariat rising against their decadent oppressors, we here heard a different version: the sailors who scared the emperor out of his palace in 1917 had actually been on a more romantic errand—pursuing the invitations of a company of drunken female soldiers calling them from the building's windows. As we closed the doors of our car, two athletic young men asked in good English if we wanted to change money. "You can talk," I said. "Come." And so, we took them along for the next five days.

I taught in the mornings, afternoons, and evenings to various groups in different private apartments. As so often before, the important people couldn't cooperate, so we had to do several things twice. Nowhere had we met such a mixture of generosity and basic mistrust among ordinary people. Seventy years with spies everywhere and jail or execution squads so very close had made it very difficult for most to communicate naturally. Every moment was fully used, however. The Russians were as concentrated as the Poles and recorded everything on tape. It would be useful for later and more relaxed times.

We put up a tent for the police to watch and then made a trip to Tallin, the capital of Estonia. I drove the stretch in less than three hours, including a meal, which must be a record. People there were as reserved and unspiritual as the Finns. They also spoke the same language. Of course the Baltic Republics should be free, but the picture is not as idealistic as presented. Being more practical and productive than Russians, the Estonians don't want to share their wealth with them. It took a while to find the professor whose address we had. Because our money changers asked in Russian, people kept sending us in the wrong direction. Later, we heard that even ambulances won't come if the caller speaks Russian. "We did not ask them here," people say.

The professor and his group managed to be both nationalists and traditionalists. Their Buddhist connection consisted of badly translated books by non-practitioners and some visits to the Burjat lama-monasteries in Siberia, where they could hardly talk to whatever monks had survived Stalin. Preferring discussion to meditation, there was not much we could do for them. Their other contact was to the Mongolian monastery near Leningrad, a tall stone building erected by the Tibetologist, Nicholas Roerich. It had survived the war but was now used by the

Leningrad—riverfront

Leningrad—war museum

Communists for animal experiments. We had been there twice and passed it every day on our way to the city.

Our only direct contact with the authorities was due to the speed limits, sixty and ninety kilometers per hour. Some misanthrope had sold radar guns to the natives and I had left my detector in America, so they earned a blessing and a few dollars. When I didn't like their style and simply said, "no," they wrote long notes which they demanded that we show at the border. Apart from not being able to keep up with our speed, they definitely had some image problems: some people had made a rough estimate and discovered that in the thirties and forties the government had killed up to fifty million of their own people. Even in Russia, it was difficult to find shoulders broad enough to carry this.

Our exit was dramatic. After leaving tapes and books for our Leningrad friends to translate, we had just cleared customs at the border when Hannah turned pale: our passports were missing. We had last used them at a hotel in Tallin, where people behind the desk were so angry that we left without talking to them again. The passports must still be there. Not to our surprise, the men standing casually around proved to be secret police and even competent. They called an office in Wiborg, which already had a file on us. They said the passports were now in

Leningrad. It was impossible to go there and return by midnight when the post closed, but if we didn't manage, there was no way we could reach Denmark before the Dalai Lama arrived. The airport where the passports were kept was situated on the far side of the city. It must have been a national secret. There were no signs leading there and no one knew where it was. But with the winding roads to ourselves and our BMW, we made it. One of our last—and lasting—impressions of Russia was a man's jubilation when a military bus and a police truck collided. He sprang out of his car and jumped up and down for joy.

We drove past the Dalai Lama's hotel in Helsinki at night and rolled off the ferryboat from Sweden in Elsinore, north of Copenhagen. It was six in the morning and three hours before the Dalai Lama would arrive with his entourage. Friends from the center had waited there all night. They had prepared everything perfectly. Though the Danish government had first been as cowardly as most others, taking no stand against the Chinese destruction of Tibet, something had now changed. They had either become idealistic or discovered that China would be exporting and not importing for decades. Anyway, the government got closer than ever to officially supporting Tibet's liberation. The Dalai Lama's public lecture, announced under the high-sounding title of "Similarities between Western Science and Tibetan Buddhism," became exactly what people needed: a loving and wise being sharing his understanding of why we should never get angry. When a more reserved gentleman asked to hear something about the announced topic, Dalai Lama replied disarmingly: "I don't know anything about that."

Brian, Stan, Sten, and other of my karate students protected the center and its guests around the clock. While thanking the Dalai Lama in Karmapa's name, I was unusually moved. I asked him to come again soon, and stay even longer.

In November, Hannah returned to Bodhgaya. It was not something she enjoyed, but she had promised Kalu Rinpoche to continue with his translation group. After amazing growth in the centers east of the Rhine, we celebrated Christmas in Karma Gon with Pedro's family. There on a mountain ridge, near Malaga in southern Spain, we had gradually built a small but well functioning village. Several of my strong students worked there and it was mainly financed by Pedro's hard work. We hoisted Karmapa's blue-yellow Dream Flag, and my brother Bjørn

The priests of Denmark

promised to stand naked and blow a bone trumpet if gawking tourists came too close. There were still some deserted houses on the ridge which we hadn't been able to afford. Maia worked in the sun on my manuscripts while Don and I flattened some decrepit buildings with delightfully heavy sledge hammers. It was the place where our first stupa would be built. On one of the last days of 1988, we flew to America for the third time that year. Once again, it was the first stop on a tour around the world.

In New York, a letter waited that would change Western Buddhism in a lasting way and become a main cause for this book. It contained painful articles from major American newspapers about Osel Tendzin, the "regent" of the Dharmadatu organization. Though he had known he was HIV positive since 1985, he had kept it secret and knowingly endangered his mostly male partners. A mother in Colorado whose boy was infected had made it all public. It was a tragic story and also made the Kagyu Lineage look bad. Though their strictly ruled organization had always evaded Rumtek's influence and built up its own power structure, these serious half-page clippings described the Dharmadatu as part of the Karma Kagyu. Our lineage really didn't deserve this.

Lisa and Tomek arranged two driveaways and we headed north through the beautiful winter landscape. It was time to talk to Jamgon Kongtrul Rinpoche in Woodstock. We would meet on the East Coast as we had last winter. He was ill due to the scandal, so we didn't go to his room. Returning for a war council the next evening, Rinpoche said, "We, the lineage holders, have asked Osel Tendzin several times to step down. He always refused. Instead, he went to Kalu Rinpoche who wrote him a letter of support. We hope the organization can make him withdraw

Karma Gön by night

before Karmapa's work is harmed even more. Ourselves, we have no means to do this. He is really 'beyond Dharma.'"

After a teaching where Rinpoche was much more formal than in Europe, we drove off. At midnight, we stopped on the snowy highway, north of New York. Passing two bottles of champagne between our cars, we celebrated the New Year of 1989. The masses in Times Square still hadn't left and thoroughly amazed our European group: they had never seen so many people of such varied backgrounds before. They were also surprised to find more police on the road than in the communist states and everything cordoned off. After a goodbye to Lisa in Queens, we drove west through the night.

After stops with our groups across the country, I held my first lecture in years at Baca Grande Ranch. It is an enormous piece of highland near Crestone in Colorado which the Strong-Marstrand family had given to Karmapa. Lying only a few hours from Boulder, the collective pain of the Dharmadhatu organization was on everybody's lips. Never had it been more evident: under all circumstances, we must stay transparent, with no unhealthy power structures or pretense.

Los Angeles was magnificent, hip, and confused as always. Two groups of friends, who should have worked together, had each advertised a different program for the same evening instead. It spread my impact but in the course of the lecture, Nanette, Richard, Yuki, and other close friends showed up anyway. Once again we stayed with Joanna Bull, who started the Wellness Institute. The waters were still stirred up after Kalu Rinpoche's weeklong visit, and I had to explain traditional Tibetan customs a few more times. Many talked about cultural imperialism and were amazed that Rinpoche had again built up a Tibetan teacher at the expense of a Westerner. The local Canadian lama should actually be well positioned in their hierarchy: he was from the first years in Sonada and had already done two of the monastic three-year retreats. Rinpoche's endorsement of Osel Tendzin disturbed people so much that we tried to organize another day in L.A. It was important to calm the rumors, but due to programs up the coast, I could only leave a tape.

Years of work across the U.S. were up in the air. Good people held their heads in pain everywhere and our basis of trust was endangered. Now, more than ever, America needed the Central European model:

mature groups of people who could cooperate and take responsibility. Sufficient information, up-to-date meditations in English, and visits by teachers with life-experience were at the top of the list.

Hierarchical systems don't function in the democratic West. Whenever employed, they attract too many bloodless yes-sayers. Expecting guidance in the simplest matters, they become jealous of each other's closeness to the teacher. In contrast, everyone is empowered through the open model which I call "meritocracy." Having a say through one's devoted contribution, and in the field that one masters, brings both development and cooperation. A central structure only works where true Rinpoches are unimpeachable in their position and delegate the opportunities for growth. Khenpo Karthar does this skillfully in America. He is a shining light among the Tibetans there, non-political and open in spite of the tight administration around him.

In Europe the same functions are performed by the Tenga, Chechoo, and Gendyn Rinpoches. The signs that a center is going right or wrong are easy to read, and always the same: if people become independent and direct, with energy for others and a robust, wide view of sex and life, this is good; bad is an unclear and indirect feeling, rumors, and a constant "quoting of authority." The Diamond Way is for the spiritual elite, and one should know this without feeling proud. Only those who master normal civilized behavior, have a surplus for others, and don't take all things personally, will benefit by following this path. As it works through identifying with the perfect qualities of one's teacher, the confidence that these exist is indispensable. Today, with thousands of students and a protective role around the world, I check a teacher of the Diamond Way like this: if the frustrated people are against him and the exciting ones his friends, he does something right. Buddha did not teach to make us sheep but to free our power. There is little chance we will bring happiness to others if we can't satisfy ourselves.

We left the West Coast for some programs on Hawaii. The manuscript for the beach this time was my *Ngondro* book. On Kauai with Janet, the Buddhas again had to work overtime. Tomek and I were both taken by a riptide on Secret Beach. As he was thrown first against some rocks and then onto the beach, he made a joyful discovery: after the Phowa, any fear of death had disappeared. Further out in the waves, I thought to myself, "Ole, you fathead, you did it again." While I caught onto the rocks the years before, together with Peter, a brave German friend who risked his life for me, this time I was saved by a surfboard. A few minutes later, I was back in the waves again.

On Maui, Jason and Dechen waited at the airport, a handsome couple. This was the beginning of our work together around the world. They organized several Phowa courses on Hawaii and are our great and graceful hosts. The contact they gave us to the environmental water filters of NSA will hopefully soon support much of our work in Europe.

Our friends returned to Germany and Denmark, and Tomek and I flew via Tokyo and Bangkok to Calcutta. It was February 2, 1989, the day we had agreed on, but Hannah was not in the airport. We went to the restaurant above and cleared our heads with their strong tea. Just as my Mos showed that Hannah was not in Bodhgaya, not on the train and not anywhere else, she came in the door, happy and healthy. There had been a strike on the way. After the overcrowded train to Gaya we took a shaky scooter-rickshaw ride to Bodhgaya where Hannah and a group of translators worked for Kalu Rinpoche. They were devoted but not many. Only a few had returned this year, although Rinpoche paid for their food, and, if necessary, for their transportation. Nearly all had done the three-year retreat of the monk-tradition twice, and we had known each other for years. As we met rarely and had somewhat differing views on how the teachings should be spread, there was always a lot to talk about. Since the wildly fluctuating voltages in India had already destroyed Rinpoche's computer, Hannah's little printer now produced the texts.

At eighty-six, Kalu Rinpoche was in fine shape. It had been much too long since we had met. With amusement, he still remembered our first drives through Europe fifteen years ago. Even the name "Roseburg" he recalled. This was where the Zen master beat his students for being late. We told him about our work around the world for Karmapa and how I put all centers directly under him. These were places where Rinpoche hardly ever went. After explaining what I had just done to smooth the waves in Los Angeles, I especially thanked Rinpoche for his letter of support. He had written it in Hong Kong in 1986, when we returned from Tibet. Due to his jealous French translator, and a strange lady in white, several had left an initiation in the ominous German

The resurrection

With Dechen, Jason and Scott on Maui

institute, doubting the closeness of our bond. This letter reconfirmed his support for our work and also stated that people in Central Europe should practice under my guidance.

Except for three lectures I had decided to give at the stupa, what I wanted in Bodhgaya was a place to work. The time had come to write the history of our lineage in the West—this book. Its aim is to avoid future mistakes and to stress the factors which bring freshness and growth. With his usual kindness, Kalu Rinpoche invited me to stay and eat with his translators. Beru Khyentse Rinpoche's staff gave Tomek and the rest of our group rooms elsewhere in the monastery.

During the day, Kalu Rinpoche preserved his strength by staying in bed. People said he wanted to live until he saw the completion of the important translation work. Now, he no longer advised monkhood or the three-year retreat at every opportunity. He praised the wisdom of these books instead. Before we left Bodhgaya to see our lineage holders at Rumtek, Rinpoche made things easier for many of us. With his last public lecture—he held a more private one for his closest students in Sonada, a month later—he removed the cause for years of embarrassed silence. His words deeply relieved those who wanted to see things the way he did but couldn't deny the evidence of their own eyes. Taking his highly praised three-year lamas down to the human level where most

Kalu Rinpoche in Bodhgaya

think they belong, cooperation became possible between his monks and our yogis and laymen. Because no group was now supposed to be inherently better, the assumption fell away that had so long pulled us apart. The field was now open for each of these paths and for every kind of talent.

At this speech, Rinpoche first gave a masterful survey of Buddha's teachings. He electrified the two hundred Westerners who had come to hear him in the monastery's upper temple. Then, with visible pain and while his translators reddened, he added, "A number of three-year-retreat centers have been established and the retreats have taken place. But, except for a few people, this activity did not bring the real fruit. The retreat centers have not brought the fruits we expected or hoped for. The reason is that people went into retreat too soon, without having really understood the Dharma. And during the retreat, they were not really able to meditate effectively. This way of meditating may or may not lead to Buddhahood. It is hard to say. For this reason, I have set up the translation committee at this point in time, to work on translating the 'Treasure of Wisdom' into different languages. I hope these translations will enable everyone to read the text in his own language. And it will be very useful for those who plan to enter a three-year retreat to enable them to understand the Dharma before they begin. It will also immediately deepen the understanding of those people who have already completed the retreat. It will be a very beneficial means for teaching the Dharma."

By permitting people to trust their intelligence, Rinpoche also removed the working-base of the most useless Buddhists, the so-called "Groupies." They are the continually dissatisfied people, mostly women, who fight for control around the lamas. Considering themselves very special, they often complain most about those who actually make the centers work. The most destructive rumors frequently had the same source: politics made in the name of teachers who usually didn't even know what went on. This confusion becomes impossible when work builds on transparency and not on who whispers what to whom.

Kalu Rinpoche's reaction to the AIDS scandal remains a mystery. We had all considered him an expert on the subject. Already in 1981, before the virus had been found, his Mos had revealed that the illness had to do with a tree in Africa. If he had gone on with his divinations, he would probably also have come upon the monkey that carries it. However, he may have thought that it was only a skin disease. When a distinguished Tibetan woman came visiting in Bodhgaya with scars from recently removed warts, he joked that she looked like she had slept with the Dharmadatu regent. This might surprise those who know that the state of truth pervades everything, but insight is an obligation and must never be used against people's wishes. The powers one achieves should never be employed to play police or spy on others. Even those with the highest realization must meet people on the level where they choose to start the contact and then help them from there. Exposing people or dissecting them usually only increases their belief in and clinging to their trips. The Buddhist way is to accustom people ever more to their true essence: to the transpersonal space and clarity of their mind. It is only of relative benefit to exchange the iron chains of negative identifications for the golden chains of positive ones. They imprison the mind just as much. An effective teacher gives no power to people's limitations but provides access to their inner richness instead. It is only common intelligence not to take one's changing emotions seriously: they come and go all the time anyway.

Enlightenment is not primarily the decreasing of bad thoughts and the increasing of good ones. This will happen on its own just by living a better life. The important thing is to stop judging one's inner states. One should experience them as the clarity and free play of the mind while reacting spontaneously and effortlessly to whatever happens. As the fearless kindness and timeless joy of the experiencer shine ever more brightly, we arrive at the various levels of Mahamudra. Then everything simply fits, and one acts directly and for the good of all.

Kalu Rinpoche's presence pervaded our two weeks in Bodhgaya. Meanwhile, Khenpo Tsultrim Gyamto arrived from Kathmandu with his Western students who were haunted by an incredible series of accidents. Hannah and the other translators often visited him and two other Khenpos in the area, getting expert explanations for their texts.

While Tomek did six to seven hundred prostrations at Buddha's Stupa every morning, Hannah and I enjoyed being together again. Then she translated and I wrote for eighteen hours with few stops. My book on the preliminary practices, *Ngondro,* was finished on February 13th. Changing from that to the book you are now reading, I had an exceedingly powerful dream, even for such a holy place: in a snow-filled landscape, I walk down a path between narrow, black sleigh tracks. In front lies a cylindrical wooden chest wrapped in torn brocade. Pulling up the arched lid, I find a golden statue of "Loving Eyes," shining so strongly that it completely blinds me. It is about a foot tall and I feel immense joy. It is of the purest style, with a trapeze-shaped—not oval—face and all four arms close to the body. Clasping it to my heart, I run up the hill to my

Loving Eyes

left, knowing only one thing, "I must save him before the people from the museum catch him." Awakening in a state of intense bliss, one thing was sure: "Loving Eyes" wants to be useful. I now had his blessing to remove the cultural barriers which keep Westerners from Tibetan Buddhism and him. This blessing, happiness about our exciting growth, and the need to always keep transparent, are my motivations for communicating even today.

When politics cramp joviality at times—an unavoidable by-product of quick development—I remember that Buddhist doesn't mean Buddha, and then compare our schisms and clashes to what I hear from other religions or schools. Then we Kagyus look excellent.

The outer frame for these weeks was again Khyentse Rinpoche's monastery at Bodhgaya in northeastern India. For that country it is a jewel of highest quality. They had used enough cement in the walls to hold the paint. On a balcony on the third floor, some rented tables offered that rarest of commodities in India: the privacy to do a job right. After writing until sunset, we followed Hannah's routine and hiked the few miles to Buddha's stupa and back. As I was doing some weeks of total fasting, it was important to keep in shape. Then—interrupted only by periodic power cuts—we worked on until early in the morning. A dictaphone collected any relevant dreams, and after some hours of sleep my subconscious mind had already worked out the following chapter. Since I never look back—there's no time for that—recalling events so massively was like a major re-wiring. It worked, however. Hannah's clear mind was a great help, and the stamps in our old passports supplied the time-frame. Step by step, it became more a question of picking what was important than of remembering details.

Noble Tomek left with masses of our luggage. Getting on the wrong train, he went to Delhi by way of Calcutta. After a magical full moon, the Kalu and Bokar Rinpoches took their translators north in a bus. The other translation group had yet some more serious accidents, and Hannah and I went to Rumtek. During those years, this always caused much commotion. Everyone was sure that now the Seventeenth Karmapa would be found. Though we like to support any collective Tibetan effort, this time we had to leave Rumtek's hotel. There were just too many old friends bringing butter tea and breakfast, spoiling for a chat. Staying in Tsultrim Namgyal's house instead, the pages of this manuscript piled up.

Our close friend Topga Rinpoche, Rumtek's General Secretary, had enough to do just keeping things together. An abbot of our lineage was at that time making his own monasteries in Hong Kong and Malaysia, bringing sleepless nights to our lineage holders. Hearing that Germany had the same problem with a lama from England, he wrote a letter asking people to stand behind us.

There was yet another important issue to decide upon: we had to clear our relationship to other Buddhist schools and to the different Kagyu lineages. Due to Karmapa's power, we had started out as nearly the only Tibetan Buddhist school in the West, the way we are today in Central and Eastern Europe. This is a situation where one enjoys being generous, and we had happily invited a wide range of teachers to our centers. Unfortunately, this benefited nobody. Even former friends suddenly started seeing us in the role of parents. They became sour when we couldn't give them everything and frequently gossiped. Only mature people can allow different things to be good in different ways. Smaller minds have to make their own teachers better by putting those of others down. Though the source of such rumors rarely lies with the teachers themselves, nevertheless, it was now time to invite only those who supported Karmapa's work.

Though painful to many, defining processes of this kind are both necessary and useful. Also, practice in Central Europe became more home-grown these years, an important sign of progress. Any Buddhist activity has only one goal, that of spiritual growth. Being strong and independent, my students couldn't help making our outer style—though of course not our transmission—more democratic and Western. It was an inevitable development and a good one. Especially the highest teachers feel more comfortable if people don't try to behave special or Tibetan. They actually enjoy our mature Western skills and powers of decision.

Our group enjoyed having ten days at Rumtek. We spent much time with Kunzig Shamarpa and Jamgon Kongtrul Rinpoche, the two lineage holders who mainly continue Karmapa's work. Hannah's transla-

Rumtek

tion schedule was fixed for the next year, and we visited the site for Gyaltsab Rinpoche's new monastery. It lies in the beautiful eastern part of Sikkim, undestroyed by Nepalese, Indians, or tourists.

On our way down through the ever more crowded eastern foothills, there was one important thing left to do: Kalu Rinpoche had emphatically asked us to see him before we returned to Europe. He now stayed near Siliguri to inspire his brave Sonada monks. They were once again involved in a giant building project. This time, it was a fully ornamented stupa about 33 meters (108 feet) tall. Only he could have come up with the idea of building something like that in such an environment: erecting a giant monument to the universal Buddha essence at a polluted road in suffering, overpopulated, and noisy north India. It would bring more benefit in peoples' future lives than during the current one.

It was a joy to see Gyaltsen and so many friends again, and their work was exquisite. As we climbed the stairs to Kalu Rinpoche's room, I understood with gratitude how much tenacity and one-pointedness we had learned from this old warrior. These qualities and the devotion of a handful of disciples had made his activity reach so far.

Rinpoche's head was shaved and his timeless face looked unearthly. It hurt us to hear that he didn't feel well. As his room was full of local people, we didn't say much. Hannah promised to do all she could for his translation project, and I told my latest plans for enlarging Karmapa's work around the world. Keenly aware that we might not see him again this life, we wished him the best from the depth of our hearts. Barely making our train to Bodhgaya, we were happy that we had been able to fulfill Rinpoche's latest wish.

In the overcrowded cafe at Patna station, Karmapa's limitless powerfield manifested once again: a pleasant and well educated Indian suddenly asked whether we knew Ole and Hannah from Denmark. Although I didn't recall his face, I had taught him the mantra "Karmapa Chenno" eighteen years earlier. Using it daily, he had done very well and was now an important politician. This time we gave him the booklet with the "Three Lights Meditation," of which this mantra is part. Maybe he will be president when we meet again.

Bodhgaya offered a fine chance to coordinate with both Shamarpa and Lama Jigmela. In Delhi, Hannah kept up our Tibetan contacts from Tourist Camp, our favorite hotel there. During our five days in that pleasant area, the rough edition of this book came up to the visit on Rumtek I just described. On the last night, we dined with Shamarpa. His Buddhist university in Delhi was now nearing completion. It was yet another example of the generosity of the free Chinese. Then our plane brought us back to Frankfurt.

We arrived a few hours late and once again I was really touched. A hundred friends were waiting at the airport. We went upstairs for a meditation and blessings. After ten days of glowing telephones and packed courses in Copenhagen and Wuppertal, that was the end of lovely Europe. With Eva and Tomek, we flew via Paris to Caracas, Venezuela. Tomek travelled on the passport of a Danish friend. At that time, they didn't allow people from communist countries. Being the warm part of the world, people had calculated our arrival for March 25, a day late. So we waited at the airport for a few hours and then took a taxi into the city at dawn.

The driver was still in shock. "They shot over a thousand people," he said. "You can still see the bullet holes in the walls. One morning in the *barrios*"—he pointed to the slums covering the mountain slopes— "people woke up and all prices had doubled. They realized that they had enough money to get to work, but not to get home. Then they fought with the bus drivers first." When the human wave reached the city center, things really exploded. Seeing the objects of their year-long savings now totally beyond reach, they decided to help themselves. The motivation of the police may have been some rough kind of social justice: they let people with one radio or television get away while they shot those carrying two appliances.

Nothing similar had ever happened in Venezuela, which prides itself on its closeness to European culture. Also a crisis wasn't even necessary then, though the usual overpopulation in Catholic countries would bring it about later: the national debt causing the price-rises was guaranteed twice over by the private accounts of the richest citizens, only these were in Florida.

We had briefly met Maria Mercedes of the Caracas center in Woodstock. She had translated our books, *Teaching of the Nature of Mind* and *Basic Dharma*, into Spanish several years before. The visit was in the nick of time. The center was disintegrating. Large cultural gaps in the presentation of the material, rare lama visits, and no incentive for people to try their strength had made Buddhism a very abstract matter. Stressing exotic aspects of the teaching at the expense of things people can understand always brings the same results: outwardly devoted but insecure people. They live on the past or future visits of their lamas but dare do little of a practical nature by themselves.

Under these conditions, it had been easy for lamas with more streamlined systems to wean members from the Kagyu center to their own groups. Four days of teachings nearly around the clock changed that, however; the audience grew by the hour. With sleeves rolled up, I blessed people till early morning and pushed the main points of the teachings again and again. As everything was recorded on audio or video, they would have ample material to work with. We also promised a Phowa for our next visit there.

After a touching farewell we took the night bus to Merida, the academic center of Venezuela. It has a pleasant mountain climate, and another Maria had booked a hall at the University of the Andes there. The questions were good, and I gave Refuge to a dozen people afterwards, mostly students of other lamas. Once again I was amazed that they teach their students Dzog Chen—we call it Chag chen or Mahamudra—without the preparatory practices or, at least, this most basic of protections.

The next bus took us along green mountain slopes to Cucuta, a gangsters' nest just inside Colombia. The main building in the town center is a massive jail, and they steal peoples' luggage already at the passport office. At the bus station, several broad-shouldered gentlemen descended upon our suitcases, but I caught them. An office in the middle of the station sold tickets for non-existing buses, but not to Tomek. Our long experience with con-men in the warm countries proved useful once again. Aside from the proneness to violence, they apparently had no trick we didn't already know from the East. We managed a dozen letters until the bus left, and the drive through the night was indescribably beautiful. The sky was luminous and turquoise green. It was so unusual that we missed most of "Indiana Jones" which was playing on the bus' video. Strangely enough, the landscape was often similar to the cleared parts of southern Sweden.

In Bogotá waited Adriana, a classic beauty, with Eduardo and some others from the center. Here also, things were going downhill. Khenpo Karthar had been away for too long. He had been busy building the monastery in Woodstock for the past two years. No other Kagyu teacher had visited since then, and a lama from Naples had filled the developing vacuum.

I want to tell briefly about our four days in Colombia: the country is a true phenomenon. It is no "near-democracy" like Venezuela, but the most violent region in the world. Its capital, Bogota, is beautifully situated at an altitude of about 2.5 kilometers. For only a few dollars, one can have someone killed there. It runs to between fifty and sixty murders nationally on a slow day. The country has never found a balanced state. The main opponents are the government; communist groups, often cooperating with the cocaine producers; and the land owners supported by the police and military. They have been killing one another in changing constellations since Colombia appeared on the map. The picture is further complicated by private armies and professional killers, like those of the M.A.S. One can only join this illustrious society by killing three unknown people in the street. Every night, Bogota sounds like a shooting gallery and Adriana thoroughly honored our protectors. In my company, for the first time in ten years, she dared walk a street. At all other times, she sat in her neutral-looking car with doors and windows shut. Everyone was marked by the constant danger. It was especially visible in the lines around people's mouths, which were often very coarse. During my lectures, people ran to the windows every half hour. That is how often one heard the alarms on cars that were just being broken into, in one small street.

Eduardo owned four farms but could only visit one. Otherwise he would be kidnapped. Two of his uncles had already been taken hostage and shot. His brother had been given scopolamine in a cigarette on the street. Though often considered a harmless truth serum, it is really a powerful nerve poison. He was found a day later in the fields, naked and with some brain damage.

The pervasiveness of the violence came very close one day; we drove behind two vans going so zigzag down the street that our conservative driver could hardly pass. "These are gangsters, for sure," he said, "trying to avoid an attack." Finally alongside them, the last van had a built-in niche with an open-air guard. He held a heavy machine gun in his hands. Weapons I knew from my time in the Danish army, but I had never seen a face like his! It was chiseled from granite.

Adriana walks the streets for the first time in years

A teaching was arranged at the best English school in the country, run by Adriana's mother-in-law. They were bright children and a joy to be with. Though already so conditioned that they had few qualms about stepping over corpses on their way to school, at the same time they displayed a mental freshness which gave hope for their tortured country. A lecture at the finest university in Bogotá drew a crowd. People were mostly over thirty, as in Venezuela and the U.S. I gave Refuge right there, and they were glad to hear of the local center which had been provided by fair Adriana. It was an exciting place to stay. A refugee camp lay next door and its inhabitants were always trying to steal something or other. Also in the Bogotá center, people were soon doing the Three Lights meditation on Karmapa. They planned to exchange their new videotapes with Caracas and Merida.

*Kalu Rinpoche's body
is carried into his monastery*

Entering the Pure Land

Before leaving, Eduardo gave a weighty gift. It was meant for our new retreat-center near Korinthos in Greece: a seventy-kilo machine for manually pressing bricks from wet clay. Though years of travelling in stingy parts of the world have taught us to take everything heavy as hand luggage, sneaking this mass of solid iron via Paris to Frankfurt and then on to Athens was quite a job. In Munich, we were called off the plane again and they checked for excess baggage. It took some real concentration to make the machine appear no heavier than the five kilos which were allowed.

A typical sign—a cut and a spot of blood

Early in May, Hannah flew to Malaysia. She was to translate for Gyaltsab Rinpoche. On May 10, Kalu Rinpoche died in Sonada. When Bokar Rinpoche and Gyaltsen had finally managed to make the meddlesome doctors leave his room, he sat up in bed and left his body. We both felt his blessing intensely then and a picture of Kalu Rinpoche fell out of Hannah's book just at the moment of his death. Gyaltsab Rinpoche flew up to Sonada for a few days and Hannah represented us there in June, on her way back to Europe. There was just so much to thank him for.

The first two weeks in May we stayed at wonderful Karma Gon in Spain. Before I had even finished giving the oral transmission of the Phowa to two hundred fifty friends, Pedro was already bleeding from his nose and had a hole on the crown of his noble head. The beauty of nature there made the jump into the Pure Realms natural. The mountains to the east were shaped like traditional Tibetan jewels and the view everywhere was tremendous.

After all reached the goal within three and a half days, we used the remaining time to fortify the village wall. There were questions during the evenings, and the powerfield of Great Joy we established then can be felt even stronger today. Nowhere is Karmapa closer than there.

I taught for the rest of the month in Switzerland and at Schwarzenberg. Then came a cleaning which was long overdue. A trust-meeting at the ominous German institute noisily demonstrated that idealistic work like ours will only function with friendship and respect. Our desire-type yogis clashed head on with the anger-type bureaucrats there. The latter had gradually taken over the centralized functions and had institutionalized their joylessness. Lovely Sys found the solution, and the parting of ways which followed was the best that could happen. Thirty-five of the then forty centers in Germany came under our organization, and the rest finally became useful: we now had places to send the difficult people.

Colombian Adriana accompanied me through Hungary and Italy. What she learned at my side would become useful in South America later. After the main German centers, I flew to Athens for a day in July. There was a public presentation of the Greek edition of *Entering the Diamond Way*. Though spiritual books rarely sell in great numbers in the West, they brought it on the market very well.

The main Buddhist event of '89 was without doubt the Kagyu Ngagdzo Initiation in southern Denmark. Six hundred friends stayed for the entire three weeks and hundreds came and went. It was given for the first time by Jamgon Kongtrul Rinpoche and was the first transmission in the West. During one of his earlier incarnations, as Lodro Thaye, he had collected these initiations. They had been brought to Tibet a thou-

During the Kagyu Ngadzö Empowerment

After the big initiation, Jamgon Kongtrul Rinpoche at the new stupa in Hamburg

sand years earlier by Marpa, the father of our lineage. In this life, Rinpoche had received the transmission from Karmapa in 1976 in Nepal. That was the last pilgrimage where we went East in buses.

Everything went well, and before the last initiation, Rinpoche did something which we had thought impossible after the Osel Tendzin affair: he praised a white teacher. Saying how deeply our lineage trusts me, he expressed his thanks for the countless centers and students which now benefit from Karmapa's blessing. Now that all battles had been won, he could speak out without becoming politically involved. His comments rounded things off nicely and we all felt good. While the hard decisions are being made, one should be alone with one's trusted men, but the gains are for all to share.

Tenga Rinpoche had assisted closely at the initiations. In August, he drove the same points home in Germany at the institute where we had just had the noisy meeting. He stressed the closeness of our bond and said that he had been present when Karmapa had made me promise to teach in Germany and the countries east of there. Then Tomek and I drove on via Passau to Vienna and flew to Los Angeles. This was the last chance to use some of our frequent flyer bonuses which would otherwise have run out. The night ride north from the airport was dream-like and we slept for some hours in Santa Barbara. Then we headed north on a 750 BMW motorcycle, our ears stuffed with cotton against the morning cold. At nine a.m., we stopped at a farmer's market and bought some secondhand helmets. Then we made a longer stop with my family in San Luis Obispo and bought some used army uniforms. The tour up the Pacific Coast after that went fast. It was especially fun to zip through the groups of Hells Angels. They didn't like that but were probably too stoned to try a chase.

In the last curve before the Golden Gate Bridge, my back wheel slid. A man in a car shouted that it was flat. We drove the last few miles through an abandoned tunnel at walking speed but made it to Point Bonita in time for the Phowa course. We still arrived before the friends who had gone up the main highway from Santa Barbara without any stops.

In San Francisco, Roland from Austria was doing better than ever. His trendy Rolo-shops were blooming and he kept them just below the size where he would have to hire people he didn't know. Beyond helping the Marin center, his vision now encompassed a representative place in San Francisco itself. As always, when we were together, we waited for each other to speak. Otherwise we much too frequently said the same thing.

A dozen Europeans had arrived a day earlier, again including the main people from Frankfurt. Also Kiffer was there, happy and pregnant. This time everyone had the Phowa sign in three days. During the Ngondro weekend which followed, a handful of new people started practicing. Once again it was a joy to do a radio interview with Will Noffke on "Shared Visions." His slot was later canceled for not being left-wing enough, but I doubt Berkeley ever had a better cultural program.

Late in August we flew to Maui for the next Phowa course. It had been masterfully organized by Jason and Dechen who had fine signs nearly at once. We meditated between a rain forest and the beach near the village of Hana, and people from all the Hawaiian islands participated. Far into my Pure Lands, I forgot the people in front of me. Letting go, there was only intensest bliss. Entering the room and seeing her teacher writhing and laughing aloud on his throne, Maia's beautiful face

With Dan on Hawaii

The world's biggest crater

lengthened considerably. It was the exact opposite of the stiff upper lip and representative behavior which are the trademarks of my teaching. Though I could get away with it there, among the now grown up flower children of the sixties, it was still a mistake, and I have been extra careful since then. Whenever an unlimited experience seeks physical expression in public, I put the lid on.

Dan was satisfied with my blessing for his job. He juggled fanta- zillions of dollars in insurance claims and got some amazing negotiation through. He and lovely Sandy wanted to donate one percent of their last profits to my work. The $2000 they gave went directly into publishing my new English Ngondro book. It was now ready for printing at Blue Dolphin. Goshir Gyaltsab Rinpoche had written the foreword and I had translated two of my popular German booklets. After Carol had edited the text, it was exactly what the English speaking world needed: a way to less spiritual confusion and more practice. Tomek and Roland gave $1000 each, and with $2500 from my previous books, we could now do the first five thousand copies.

Eight wonderful days with Jason and Dechen were the closest we had been to R and R, rest and recreation, for years. There were only lectures in the evening, and it was wonderful to do manuscripts on the white, open beaches. We also took time to walk to the bottom of the impressive giant crater there. Back in Frankfurt many friends waited at the airport and after a stop at the Hamburg center we arrived in Copenhagen at an auspicious moment. In five minutes Gyaltsab Rin- poche would give the first Western initiation into the Fifteenth Karmapa ever. Among the beneficial actions of this Karmapa, his women had borne twelve high incarnations. This was something strong laymen could understand. There were constant requests for this initiation as well as for that of Marpa, another powerful master of life.

The next morning, Hannah, Pedro, and I flew to Karma Gon for a week. Pedro talked with the local people about buying more land, Hannah translated texts for Kalu Rinpoche's foundation, and I had some time for the German edition of this book. Then Hannah went back to driving Gyaltsab Rinpoche through Germany. Filling some cars with friends, we did another of our yearly high-speed tours through Central Europe. A week in Greece at the invitation of Magnus and Georgia brought a pleasant surprise. Greeks read books! *Entering the Diamond Way* had caused a new wave of interest in the centers I had started there over the years: Athens, Thessaloniki, Ceres, andour magnificent new retreat near Corinth; all showed many new faces.

From the middle of October '89, Hannah was free again. For the next two weeks we had planned one of those big events we prefer to do together. There was now time to really get things going in Russia. For the first time, both back-up and logistics should be tops.

Goshir Gyaltsab Rinpoche

Our Kagyu Center in Hamburg

Goshir Gyaltsab Rinpoche blesses Karma Berchen Ling in Greece

Teaching with Namkhai Norbu Rinpoche in Greece

CHAPTER SEVENTEEN

Across All Borders

ONCE AGAIN WE LEFT THE CAR in Berlin. Gas and roads in east Europe were not good enough for my Porsche-and-Mercedes-hunting lowered Audi quattro turbo 200. In Warsaw, my heartson, Wojtek, and another close student joined us. An exciting evening of teaching there was followed by thirty hours in a posh night train to Leningrad. For long stretches of the way, nothing seemed to have changed since the war. Though Stalin had pushed Asia five hundred kilometers west into Europe, much of the original population had stayed. Politics in the Baltic countries now feature frequently in the Western press, so I don't need to say much. On the level of the environment, dream-like groves of pine and birch alternated with loveless heaps of trash.

Until a short distance before Leningrad, only the officials spoke Russian. Right after the border, I saw a woman of unbelievable beauty. Wearing a uniform, it was doubtful what karma she was collecting during this life, but the last time she must have done something right. Our friends were at the train station in Leningrad, and people's interest had grown. Vitali worked for a TV network, and with lovely Marina and a group of friends they had kept things together. It was simply great to be with them again.

We were installed in one of the grey, one-room flats used for storing a majority of the country's families. The meetings were mainly at Vitali's place. Exciting people came and went, mostly actors in possession of a

Celebration in St. Petersburg

rich inner life. During the first thirty minutes of our interview for Russian TV, the sound cut out. It was on "Fifth Wheel," the only network without marching soldiers and hours of dreary productivity rates. This was a pity as it was really a good interview. Today, TV is a major conduit for our work in Russia.

While our friends digested my condensed lectures, it was time to visit some more traditional groups. The Buddhists in Russia have a past which makes one's hair stand on end. Whoever lives today has survived decades of evil oppression.

Early Russian Buddhism was mainly influenced by the Burjats and Kalmuks. They are central Asian tribes of Gelugpa orientation whose scholars were educated in Mongolia. During Stalin's days, they were nearly extinguished. Another invitation was from a small "Dzogchen" group which also had its roots near the Baikal lake. They had not fared any better. What they had to say was enough to make one ill. For example, one day during the thirties, the secret police raided the East Asian Institute. Unable to read the characters in the texts, they assumed the staff were Japanese spies and shot half on the spot. The rest were given twenty years in Siberian labor camps. Only thirty out of two thousand Gelugpa scholars survived the carnage, and when they were suddenly released during the fifties, they had no energy left for a new start. Now, they expected power from dynamic Europe, the historic source of whatever quality entered their country. "People will accept it from you, Ole," they said. "Please, come as often as possible."

Leningrad was as dreary as last time. Not even the sun was shining, but that freed energy for learning and making friends. As hundreds came and went in the small apartment, we were aware of making Buddhist history.

To protect our hosts, we went to have our papers stamped by some authorities. It was a fascinating experience. Coming upon the office in a converted movie theater, we found three solid muses in full battle formation. The youngest sat somewhat back from the bar which restrained the visitors. The second showed a broad back and was half hidden behind a shelf to the left. The third and most dangerous of the species could only be surmised behind a half-opened door to the right. Obviously, their goal was to facilitate nothing at all and to prove their power by putting down whoever came. This they managed very well. While we waited, they drove a dozen people to desperation by going at them systematically, each taking turns. The system proved its absolute rightness by yielding nothing, and the scene was totally surrealistic. It took us awhile to understand that we were not watching theater of the absurd. As people crept backwards out of the room, I regretted not speaking Russian. I would gladly have done something for the improvement of those three ladies.

We took a day to visit some friends in Moscow. On the night train there, my dreams didn't stop. When waking up, they continued on as strong wishes: the average Russian woman has about six abortions. It was time to get them to the adoption-hungry families in the West. The mothers should somehow be paid, and since the children were very European, they would easily integrate. It would take a deep shift of consciousness but could be done. My friend Daniel Susott from Honolulu has managed the same with Cambodian babies for years.

Moscow was very different from Leningrad, a real mish-mash. The tall and blond people were army or police officials, often with an aura of amazing power. The fat or worn ones were workers, while the Asian segments of the population obviously got by on illegal trade. To get a reasonable price, we had to pit the taxi drivers against one another, just like in India. Then followed an impressive ride along broad but deserted boulevards. Ludmilla's flat had one room more than usual and was really well kept. She spoke English and wanted to translate my books, starting with *Entering the Diamond Way.* In Russia, editions are not counted by the thousands but by the hundreds of thousands. People can still read, and my books will probably have a greater influence there than anywhere else in the world.

The Moscow group was more political and traditionalistic than the one in Leningrad, and less homogenous. People looked very different and everyone pulled in their own direction. A Burjatic Gelugpa office publicized and tried to direct any developments. Though well-meaning, they badly missed the market. The traditional structures they wanted to rebuild belonged to the past and were no longer relevant. Also Russia needed lay Buddhism: understandable teachings and meditations which are closely connected to people's everyday lives.

In Moscow more than anywhere else, it was important to make people partners in their own development. Several times, I asked them to trust their own experience and employ it for the benefit of others. Groups with such a split base never become large, but I gave Refuge to the thirty who appeared. Although they had eagerly consumed Buddhist snippets for years, apparently no one had explained the importance of Refuge to them.

Sitting around tables of very different heights on even more unequal chairs, the architectural office of one of Moscow's oldest churches was a fitting frame. While the Russian cognac we brought disappeared, our information from the wide world fused everybody's views. With this group being so traditionalistic, however, the Western zap would not last. Hannah's years of experience with people like that told her one thing: they needed to have everything officially confirmed by a Tibetan lama soon.

For a mere $50—the official rate of $1.7 per ruble had fallen to seventeen cents the very day we arrived in Russia—we could take nine Muscovites to Poland and back. There they could meet two of our most important Rinpoches. Hannah would translate for them. It was amazing economics and we could hardly wait to also invite our Leningrad friends.

The train back was several hours late, but the people knew how to wait. We spent another two days in Leningrad to deepen the work. As we stepped on the train, Olga, a super-sweet girl handed me a large, irregular, disc-shaped lump of copper. It was a five kopeck coin from 250 years back and it somehow represents Russia's timeless power to me.

Our Warsaw group found a nice flat for Gyaltsab Rinpoche. His Mo confirmed Maia's intuition that I should bring a gun on our coming journey across South America. "Monks in Tibet always carried a rifle when they traveled," he said. Hannah first translated for Rinpoche there and then in Greece. After that she returned to Poland where Beru Khyentse had arrived and helped him for another week.

My own unique bond with central Europe once again found an amazing expression. Though uninformed about the latest political developments, I crossed over to West Berlin on the morning of November 10, 1989, just as the Wall came down.

The sour East German police were totally overwhelmed. Many of these massive men had tears in their eyes and could only shout, "Passports left, ID cards right." The milling crowd was endless. I will never forget the faces of the East Germans as the West Berlin train started and they realized that their authorities could now no longer reach them. Maia had seen people sitting on the wall when she arrived from Copenhagen.

There was a lecture planned in Passau near Austria but no chance to make it. After taking the necessary time with our growing Berlin group, a back-up of smelly two-stroke cars caused a six-hour delay at East Germany's southern border. Arriving at midnight, the wise Buddhist healer, Theresia, had kept two hundred friends well occupied. The following hours of teaching focused more on Gorbachev and Europe than on Buddha or Karmapa.

The rest of the month was spent in north Germany, and for the first time, things functioned in Holland. Jolanda had organized a well-attended three-day course in Groeningen, and my student Marja had translated *Entering the Diamond Way* into Dutch. It was great to have two days in The Hague with Franz and Gülfen. They had been great supporters of Schwarzenberg and my work for years. What had happened to the centers of formerly cultural Dutch towns was a real shock, however. An influx of Africans and Asians from former colonies had made them much like American ghettos and a great drain on society. This was something the rest of Europe would absolutely have to avoid.

The beginning of December saw a retreat with our Swiss friends at a mountain hut near Bern. Then followed time in Karma Gon, Spain to work on this book. The centers in Austria were family, as always, and Christmas was in deep snow at Schwarzenberg. New Year we celebrated in Copenhagen. Hannah was there and all danced the whole night through. It left few hours to prepare for our most exciting tour so far: an overland journey across South America. We would travel via the southern hemisphere around the world. Since Tomek had organized it, every day would be used to the hilt.

We landed in Caracas at five in the morning. After the recent changes in Eastern Europe, Tomek could now travel on his own passport. The customs officer wanted to see only one thing: the suitcase with my

In the Swiss Alps

The Caracas Phowa

gun. When all attempts to divert him had failed, he was suddenly called
to the phone and we quickly walked through. I remembered Gyaltsab
Rinpoche's Mo and it was all very funny. Pedro also got his video camera
in. Danish TV had asked him to do a documentary "with the white lama
around the world." Though really sick from a flu which was then ravaging
Europe, there was no time to be ill. Thirty-five hopefuls were waiting at
a beautiful university site to do the Phowa. I had exactly two and a half
days to create the necessary bond and take them through.

During the final session, I gathered the last seven very closely
around me. To our enormous gratitude, they then got the result. During
the next two days in the Caracas Center, fifty took Refuge. Though the
staying power of the general population was not the greatest, at least the
distribution of information was now clear: the three powerful Hoogen-
stejn sisters would handle that. The teachings from my first visit were
already printed in cheap booklets and could reach many. This fact plus
the intuitive openness of most made it possible to shift many karmas on

An author's hard life

short visits. Whoever had a ring for the compassionate hooks of the Buddhas was given a good chance. Ulla and Detlev, close friends running the Munich center, joined us here. Their excellent description of the next five weeks in South America is included in my German book. As this English edition contains a later visit to the area, I bring up some points as a shortened travelogue here.

The Colombian Phowa retreat was with forty people and happened near Tunja, north of Bogotá. Adriana had been born in the stately mansion where we practiced. It lies in the famous Emerald Country. The wars in that region were due to these fine gems and not to cocaine, but still they cost many lives. Something was changing in the general karma of the country, however, which my dreams showed.

The year before, I regularly spent my nights storming houses to free hostages and set things straight. As the doors came off the hinges this time, however, people were sitting peacefully around tables and talking. Some days later Pablo Escobat, the biggest drug boss, started negotiating with the government, and "M 19," one of the three main guerilla organizations, became a political party.

After a warm farewell from Adriana and the group, Eduardo accompanied us on the bus through southern Colombia to the border of Ecuador. Tenga Rinpoche had advised us to fly there, but since the situation had now calmed down, we decided to risk the twenty-hour bus trip.

Ecuador is completely different from its neighboring countries, Colombia and Peru: there is little violence and the Indians, Incas, are unbelievably small and quite spaced out. It is the place to buy leather goods. There was a monument marking the equator and we stayed in a cheap hotel in Quito, their capital, enjoying both the architecture and their prices.

Colombian Phowa at Adriana's birthplace

Sitting on top of the world at the equator

On our way to Guayaquil, the second largest city, Pedro almost lost his camera. Eager for some local color he had filmed a policeman with his hand out to receive a bribe.

Quite a few things were out of the ordinary there. Some attractive ladies who praised my virility in the street were apparently men. The biggest surprise of all, however, was on the part of our host. Though never remembering any dreams, this night he saw nothing but men in red robes and giant mountains. Karmapa's blessing had apparently awakened some deep memories in him, and he was already on his way to the Himalayas.

The road passed through banana plantations to the border of Peru, which simply closes at six p.m. With the usual delays, we didn't make it. We had no intention of staying in the unpleasant border town, however. Dashing through the city towards the offices was an archetypal

At the pauper's market in Quito

Our host at the table

experience. Clapping their hands, bands of hostile people chanted: "Run, white men, run! The border is closed anyway!" But the problem was easily solved. Ten dollars for the official in Ecuador and fifteen for the one in Peru got us the best of personalized service.

We avoided one of the worst customs-checks in South America by sheer luck. Since there was no bus to Lima, we chartered two run-down taxis. The drivers looked seedy and it was a five-hour trip through the desert, but we didn't want to stop. Dozing off as I so often do when my protectors have a complicated job and want no interference, we were again very lucky. We drove parallel to the Pan American Highway at the very points where hold-ups were being staged. When we reached the city next morning, one could see the relief on the drivers' faces—they'd been real heroes. Several buses had been robbed on that stretch during the night and a female tourist shot.

For the trip on to Lima, we got the worst bus in South America. After a hundred yards, the engine died and there was thick diesel oil on most seats. It missed no hole in the road. The signs of the desert eating

Ricardo in the middle

My true self

up the arable land was instructive: Pope or no Pope, the poor countries
will have to control their populations very soon.

In dry Lima, by the deep blue Pacific, we were welcomed by
Ricardo. He had become my student in '85 while studying in Poland and
had kept the bond. He now taught art and wanted to offer his town a
Buddhist center.

During three days of teaching, Ricardo's home in the once-posh
Miraflores district filled up. Dozens took Refuge and a small Dharma-
group appeared. Ulla and Detlef saw more of third-world slums here than
they had wished for. Getting off their bus a stop late provided some
radical education and somebody very nimble-fingered stole our passports
from Hannah's purse. Nobody had managed that in the East.

In the opinion of experts, Lima is as dangerous as Beirut was.
Guerrillas are the main concern here: a Maoist group called "Shining
Path" controls large parts of Peru. Their name may be nice but their

methods are like those of the "Khmer Rouge" in Cambodia. They had then already killed eighteen thousand people and currently prefer targeting tourists. By causing an economic crisis, they hoped to drive the country into a civil war. Two weeks earlier they had pulled two French girls off a bus and shot them right there for their white skin. This was the region Tenga Rinpoche had told us to avoid at all costs. So we took a local plane to Cusco, the capital of the former Inca domain.

Gerhard picked us up at the airport. He is an idealist and a powerful childhood friend of Kurt Nübling. Working for five years as an adviser to developing countries, he knew the region inside out. He showed us the Inca forts and temples in their holy valley, which lies at the same breathtaking altitude as Lhasa. Staying with him and his Peruvian girl friend on a mountainside overlooking Cusco, we made several short trips on horseback into the mountains. The area had everything: Indian farms, mountain creeks, and guerrillas. Their zone started just behind the mountains. Here they killed any official and dynamited the cattle. The ring around town was narrowing and tourism had been badly affected.

Cusco

The last binge

This was very hard on the locals whose enormous families depend on foreigners for their livelihood. I used my revolver for the only time on the tour, target shooting, and got so sick from gallons of fresh sugary wine that I stopped drinking for this incarnation. Life is simply too short for hangovers.

Buses to Lake Titicaca and the Bolivian border were not advisable, so we took a local train instead. It was overcrowded with Indians and merchants and crossed the Andean plateau for a day at an altitude of four thousand meters. There was an amazing view over wide arid plains and herds of funny-looking alpaca and llama, often with snow mountains on the horizon. Shortly after dark, the train suddenly stopped. Getting off hurriedly, the local people said: "Now the robbers come." The engineer seemed to get his cut from them: he drove to a side track and turned the lights off. Then quite a scene unfolded: groups of small but muscular gentlemen in blue sports jackets started moving up and down the corridors, openly sizing up passengers and baggage. Though they were probably police out to improve a subsistence-level wage, they apparently had no weapons, and seeing our blue eyes and Nordic dimensions, they decided to go somewhere else. Tomek blinded them with a flashlight, Pedro nudged them between the ribs with a bayonet and Detlef and I bounced them to and fro with our bellies. With Hannah and Ulla at the windows, we had eyes and ears. Except for bad headaches from the night before, we had only fun—but two other cars were raided.

Pedro eyes people leaving the train

Lake Titicaca, the world's largest body of water at such altitude, was an explosion of blue colors. The capital, La Paz, was a pleasant surprise. There were hardly any slums and the surroundings might have been Tibet. They openly sold charms and objects for casting spells, right in the center of town, and had the same cheap Chinese trinkets on display as in Nepal.

After two days there, Tomek and Pedro joined the dry brigade. It was much more fun to be clear and straight. An unbelievably luxurious train took us south to Argentina, where Kagyu Buddhism was a mess. Though the state of the centers is primarily the karma of the countries involved, here foreigners had contributed generously to the confusion. The few who had the courage and maturity to see space as opportunity and richness, the main prerequisite for a successful practice of the Diamond Way, had been left high and dry. A Bhutanese lama from Kalu Rinpoche's organization in France had started the center in Cordoba. Also due to some bad accidents, he had never once returned. Later visits by lamas of the same school had not been coordinated, and worst of all everybody was kept waiting, and as usual nobody empowered the local

Lake Titicaca

hopefuls. As in Caracas, a Rinpoche from Naples had then come visiting and several from the dying center had joined his organization. It was the best possible solution under the circumstances. Things stayed in a Buddhist frame. But it was a pity that people who had had the good karma to meet Kalu Rinpoche's lineage—and through that got a connection to Karmapa—were now losing that chance.

From here, Ulla and Detlef left for Europe. Kindly they took our warm clothes, my gun and the German tapes of this book along. After a touching goodbye from our friends in Cordoba, where the economy was daily going down and interest was hardly big enough to support two groups, we took the bus west to Mendoza at the foot of the Andes. In the last century, the hero San Martin had led his army across the high passes from there, bringing an unpleasant surprise to the Spanish troops in Chile. Though the slope down to the Pacific was barren as the moon, one could still feel that Chile has the healthiest economy in South America. The election had deposed Pinochet's military regime was eminent. In Santiago, a medical student found my blood pressure to be that of a twenty-year-old man. According to her instruments, Hannah must be around fifteen.

Goodbye to Argentina

Chile descending toward the Pacific

After two nights in a strange hotel which apparently catered to some sexual minorities, we switched from six weeks in buses to the friendly skies. Six hours west across the Pacific is Easter Island, a third of the way to New Zealand. It is a Chilean National Park. Lying more than 3000 miles from the nearest continent, its nature totally blows one's mind.

Hannah's beauty

From the first moment, the giant stone torsos of the island were intensely sympathetic. They dot its shores and I think they are in fact Buddhas. Though they don't much look the part, the vibrations fit. Gazing inland, they radiate powerful good energies. Also some details cannot be coincidence. The proportions of their ears fit and the posture of their hands is similar to what Tibetan yogis like Milarepa used when practicing the "Inner Heat."

Fifteen hundred years ago, Polynesian fishermen had probably looked in awe at some Buddha statue in Indonesia. Moving east across the Pacific for generations, they had passed this experience on, and Easter Island had the stones for giving it life. Pedro had his first driving lesson there, learning fast. Placing Karmapa relics near an impressive crater, I had some moments of real wonder: what would be the long-range effects of thus blessing billions of fish?

Buddhas?

Our Tahiti hosts

Six hours further west lay the Tahitian Islands, probably the most expensive region in the world. Everything is imported from France, and by plane. A newspaper may cost $10. A cyclone tossed us around and passed just when we landed. The sun was black and the sky a brilliant yellow.

Fortunately, we were expected. Chinese Marie Claire, a friend of our artist friend Xolotl, picked us up at the airport. She drove us to a beautiful hotel on the beach. Working in the tourist branch, she knew about that, and she and her Japanese husband, Moriya, were wonderful hosts. For three days they feasted us or drove us to their friends on the island, where I taught in French. The island resembles Hawaii but is more tropical. Several beaches have black sand and a worse undertow than even Secret Beach.

New Zealand is northern England placed in the southern hemisphere, before the world got crazy and their former colonies moved in. Though there were more sporty red knees than erotic vibrations—even officials appeared in shorts—the country was still refreshing. Everything was clean and people were tall and strong. They were consumed with

With Tomek and Pedro in Auckland

Typical New Zealand coast

building skyscrapers everywhere, and their colored glass reflected the
moving clouds. Nothing happened in the Kagyu center near Auckland
on the northern island. After a night in a youth hostel, we went by train
and ferry to the South Island instead following an invitation by Ron and
Lisa. Landscapes on the way were unique and they lived among amazing
geological formations near Christchurch. Though the interview advertizing my first lecture was a day late, all chairs in the hall were occupied.
People had European powers of concentration, and the next day I gave
Refuge at Maureen's house where we stayed. A dozen good people became
the start of the Karmapa group there. After an experience of our transmission and lineage, the next point was giving them the Three Lights
Meditation and self-liberating teachings for their lives. Due to good luck
we avoided Numea, another expensive French colony with no Marie
Claire. It gave us two extra days in Australia and felt just right.

John waited with a yellow jeep at the airport. He is the angel of the
Sydney slums and saves scores of homeless boys who would otherwise
really go down. The city's architecture is a mixture of European styles

Maureen, Lisa and Ron in Christchurch

With Lama Trijam in Sydney

and three million live there. Again, we were in luck. Jytte and Peter invited us to stay with them in luxurious Mona Vale on the northern coast. It was the best possible place for working on my manuscripts, and Jytte Marstrand is our friend from wonderful times with Karmapa. They, themselves, were busy with telephone and fax around the world and around the clock. The beach was only a few minutes away by car, and from its high ridge the house offered an amazing view over kilometers of coast both south and north.

It was also a pleasure to meet Lama Trijam. He was our friend from the early seventies in Darjeeling and Karmapa had given Australia a great gift by sending him. Unfortunately, with the usual Tibetan delays, he arrived four years later than planned. It had sorely tried the devotion of the waiting group. Like in most places with traditional teachers, our job would be to diminish the cultural gap between him and his students. We wanted many to benefit from him.

Everything was bathed in the clear light of early March—their autumn—and my first lectures were at Sydney University. Some dozen took Refuge. A professional heckler tried to disturb the teachings there.

He was well known for this but only tried once with me. As a residue from my bad old days, the few times I have to cut willfully unpleasant people down to size, I rather enjoy it. Actually such people are useful: the only reason for the Buddhas' teachings are for us to live better, die better, and have better rebirths. Therefore, it is very important to show the invulnerability of the teachings and iron things out while together. Sending people into the hard world with some sweet words in their ears offers no protection. The process is only awkward when the "enemies" are people one has blessed or shared initiations with. Also here, I came to share some very committed students with an English-educated Rinpoche. He is strongly influenced by Trungpa Tulku. People attracted to his graded system of study retreats and good P.R. often come for my hardy example and blessing. Adding a father to the mother they already have, they find that many things fit.

A garden party at the center developed into a long interview. A woman journalist who had also managed to catch Lech Walesa in Poland wanted something for Australia's largest weekly. Then the group had prepared a Phowa course near the Blue Mountains, which lie an hour from the city in Peter's Porsche and are in a league with the Grand Canyon in America. Either all participants at the retreat were yogis or the power of my transmission had increased—everyone had the sign after two days of

Phowa in the Blue Mountains

With Jytte and Peter in the Blue Mountains

practice. During the breaks, Peter and Jytte showed us the ancient landscapes in their Maserati. Apart from our new friends, we also had old bonds to Australia. We knew Carolyn from early 1970 in India and Viviana from the smuggling sixties in Copenhagen. Both were fine and Carolyn had worked for years on a Theravadin retreat place.

In the middle of March, I rounded off our stay with two days at Sydney University. After promises to return at the airport, we were in Singapore in the evening. Hannah's Chinese friends had come down from Malaysia. They had not received Tomek's flight information, however, so we ended up in a hotel. The city is one giant shop, and Pedro bought a video camera for Kurt. The presidents of Karmapa's Singapore group— former and current—drove us to the center, the latter's bowling alley. Apparently they had heard about my flagrant yogi lifestyle and were, at first, a bit on guard. Lineage and blessing quickly proved more important than monogamy, however, and suddenly they wanted a Phowa course. Organizing that would not be easy. Malay laws allow for no extra vacation time, even when paying for a stand-in, and they only have a few days off every year.

Early in the morning, Hannah's friends waited in another apparently indestructible Volvo. The bridge to Malaysia was grid-locked and during the next hours north we saw only plantations for palm oil and bananas. Then came the Patubahat center where Hannah often translates and for long periods of time. It was only for the Chinese. Malaysia is Muslim by law and people of Malayan race were forbidden to visit Buddhist shrines. They also have affirmative action legislation like in America. Laws regulate what the proportion of workers from different races has to be. Though they pay them very little, the busy Chinese still feel exploited by people who do not work very hard.

I blessed a hill in the vicinity for a later retreat center. It had a fantastic distant view of the ships in the strait, but close up it was the tragedy of the tropics: marvelous trees with irreplaceable hardwood had just been cut down and left, partially burnt. The soil was already so eroded that something similar could hardly grow there again. In the evening, I taught Buddhist self-defense. The center was filled to the brim and I taught things that help one be comfortable in a hostile culture. Sharing experiences from the sixties in North Africa and the Middle East, I told of practical ways to ridicule and deflect Muslim fanaticism.

At midnight, they brought a birthday cake for my forty-ninth year, and the next morning we were off by bus to Kuala Lumpur, the capital of Malaysia. Peggy and a friend, both supporters of our highest Rinpoches, picked us up in real Mercedes cars. After a Chinese dinner of countless courses with the center leaders, we stayed in their large and beautiful temple. Peggy and her genius of a husband, Eugene, even sponsored our airline tickets to Bangkok.

After a boring night there—I dislike the town—we flew on to Calcutta. Here, the Indian customs officers were on a trip. They kept asking for video cameras. Discovering Pedro's they put him in the line of people who merited special examination. They said they would confiscate whatever else they found. This was not good, since Pedro also had Kurt's video with his luggage. For once I detected a slight strain on his noble brow. With a trick which would not have worked anywhere else in the world, I simply took it from his cart and put it on Tomek's. Ten gentlemen in uniform watched this, but apparently didn't get the message. They had no slots for behavior like that.

Birthday celebration

*With Kurt—
busy as always*

Tsultrim Namgyal, Maren and Brian near Rumtek

The way from there to Sikkim was proof that the last twenty years were well spent. The European division of Karmapa's powerfield manifested everywhere. Thomas of Joy Publishing was at the airport. Sitting in "Sikkim House" in Siliguri after the night bus north, Maren and two Brians from Copenhagen arrived. At the border to Sikkim, we signed right below famous names from Primavera, Schwarzenberg, and Logos: Ute, Susanne, Kurt, Suscha, and Mathias. Late that evening we were finally all together in Rumtek.

Though Jamgon Kongtrul Rinpoche and Gyaltsab Rinpoche were in retreat, they took daily time to talk. Everything was possible and up in the air. The area was now really changing. The 17th Karmapa would soon arrive and Sikkim was being opened to tourism. With real hotels planned, a new priority had appeared: the powerfield of the hidden world in which we had learned must now be spread in the right way to the rest of the world.

CHAPTER EIGHTEEN

Opening the European East

*L*EAVING EARLY IN THE MORNING from Rumtek, we stopped at Kalu Rinpoche's monastery in Sonada. We wanted to pay our respects to his now mummified body.

Darjeeling was badly congested. The masses of Nepalese children of twenty years earlier now had masses of children themselves, and the quality of life was markedly down.

We marveled at the progress of Kalu Rinpoche's last project, the thirty-three-meter stupa in the lowlands. Gyaltsen took us from one magnificent story to the next. In the train near Patna, some little tribal ladies managed the impossible: they stole Hannah's suitcase while Tomek was sleeping on it. Pedro and Tomek got off near Bodhgaya and in Delhi, H. E. Shamarpa was glad to see us at the airport. Napping on the plane, he had dreamt that we would wait for him there.

March 31, 1990, we landed in high-powered Europe again. There was massive growth everywhere east of the Rhine, and it was a joy how independent everybody was becoming, how well our centers cooperated.

Über alle Grenzen, the German and first edition of this book, took final shape in June. It was all in the family. Susanne, now from Forum Essencia, gave her home. Sys, Paul, Erik, and Nina improved my German. Paul chose the pictures. I never do that myself or there would be very few with my face on them. Markus from Zürich did the graphics and brought it all together, while Thomas from Joy Publishing would print it. In

*The Stupa
near Siliguri*

mid-June I promoted the Dutch edition of *Entering the Diamond Way.* I was amazed that a book with such a clear message would arouse any interest there. To a shocking degree, the liberal Dutch immigration laws had already made the centers of their main towns into unpoliceable third-world slums.

While digesting this bad omen for the future of lovely Europe, five of us landed in Miami. Mark, a descendant of the imperial Russian house of Romanoff, was waiting in the unbelievably humid heat. Two days of teaching surrounded by deserted banks with no cocaine money to launder brought a score to the Refuge. Some Gelugpa Geshes teaching in traditional style fight an uphill battle there to keep things centered and Tibetan. I surely don't envy them.

Finishing the German edition of this book with Paul, Erik and Detlev

Bob, Melanie and latest offspring

The Albuquerque Phowa

The first Phowa in America this year was near Albuquerque, New Mexico. Bob and Melanie had organized it. A political Tibetan at Woodstock had tried to block an article where they praised our work. He supported the Dharmadhatu and disliked our European common sense approach, but that didn't matter. Harold and Ariane let us use their beautiful home, and though the group was once again only American in size—thirty to forty—there were masses of blessing to share. As I gave the interviews in the burning sun, people only said what was important, and that freed time for a visit to our land at Taos. The second plot of high mesa which Norbert had added even sported some trees, and it was right next to Yongdu's. We also held a shooting session there. Harold's mental patients often gave him the funniest guns when he helped them decide against suicide.

Though we started for Phoenix at two a.m. to avoid the worst desert heat, the engine of our giant pickup would hardly run. On the way, the largest crater in the West was an amazing sight, and touching the metal of the meteors was a total thrill. A Mormon lady in a pool threw water on us to "ban our bad spirits," and for days no flights could take off because heat made the air too thin. We shared two wonderful evenings with Erma, Jerome, Bill, and our group, invited by Stan to his luxurious Fiesta Inn. Then Maia and I flew to San Francisco. Here Tomek and Roland had organized a true joy: a tour down winding Highway 1 on my old but fast BMW motorcycle. The woods around Santa Barbara were burning and we stopped to see "Total Recall," an impressive film. At my lecture in San Diego, my brother Bjørn also joined our happy company. For the first time in years, our group stayed with Bill and Cathy at the Encinitas center. Two days in L.A. drew the largest crowd since the scandal. Yuki, Nanette, John, and other close friends from the late seventies came. We stayed with Karin, my student from Austria and a close friend of Roland. She is an expert make-up artist for important films. Also bright Annette from Hamburg was there, a specialist on film locations. In Karmapa's Los Angeles center, Isabelle from Paris represents common sense. Some people were amazed about my frank answers to questions about the Dharmadhatu, but I see no other way. Only by coming clean can we avoid festering rumors for years. The necessity of being straight and non-sticky is probably the last thing some Tibetans will understand about the West. If even year-long sponsors like my old friend Lex calls us "Catch-you-pas" and the reformed school "Glue-pas," there are some things we absolutely need to learn.

Carol had arranged a Ngöndro course at Point Bonita with our Marin group. She was now teaching four classes at the University which were always full. After some well-attended public lectures in San Francisco, Bjørn and most of the group flew back to Europe. Tomek, lovely Annette, and I went on to Hawaii.

On Kauai, our Hawaiian friend, Angeline, who had come to the Spanish Phowa, had established a center for traditional Lomi massage. Again on Secret Beach, but this time in summer, we experienced what is a life-long dream to many locals—we swam with the dolphins. Half an hour out from the coast, about forty came from all sides to play. Much larger than I had thought, they jumped over and around us, taking us ever further out until they disappeared.

We placed our last brass statue of the Eighth Karmapa with Dan and Sandy. We had already given six others to centers and friends across the U.S. On our way back from the Napali coastline and its fantastic caves, a powerful storm shook our boat until it really hurt Dan's back.

On Maui, Jason, Dechen, and Prema had organized a three-day program at Hana, near beautiful pools. On our way to a meeting with Lama Tensig, a native gentleman—apparently on some drug—performed a mono-syllabic war-dance around the car. I gave him that satisfaction. We had apparently splashed his family, in their Sunday-best, with mud when driving through a puddle. The skill of Prema's young students was amazing. They performed traditional Buddhist dances in perfect Orissa style.

Adriana from Colombia was already on the island, in fine shape as always. It was a joy to see her again. July 22nd we flew back to L.A., organizing future work there during a stop-over. Tomek left for a romantic adventure in Colorado, but ended up in a well-insured accident instead. To nobody's surprise, he is using the financial freedom this gives him to work even harder for Karmapa and me.

Arriving in Amsterdam, mail and organization were all done on the flight, but I had not slept for a week. Friends from Wuppertal waited, and we were in Germany in no time. I still functioned for the lecture but was not very useful after that. This time I had really gone too far.

Passau on the border to Austria was overflowing with people and activity. They are a true example of a regional center, giving growth to the whole area. Theresa and Charly are excellent. They can both teach Buddhism and heal without getting the absolute and relative mixed up. Beautiful Doris came along to Hungary, where our group is in an unusual situation.

Unlike the rest of central-eastern Europe, there already was Buddhist activity when I first came. Speaking a Mongolian language, Hungarians have always had a romantic orientation towards central Asia. They think the name Budapest comes from Buddha, and over a hundred years ago the famous Alexander Choros went to Tibet and wrote a dictionary which is still used today. A German lama, Anagarika Govinda also had influence there. Luckily I had met him and his artist wife, Li Gotami, a year before he died. One of his "Arya Maitreya Mandala" organizations had built a fine stupa on the outskirts of Budapest but otherwise didn't seem to cooperate.

Our new Karmapa Center in Budapest

Also Lama Ngawang from Sweden had a group. There were students from San Sa Nyim, a Korean master, and Sakya Dorje, a Nyingmapa. Josef, Hannah's and my host on our first visit, was actually from the Sakya school. The Karmapa centers we added over the next years would thrive on the strong yogic tendencies of my students and excellent ties to our Witten center in Germany. Kept informed by Suisza, the graphic designer, Istvan, takes care of P.R., and groups of powerful young people regularly come to practice. They follow the pattern in newly opened countries everywhere: when strong karmas from past lives bring people together again, the next and lasting step—after motorcycles, karate, hash, or political activity—is to reconnect with one's spiritual roots. Many who stole horses and made stronger wishes for development than for consumption in their former lives were reborn this time in the East Block. It brought the character-forming factors of an easily identifiable enemy and a non-commercial education. Above all, it taught the precious quality of solidarity. The mature and open atmosphere we first marvelled at in Poland, we later found everywhere. Painful to Hungary is its amputation by Stalin after the last world war, but the extra suppression has been useful to our practitioners; Paul, Martha and others who grew up as minorities in Romania and Yugoslavia have the strongest motivation of all. Though by the laws of karma a birth in a poor place is not the best, my East European students have made excellent use of their situation. Today they look very together and centered compared to some over-individualized and "flaky" practitioners in the West.

Back in Vienna, lovely Hannah waited. I was alone teaching in Europe and we gave the courses of summer '90 together. First, Magnus, Georgia, and Panos organized a long-promised Phowa on our land near Korinthos in Greece. I have dedicated it to Black Coat, our protector, and it complements the center near Malaga in Spain as our other European leg. We will also build a stupa there against Muslim influence. Here we heard about Saddam Hussein's occupation of Kuwait. Situated on a promontory at 1,2 km altitude with a view of two seas, the area is protected and nobody may build near it. One hundred seventy attended, in spite of the bad road through Yugoslavia, and once again Karmapa's

Pillars of our work in the East, from right:
Marzena—Poland, Zsuzsi—Hungary, and Tatyana—Russia

Berchenling in Korinthos

Phowa in Greece

The sign of successful practice is found—Greece

blessings worked wonders: the forest police decided that we had bought twice the land we originally thought. The Austrians were family as always, but the Romanians, who now came in droves, were not popular. They had been eating the swans in their cultural parks, thinking they were geese. The main program in the country was a Ngöndro course in Graz, ten wonderful days with masses of friends.

At the Phowa in Poland right after, five hundred fifty had fine and quick signs. At every visit now, the country became more like Europe and it was a joy how meditation kept our friends sharp and on the cutting edge. For a dozen years already, my mountaineering students there had been earning good money. They left Poland in droves to fix chimneys and high roofs in Norway and Finland, giving the centers a steady twenty percent of what they earned. Also, several who stayed in the country were entering financial conditions from which they could support the centers. The first practicing Buddhist yuppies were blooming in our groups.

Once again our friends welded thick Polish iron-plate to the rusty body of Hannah's old BMW, thus prolonging its life. Then Woytek, my

Phowa in Graz—1991

Phowa in Poland

right hand in Poland, and Maren and Michael from Kiel joined us on the train. Arriving in Leningrad, now Petersburg, everything was in chaos. Telephones to the outer world barely functioned, mail took months, and couriers had missed their contacts so nothing was organized. The hundred-odd people I had given Refuge to were nearly all actors. Hearing absolutely nothing from us, they had no choice but to sign up for their summer contracts. They were now spread all over the enormous country.

Vitali, Marina, Andre, my expert translator Vagid, and some other friends had organized a run-down mansion a few hours from town. It lay on a hill near a historical church and overlooked the first fort which Swedish Vikings had built on their way south through Russia. Being twice the strength of anybody else, they were hired to protect the East Roman Empire against the Moslems for centuries. First rowing as far south as they could and then carrying their boats across the water-divide before going south on another stream, the Vikings very understandably called those vast expanses "the land where one rows," "Rus-land," Russia.

So having the place but no people, I gave two high-pressure lectures in St. Petersburg and simply told the listeners, about seventy of them, to come to the mansion for the planned Phowa. They were totally without preparation so it was both premature and on the border of what was

Vitali, Marina and Polish Woytek

The Viking fort

Phowa in Russia

permitted. Things had to happen now, however. Our future work must not stay on the sidelines or be wasted in squabbles. In spite of so many years of suppression and internal spying, the Russians had to trust each other and become a group. It couldn't happen fast enough.

The bus stopped at the uncared-for but powerful site where the most unkempt soldiers we had ever seen occupied the lower floor of the building.

Though grateful for help during two world wars, Europeans are frequently amused by the American army. The general comment is that half the soldiers are from the ghettos and cannot read and write. If this was the enemy, however, things didn't look too bad: sitting among broken-down military trucks and searching for lice in the seams of their ill-fitting uniforms, the great Red Army did not look much of a threat.

Never have I worked harder. The job was to give seventy chronically disillusioned people their first introduction to Buddhism, Refuge, a trustful contact to Karmapa as the Buddha of Limitless Light and a hole in their heads—all in five days. During the third afternoon, the change happened and we gained Russia. The blessing suddenly *took*. People who would habitually rather avoid one another, contact-shy after too many years of fearing spies and being stacked together in ugly minuscule flats, eating bad food, suddenly became Karmapa's students. They were proud of the power they felt. It happened within a half hour and one could see the faces change. Rudimentary, untried smiles and a willingness to share new-found richness found their first expression everywhere.

A TV interview and a last night of teaching ended the programs. With my books expertly translated by Vagid, things were now ready for spreading Buddhism across the vast continent. It was the eighth Phowa of 1990 and it left me in a state of indescribable bliss.

From the joys in Russia, Hannah and I went to a deep experience of friendship. Topga Rinpoche landed in Copenhagen. He is a highly educated former Tibetan King whom Karmapa had first made Dorje Lopön and then entrusted to be General Secretary of Rumtek. We had invited him for years. He had worked with Lopön Chechu Rinpoche to get our last group to Bhutan. Humble as he is, he had actually doubted that he could be of any use in the West.

He fathomed our formula of success—common trust—on the high-speed stretches between the central European centers. As we were

Topga Rinpoche

Topga Rinpoche at Schwarzenberg

organizing, he saw the people who actually do the work. Everybody else meets those occupying the official seats. Twelve days in Copenhagen, Hamburg, Wuppertal, Heidelberg, Schwarzenberg, Munich, Passau and Vienna produced a series of working contacts and friendships. For many of our people, cooperation with Rumtek moved out of the abstract sphere. Cultural differences were no longer holy cows to be sanctified and marvelled at, but energy to be either enjoyed or discarded if useless.

The autumn of '90 became the time to delegate our Eastern work to our Western countries and groups. The strongest karmic connections were becoming visible, making it possible to combine the useful with the natural. Switzerland—especially my kind sponsor, Annemarie in Zürich—Kiel and Denmark would be the main contacts for Russia. Organization for Poland, especially our retreat at Kuchary, had been done expertly by Manfred of Villingen for years, and the Witten center holds the key to Hungary. In Vienna, Tina, Alex, and Thule put much power into finding a major site for courses in their country, and being comfortable with working steadily and methodically, I gave them Czechoslova-

With my great and kind sponsor, Anne-Marie

Manfred, one of my true young lions, together with Beate

kia, the slowest of the countries in the East. We have a good friend there, Sasha, the secretary of President Havel. From Hungary I would start groups in Romania and Yugoslavia, and we had a first contact in Bulgaria. When that also matures, there will be Karmapa groups all over Eastern Europe.

Hannah translated for Shamarpa for some days, and between Germany, Switzerland, and Denmark, she came to the book fair in Frankfurt. H.H. the Dalai Lama came to represent a major new book, and my German edition of this one, written to give direction to our work, was in everybody's hands.

As expected, my fresh Danish style was not to everyone's taste. Some gentlemen from the Gelugpa government had obtained early copies and apparently complained about me. We will never learn from pretending not to make mistakes, however, and it is the clearest sign of the basic health of Tibetan Buddhism that we can make good-humored jokes about our differences and learn from the past. When we met at the conference, the Dalai Lama, the representative of all Tibetan schools and not a Gelugpa, as many think, showed his trust in us as always. The only criticism a dissatisfied politician could bring forth—the many pictures

*Kunzig Shamarpa
at the start of
the University project*

of Hannah and me—I could easily deflect: I don't choose the pictures in my books myself.

Actually, the state church can afford a more sporting mind. They have nothing to complain about. Whenever they can, the Gelugpas speak for all of Tibet. They quickly fill any religious- or power-vacuums inside and outside the country and control the information to Western universities. In exile, they have received nearly all the official aid. One reason for the advertisements employed by lamas of the old, yogic "Red Hat" schools, the Nyingmapa, Sakya, and Kagyupa, is exactly this: we are, to a high degree, left out of official presentations like expositions in museums and other public displays. Though most may not know the difference, and enjoy the simplification that everything Tibetan is the same, it

Karmapa's institute in Delhi

With Marion and Peter in San Sebastian

was a fault not to mention Karmapa, the first incarnate Lama of Tibet, at the recent enormous exhibition in San Francisco. He is their greatest yogi and has hundreds of centers in the West, a vast majority of the Tibetan Buddhist ones. In that town alone, there are two—those of Carol and Roland. Also, Kalu Rinpoche has one. The university which H.E. Shamarpa has made for His Holiness Karmapa in Delhi is one effort to balance this trend. Besides their intellectual view of emptiness, the world deserves the joyful yogic teaching that space is naturally fearlessness, joy and active compassion, and that these qualities cannot be removed from it.

October 12-15 we spent in beautiful Spanish autumn, first with Marion and Peter in the north and then a few precious days with Pedro on Karma Gön. We were glad to see the growth in San Sebastian, but in Madrid and Barcelona the feeling was more cultural than dynamic. They

*Pedro translating
in Malaga*

had made themselves into churches. As in most of South America and several places across the U.S., at least one of our hands was tied. We were visiting the centers of other lamas—here Kalu Rinpoche—and therefore couldn't prescribe the necessary jump-start. The island of Ibiza was a true deja-vu, the sixties in nearly original packaging, and there were dozens of friends from the old smuggling days. It was our first visit since '67 and was a real welcome. Also here, we had remained in the gossip-columns, and dog-eared copies of my books had been passing to and fro. My friend Ulli from Heidelberg had a house there. She had activated Harald, who had then gotten things going. We stayed in Santa Gertrudis with Paul and Lola.

Some Gelugpa lamas came from Barcelona once a year, so we started out with the lowest possible profile. Under no circumstances would we behave like the teachers I had been stopping for so long, who split and take over the centers of others. Ibiza, however, was a special case. Unable to handle the wild people who frequently still smoke hash, the lamas had only lectured there. Nobody had been given Refuge or a meditation practice. Karmapa's broad shoulders were used to carry that load, however. We started over fifty people and the Karmapa meditation was exactly the zap they needed.

In Copenhagen we bought the beautiful neighboring mansion and twenty-three friends now live in the center. It was the fulfillment of a wish by Karmapa back in '77. Also Berlin was exploding. Since the wall came down, things there happened very fast. Mid-November saw my first lecture in formerly communist eastern Germany. It was painful. My lowered Audi 200 Turbo suffered on the miserable roads and everybody was extreme. Either people had wintered the uncouth style of the former government by becoming totally bourgeois and intellectual, or they were now Bhagwanese. Jenny from San Francisco and Eduardo from Colombia, both with us since Zürich two weeks earlier, had a glimpse into a truly unbelievable world.

After an enjoyable time together, Hannah's services were again needed, and she went to the Delhi Institute for a month. Eduardo left and Tomek, my secretary of the exterior, drove Jason and Dechen to Wuppertal November 15th. They brought an answer to years of strong wishes for a better economy in our centers: some tenacious friends from

The two mansions of the Copenhagen center

our groups would now distribute the water and air filters of the American company N.S.A. The success of Primavera, our company for essential oils, had already proved the power of meditation and common trust in the market place.

It was family that met. Seeing central Europe at 140 mph—240 kph, Jason taught about the filters at every stop, and he and Dechen made many friends in our groups. Jenny was a great joy to have along, always an eye-opener and a fresh breeze of inspiration from the West Coast.

Maia only came along for a while this time. Though so young, the years of travelling had been hard on her delicate constitution and she had often been ill. Also her son needed more care and her sweet sister was busy with two kids of her own. We had shared much, and it was now time for an education and a family situation in Copenhagen. Having learned well, she would influence people wherever she went.

The year ended with major courses at our three German pillars: Schwarzenberg, Wuppertal, and Hamburg. There were hundreds of friends everywhere. Caty in Hamburg was the best of Christmas gifts. She had now moved so far towards completing her M.A. that I could ask

Sharing a great idea with Jenny

for her help, and she gracefully accepted. She is an amazing woman. She won the hearts of all in Copenhagen at the New Year's feast.

Tomek and I left for San Francisco the next morning. This tour around the world would be even bigger than the last one. We spent the first eight days in San Francisco with Carol, Roland, and Jenny, working on this book. Everybody was distressed after a five-year drought in

With Carol in front of her Marin house

California, and as I asked the Buddha of Limitless Light for rain, to our amazement we woke up to dripping trees.

Hannah came to Miami, and with Roland we flew to Mexico City for five days. To my intense joy, Cesar and Yoshiko were in the airport and in fine shape. The manhandled Toyota and the differences in culture had melted away in the sunrays of immeasurable blessings, and we were family as always. Close friends from Germany, Jens and Karin, had organized. They drove us everywhere and treated us royally in their Spanish-style house.

Antonio does an amazing job there and became our close friend very quickly. Though he had seen many strange things during some years of studying in Boulder, it had not shaken his deepest confidence. His interest was to help people through Buddha's teachings, and his refuge was Kagyu, but the center's stature as "Tibet House" had given him many political duties also. He enjoyed the external ones, spreading awareness of the cultural richness and deep suffering of Tibet, but thoroughly detested the internal one. The in-fighting among the virtuous monks of the official government made our occasional Kagyu clashes look like a child's birthday. Though the Dalai Lama had forbidden it, a political geshe in Guadalajara had invoked an unenlightened and much-disliked spook which was now causing them trouble. In Tibet, it had mainly bothered the other schools.

Near the sun and moon temples, a group of Indios had prepared the town hall. They were great hosts, and after many dishes we had hardly tasted before, I taught, and thirty took Refuge. There was a strong energy in the room and for a moment I imagined our centers with more brown and black faces. They are conspicuously absent even in mixed-culture countries like America.

Being modern people, Antonio and we wanted the same: for people to take the teachings into their lives. Spending some weekly hours in Buddhist "church," and hoping for help from the outside while continuing their habitual thought-patterns would not do. Meditating on and identifying with Karmapa was exactly what they needed. Before leaving, we decided on a Phowa there in November, 1991.

Returning to our posh art-deco hotel on South Beach in Miami— Roland had been generous, as usual—we switched on the news network

On top of the Sun Pyramid

My Indios

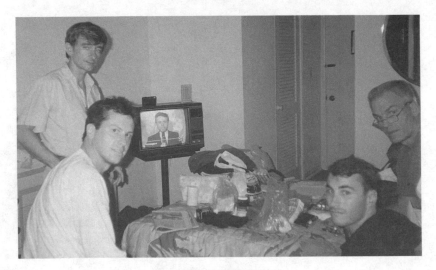

The war in the Gulf starts

of CNN just as the first bombs stuck Baghdad. Knowing that neither Russia nor America could afford their present level of armament, I was immeasurably relieved. When everybody else gets peaceful, the world must not be left with a powerful Arab state. Only one thing amazed me—that Schwarzkopf wanted so many men. The traditional ratio is one European soldier to ten Arab ones.

After one night there, we flew to South America, again with Eva from Munich. At that time, Aero Peru offered a package of seven flights in their ancient planes for $700. During the next three months when the Arabs threatened to destroy Western planes in revenge, we enjoyed forty-three remarkably empty flights around the world.

In Lima, where the terrorists of Shining Path now controlled the slums around the airport, Ricardo and Jota had held our group. They had been fine teachers; the basic trust of the group showed that. Otherwise, there was not much to rely on. The Inti, their money, had gone from 15,000 to 500,000 to the dollar in one year. We stayed three days there, teaching at Ricardo's house and in a beautiful hall, and saw his art gallery. Then we enjoyed Jota's beautiful house in a protected settlement. His lovely wife could never leave at the same time as he. The house would be broken into at once. A lasting memory from the desert were some especially evil mosquitos. The holes they bit didn't heal until late in Brazil.

A story Jota told was so funny that I will include it here: The mayor from Lima visits the mayor from Washington and asks how he can be so rich. Pointing to a large hospital, the latter answers, "Do you see that hospital? I took 10 percent." Returning the visit, he discovers that the mayor of Lima is even richer and asks how that can be. Driving through town, the mayor from Lima answers, "Do you see the bridge over there?" "No," says the Washington mayor. Patting his pocket, the mayor from Lima says, "100 percent."

Argentina was another economic disaster. The rate fell from 6,000 to 9,000 australs for a dollar while we passed through. The group in Cordoba was hopeful, however. The fine Lama Trinle from Portland might be coming down to stay. Some Allied pilots I have given Refuge were probably active over Iraq right then, and I frequently dreamt of protecting them. The Iguazu Falls on the border to Brazil were amazing. Nowhere in the world does more water fall more impressively than right there in the Amazon. Standing at Devil's Throat, seventy meters of roaring water, I quoted Tilopa to Tomek, "If I had a good student. . . ."

Our Peru group

Breakfast in Rio

The whole area is incredibly biologically rich, and one somehow senses that. Eighty percent of the world's genetic information lies in and behind the deep foliage of the trees, containing possible cures for most of the world's diseases.

The bus up to Rio took a night and a day. Here Nina and Ramon picked us up and took us to their idyllic colonial-style house in Santa Theresa. She was a German free-lance journalist and he a labor leader, and they did not have a boring life. Just covering the destruction of the Amazon, they had barely escaped several murder attempts. One of the most painful stories they told was of Indian tribes which some Protestant sects had aggressively proselytized. Feeling lost between two cultures, a few were now hanging themselves every week.

Rio in Brazil

The authorities were only a problem. The charming young president jogged on TV every day, and they frequently froze people's assets in the banks. Every time the police went on strike, the murder count, a daily average of fifty, went down to nearly nothing. It rose to over a hundred when they were negotiating for a raise. The country, though rich in raw materials, is a total racial and cultural mix up, with masses of children. I give them even less of a chance than India for ever catching up.

Martha, a nun, drove us to a small monastery she had built north of Rio. Her parents were impressive people. Their ancestors left north Italy during the Inquisition. I also taught at the Gelugpa center, and we were guided through a hill of *favelas,* absolute slums. After the last teaching at Nina and Ramon's house, the lady president of the prostitutes' union promised to show us the town's funniest transvestites. When I finished at three a.m., however, they were all gone. One misses out on a few things if one always puts work before everything else.

Another age-old plane took us north to Colombia. Adriana, Eduardo, Miriam, and others waited with jeeps. We drove straight to the one of his four estates which Eduardo could still safely visit. It lay in beautiful surroundings and was warmer than Bogotá. Thirty people were waiting here for a two-day course during which we used every moment. Adriana had an often-heard complaint: the three years of retreat her

In Colombia, Adriana and Eduardo to the very right

husband had just finished had drawn them seriously apart. Strangely enough, few understand that it is for monks.

Our friends are the cream of Colombian society, on the straight side. They don't export cocaine. They strongly warned us against going overland to Caracas, our next stop. Also our group wanted me to do a divination, but I asked how much the tickets were instead. With the bus costing $20 and the flight $200, I kept my beads in my pocket. "We are travelling on the donations of our friends," I said, "and cannot spend their money on luxury." My respect for the generosity of my students soon caused our protectors a lot of work. In the morning, between a town called Bucamarance and the infamous Cucuta, Hannah saw girls with machine guns; a tank truck blocked the road. A moment after, two sweaty-faced soldiers with worn machine-pistols stood in the door and asked people to get off the bus. Everybody complied. They were so nervous that nobody thought of discussing with them. Having looked for weapons—I hid my bayonet under the seat, it would not be much use there—people were told to move up the road towards a village they had occupied.

In the middle of the street stood the commandante, a small, strong man with a beard. He declared the fifteen, mainly masked figures, to be

Dining in style with Gonzalo in Bogotá

In the bus again

the Simon Bolivar Guerillos of the National Liberation Army. They were right now in a major attack, blowing up bridges and roads across the country. So they were from the left and not the right. It meant our lives were in danger but not our things. The other side would steal our luggage and might or might not shoot.

I decided to freeze them out. They were a total waste of our precious time, and I showed that I was not amused with this strange local habit. The commander made a three-hour hateful and repetitive speech: we gringos (white people) were the cause of all evil. He denounced the class of Colombians in our address books as being the worst of all. While all this went on, there were some things to do. While finishing the last pages of my *Mahamudra* book in English, I was checking how their machine guns worked and deciding whose to snatch in case of trouble. The worst problem would be the soldiers who must be hiding in the hills behind. In true Huckleberry Finn style, I asked Tomek to eat the most incriminating page of addresses but he quickly put it in a fire place instead.

The great honor for dissolving the mess goes to our protectors. It was amazing how they worked. Though we were only a few meters away, the commandante just couldn't see us! Every time one of his men pointed us out in the crowd—we were the only four blond heads among all the black ones and had big Buddhas on our orange and red T-shirts—his eyes reached right, left, up and down, but . . . could not focus. Once when several pointed us out at the same time, a grey-haired gentleman with a beard asked a question. That distracted him once again.

People in the last town didn't know what was happening. Cars and buses were still coming up the hill and being stopped. When the guerrillas had more hostages than they could handle, they sent us away. Their last greeting was a promise to kill whoever showed up on the road again, and that convinced even me to get on a flight. It had been an interesting experience but even the best protectors should not be asked to help one around the clock.

Our friends in Bogota knew how lucky we had been. They were happy to see us again. It was impressive to watch TV: we had been involved in the biggest concerted attack in thirty years. Over four hundred had been killed in a single day, and Bogota was cut off from the

Celebrating our freedom

country on all sides. They also showed the haggard faces of some Englishmen who had been held hostage for three months. While most were killed, they had just been freed for a very high ransom. We could not complain: the hours with them had given inspiration to the last pages of my *Mahamudra* book.

Caracas only got two days, but they were important. It was the time to give the center functions to those who were really Buddhist, not just New Age, and who felt a bond to Karmapa. Again it was the central Europeans who saved the day. Their spiritual power and consequence gives a backbone to most of our centers around the world. The three tall and impressive Hoogesteijn sisters had had enough *mañana* culture and would now take things into their hands. They would arrange a Phowa with Bogotá in April, 1992.

Landing in Lima for a night, the area around the airport had just been car-bombed and cholera had struck. It was the first time in 150 years and half the water in the city was contaminated. A popular dish of raw fish was considered its main carrier. To calm demonstrations by angry fishermen, the president had ordered his minister of health to eat it on TV. The next day he was taken to the hospital with symptoms which looked suspiciously like the disease. We felt bad about leaving Ricardo, Jota and our now thirty friends in such a mess, but they knew how to cope. In the airport there was one last bit of local color: not getting any pay, the Aero Peru staff had actually been on strike every other day during

The three power sisters—informal

the last few months. With our luck, this was the first time we even heard about it.

In Miami, I told people that I had nothing personal against the Dharmadhatu. My wish was to support the reformers there and make sure that nobody would try any absolutist trips in the future. Buddhism just couldn't afford that. Then followed L.A. The first program was at the Mandala bookstore. Some alternative people there disagreed with my "hit Saddam" view on the Gulf War, but had to accept that I knew what I was talking about. Europe is close to the Middle East, and the more one knows the angry people there, the less one likes them. A lawyer from the early days of Buddhism in California invoked a ghost. He demonstrated once again why our teaching has trouble growing in that otherwise rich part of the world: inviting teachers from all kinds of lineages to the practitioners there, he would only confuse them more.

A nightly talk-show on an alternative radio-station in Los Angeles became quite bizarre. Our dozen Europeans sitting outside the studio seriously asked themselves if Americans from the ghettos go to school. If the callers were not claiming that Danes were Mongolians, they insisted that Buddha was black and that all civilization came from Africa. The classical texts say that he had blue eyes, but I didn't mention that. It would have blocked their entry into the teachings for many further incarnations.

My most useless radio interview

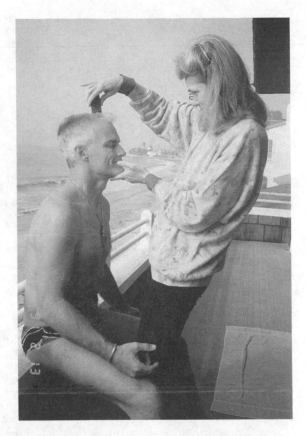

*The Nydahls in
private—Malibu Beach*

Van and Carolyn had prepared one of their fantastic meals and our
center north of San Diego was on its way to sustained growth. Cathy had
been guiding meditations in English, and also Bill had decided that in
the West one had to be understandable. Holy means functioning, not
exotic. Now also Southern California had a timeless offer for clear minds
and accepted the practices we use everywhere.

The flight was only $20 to Albuquerque. The next day the Phowa
started in Phoenix. The site was a fantastic mansion offered to Karmapa.
Cesar and Yoshiko came, warming my heart, and Ira Green from Dean
Witter investment shared the insights of highest finance. They were not
rosy. Forty of us once again enjoyed the hospitality offered by Randy and
the Phoenix group. After all had the signs, the Buddha of Limitless Light

Leaders of the San Diego center—Bill and Cathy

With Randy in Phoenix

The mansion for the Phowa

granted another prayer. This time he blessed the earth with a day and a night of rain.

Southern California was burned brown from the sun. We drove Roland's Volvo north to San Luis Obispo. My cousin Dudley had arranged a major lecture at the Unity Church. It was the largest audience in North America since the Dharmadhatu scandal broke. Visiting the farm of my family near there, it was evident how bad the five years of drought had been. With amazement, I once again heard my voice declaring publicly that I would ask the red Buddha for rain, that He would surely be kind also a third time. It felt strange every time that happened. The logical part of my mind always said, "Stop. You cannot put the Buddhas in a squeeze like that. You represent them and if they don't deliver, you make them look bad." I found myself making the statement several times up the coast, however, and increasingly a small "personal" addition crept in which made me feel even stranger about the whole thing: my altruistic prayers for the beings and the land were frequently accompanied by the typically "Danish" wish that the rains would not start until we had left California.

February 25th, eight of us landed in Hawaii. Jenny could stay for two weeks but the rest of us only had three days. We stayed one night

Members of my family in San Luis Obispo, Dudley to the right

with Daniel and Laureen in Honolulu. They adopt away orphaned
children and it would simply be wonderful if large scale adoption from
Russia could work out. Watching the news on Maui with fair Deborah,
our eyes nearly jumped from their sockets: thunderstorms had hit Cali-

With Daniel Susott, overlooking Honolulu

At Dechen and Jason's place with Hawaii friends and our group

fornia and, as I later learned from several thankful letters, it rained for
weeks and weeks.

Crossing the time zone, we landed in Christchurch, New Zealand
on March 2. Maureen and Manfred had organized three lectures, one with
the Theosophists, and Ron and Lisa took us to their amazing home on
Bank's peninsula. The native flora of the south Island was original and
scarce. Prehistoric trees in unbelievable shapes and with incredibly hard
wood stood wherever nobody had noticed them. A law passed during the
last century to increase sheep-holding had resulted in the trees' destruction in all fields. As the wood didn't rot, their strange whitish forms now
give the age-old landscapes a Goya-like impression.

In Auckland, the capital on the north island, we only met a kind
Buddhist family, but Sydney in Australia was a joy. They had used my
instructions from the last visit and now asked for more. Once again the
experience from twenty years on the road and a hundred well-running
centers brought direct benefit. Up the Australian coast, I destroyed four
retread tires on Jytte and Peter's car. A thousand kilometers at high speeds
was all they would do. Nature on the way was timeless, with floods,
exciting curves and way-out trees. At Surfers' Paradise, possibly the
world's best beaches, we enjoyed meeting Terry James. He organized

New Zealand near Christchurch

some first meetings with small groups of people, and there was ample time for writing. In Canberra, their capital, our old friend Lee worked for the Aborigines. Though deeply deploring their losses at every encounter with Western culture, he also contributed some touching pictures: many enjoy driving immensely. They step right from the social office and into a taxi, only leaving it when the week's allowance has run out. In Wollongong I taught a Theravadan group. It was led by a monk who was

Australian gridlock

My fiftieth birthday in Sydney

the mirror-image of Jamgon Kongtrul Rinpoche. He did a fine job. From March 21st we enjoyed a retreat in the woods near Sydney. The land belonged to Ayya Khema, a German nun. Her main center is near Schwarzenberg, and this beautiful area was run by an English monk, a bhante. He was thinking seriously of entering the Diamond Way.

In spite of Kunzig Shamarpa's wishes and several letters from Tomek, the Chinese were unable to organize a Phowa. Both Singapore and Malaysia were restructuring their centers. It gave Australia another week and us a chance to catch up on the action films of the last few years. Stopping at the local BP station after my lectures at night, we picked up videos which kept us in blood and gore until the early hours.

Early in April we left Peter and Jytte's wonderful home. Taking the night bus to Melbourne, which is very English, we flew from there. In Kuala Lumpur in Malaysia, kind Uguen and Peggy picked us up. They had already hosted Markus and Kasia from Zürich for a week and their hospitality was once again beyond words. The year before they had sponsored our tickets on to Bangkok.

It was again impossible to avoid a stop-over in Bangkok. AIDS was now really spreading there and the tourists were becoming wary. Though nothing had been planned from our side, the times for visiting Rumtek alone were clearly past. Having offered twenty percent of their Norwegian-earned money to the Kuchary retreat center, several of our enterprising Poles now wanted to travel. They found out when we would arrive in Sikkim. This time we were there with thirty friends.

The road west to Kathmandu was worse than ever before. The infrastructure of Nepal was disintegrating and our friends who had experienced the recent riots had a lot to tell. Unpolitical Shangri-La was truly a thing of the past. We stayed with Lopon Chechoo and his attendant, Lama Kalsang. Every day there were exciting developments to plan. Tenga Rinpoche's success with educating the little monks in his new monastery was a thing to see. My lectures in the Vajra Hotel were attended by some English-speaking lamas of the Sakya school. They enjoyed seeing how fully traditional teachings can be made interesting to modern people and I was thankful for their praise. Visiting the V. Ven.

With Pawo Rinpoche

Tenga Rinpoche's monastery in Kathmandu

On top of Tenga Rinpoche's monastery

Pawo Rinpoche shortly before his death was a great and lasting experience.

Hannah flew to Hong Kong to translate for H. E. Shamarpa and Tomek and I went on, hopefully, our last Indian Air flight. We were thoroughly tired of their confusion, pedantic checks on the weight of one's luggage and total lack of generosity. Even the flight attendants seemed to consider it a personal victory to give the absolute minimum of everything. We would now take other airlines even if they cost a bit more.

Arriving six hours late in Frankfurt airport, eighty friends were still waiting. After news, blessings, and a short meditation upstairs, the well-known film producer, Clemens Kuby drove us north to Wuppertal. Reaching the center at eleven p.m., the street was packed with friends. I first thought everybody had a break for fresh air, but it was not so. Every inch inside was completely packed. Over four hundred had come for a single evening and had waited for five hours. I was deeply touched. It was really home after three and a half months around the world. After twenty-four hours of interviews, helped by Caty, we drove to a program and Refuge in Berlin. The town had really changed. It was much less chaotic than before the wall fell. People who had been matting their hair for years now cut it off. Michael, Gunda, Ali, and Eva did a good job there, and now we needed a larger center.

The train east was of the traditional Russian kind. It featured a wood-stove for heating and tea. Gaby and Danish Lotte looked in amazement at the shoddy out-datedness of everything, and Tomek and I had to explain why the personnel were so jumpy. They just weren't used to unexpected situations or answering questions.

In Warsaw, forty of my Polish students outsmarted the train attendants and stayed on for an hour to receive blessings. They had good news: 20,000 copies of my book, *Entering the Diamond Way,* were now in print. Woytek's translation was excellent though the printer had allowed themselves to soften some of my views. Here Michael from Kiel joined our group. After a day and a night of rolling through fertile but dreary, formerly Polish, and now Ukrainian landscapes, we were in Kiev.

Stepping off the train, a powerful gust of warm wind enveloped us and in front of me stood lovely Tatjana, Vitali, and close friends from the

With Caty, in good hands

Petersburg group. During the next weeks, she would give me the essence
of Russia and all would become a perfect team. Vagid, my translator, is
a self-taught language-genius. Since we met, he has moved far from his
roots in Baku. He used his years in the Red Army gaining some stars on
his shoulders and learning English and German. His goal was translating
my books into Russian, and, except for this one (Autumn, '91), they all
are.

Kiev is the original capital of Russia. We heard at once that there
was heavy rationing. Only Ukrainians could buy the few shoddy items
on display. An amazing amount of historical buildings were still standing, and looked like they had missed out on the scorched-earth strategy
during the war. In the low-ceilinged room of a colorful art gallery, only
a few dozen found a seat, but guiding a meditation, I had a unique
experience. The local gods and other energies came. They showed me the
holy places of the land, the hidden birch groves and charged up rocks
which centered their powerfields. There was no doubt they liked us and

would support our work. The feeling of deep yearning they instilled in me fused with several similar experiences from the country's north. So much feeling for every little bit of articulation there. There were other signs that Russia would become a major activity in my life. As in several places I opened to the Dharma, I bled—here, from the intestines. A meal I had eaten and Tomek had avoided on our flight from Nepal had apparently contained a bad batch of amoeba which a handful of Russian tetracycline could not take away.

After another two and a half days on the train, we arrived in Zaparoje, the heart of Cossack country. A bus awaited our then humble group of fifteen—across Siberia in January '92 we would already be sixty. On the way they showed us some of the historical places which are still so alive in their collective imagination. They clearly wanted to give and not just take. Except for the teachings where five hundred intelligent and deeply interested people didn't stop asking questions, above all we were their guests. We stayed in a vast sports hotel, rode their fast horses, and saw their sights. Here, at the mouth of the Dujepr River, lies an island with a terrific view. The Vikings made a last stop here on their way to protect the East Roman Empire.

With two hundred wishing to take Refuge, it was only possible to give collective names. I decided on Karma Dorje (Diamond) for the men and Karma Pema (Lotus) for the women. Expressing the essential male and female qualities, they should have the added benefit of bringing the two sexes close together. As people filed by the table we stood on, I blessed them. Gaby cut their hair. Lotte and Tatjana distributed charged-up blessing strings, and Tomek and others kept things flowing. This became the pattern in every town until Petersburg, and once again we saw with amazement how nothing is coincidental: the Buddhas can count. Like in Poland and South America, the exact number of people came that I had Refuge cards for. The last of the twelve hundred received in Kiev were given on the final day in the country.

Kharkow, a capital the Russians imposed on the Ukraine to better be able to control them, was humming with the same interest. Another two hundred took Refuge here, but our main contact had ruble-signs in his eyes. He thought too much of what could be earned from the Dharma. A real group will have to form around somebody else. Volvograd, formerly Stalingrad, was our first stop in Russia itself. Being the guests of the youth communist group there, not many came. They expertly separated Tatjana, Tomek and me from the rest to have more time with us. We got a good impression of their empty but privileged lives, however, and of the town's atmosphere. It was still in shock. The park containing the war memorial was larger than anywhere else, and the hill overlooking the Volga River is indescribable. This is where the most decisive fighting of the Second World War took place. Here Stalin kept sending new troonps over the river and executed the ones trying to retreat, while the Germans first ate their horses, then their boots, and finally succumbed to a wickedly cold winter.

Samara on the Volga is the next stop. It is just regaining its pre-communist name. The signs that grace it with the proud epithet of a former police chief are being pulled down everywhere. Here, more than anywhere, we wince at the way rows of beautiful old block houses are torn down to make room for uninspiring concrete boxes. We stay with a lovely Burjat (traditional Buddhist) family and enjoy their circle of academic friends. The father is true lama material so I ask him to guide the group. The local KGB officer for religion, empowered according to Gorbachev but non-existing according to Yeltzin, actually impresses me. He mentions how much money the proselytizing Protestant Christian sects now bring to his region, but is privately pleased with my more idealistic promise: not to put any religion above the mental freedom of the people. After my briefing on how Buddhism transcends philosophy, psychology, and belief-religions, we gain a friend. He even walks us down interminable corridors and stairs to the heavily protected main door. As we stand in the wind and sunshine on the banks of the Volga, pictures of the countless police stations of my youth float by. How much nicer they are to visit on one's own accord.

After another few hundred take Refuge, we get on the boat to Lenin's birthplace. Formerly Simbirsk, and now Ulianowsk, in honor of his family name, it had been receiving more than its share of the socialist pie. The boat keeps breaking down on its way through the frequent sluices, so we are two hours late for our crowds. They wait in a beautiful hall overlooking the river. To my amazement some high officers in the audience seem pleased with what I say. They even like my joke from the

Teacher of Samara Hep

years of emergency rule in Poland that they should be glad their system doesn't work. It helps them develop spiritual values instead of just consuming.

The next day is historical. We spend the last communist May 1st, the day of the working class, in Lenin's birth town. Police stand around in small embarrassed groups, and the main streets are cordoned off for the jubilant demonstrations which no longer materialize. On our detour to the hall where I am to teach, a man carrying a banner in front accidentally strikes my jaw with its pole. On my way up to catch him by the neck, with amazement we see the result of this latest Buddhist-communist confrontation. This time we win. While their group looks on in amazement, sickle, flag, and ornaments break off the staff and fall on the ground.

Ulianowsk is fresh, new territory. Another few hundred begin practicing here. Vitali and our Petersburg group have also organized this stop perfectly. After a great disco night in the youth club where we have our rooms, we get on the train west to Moscow. The capital has little of this pristine quality. It is a mix of everything, which doesn't bring out the best in people. Meeting our group in front of the Kremlin, Tatjana and I hear that the police evicted them from a mixed-spiritual center during the night. With typical Slav hospitality, however, some people they met in the street just invited them home. Things like this happened along the whole tour, and we all agree we have never met a kinder and more caring population than in this enormous country. Leaving the last teachings in a museum where Tatjana's grandmother and mother both take Refuge, it dawns on us what has happened during the last weeks. It was a landslide bigger than anything before. Thousands from all over Russia have been touched and inspired. I have started six new centers and given over a thousand people Refuge. All have been told to bring their friends for Lopön Chechoo Rinpoche and lovely Hannah, who are arriving from Nepal tomorrow. In every group, preparations for the Phowa are the main point. It will start near Petersburg in a few days.

While teaching in that beautiful town, friends come from every station on our tour, and it is wonderful to be with Rinpoche and Hannah

V. Ven. Lopön Chechoo

again. All together three hundred of us go by bus to a large communist pioneer camp north of the city. It lies in those fir and birch woods which I love so much. Here, in the intense blessing-field of the lineage, all get the signs in three days. Then Rinpoche blesses Russia with a series of initiations. They are the first Kagyu transmissions ever and leave all deeply thankful.

Though I sit next to Rinpoche on the podium, and don't think that a lama should show emotions in public, his last words leave me with no choice. With something like dry heaves moving up through my body, and hot tears of thankfulness that I try to hide, I hear words which explain so much: "I often state that Ole and Hannah are activities and even emanations of Karmapa," he says. "And I will tell you why. It is not something I say because I like them so much, but I have that from Karmapa himself. I was present when they met His Holiness first. After a Crown Ceremony in Kathmandu they came up for a longer blessing in Karmapa's room above the Swayambhu Monastery. When they had left, he asked who they were. Without thinking, I answered, 'They are my students.' 'Now they are mine!' Karmapa said. 'They will express my activity in the future.'"

Our Russian Phowa friends

At the Phowa place, Gabi, to the left, is now streamlining Russian practice

For once I have nothing to say

The seat for the seventeenth Karmapa in Rumtek

Explanations to the Names
of the Buddha Aspects

Almighty Ocean (Tib.: Gyalwa Gyamtso / Skt.: Jinasagara): Red, sitting four-armed form of Loving Eyes in Union.

Bearer of Black Coat (Tib.: Bernagchen): Main protector of the Karma Kagyu lineage.

Black Coat: see Bearer of the Black Coat.

Buddha of Limitless Light (Tib.: Öpame / Skt.: Amitabha): His mental realm is the pure land of highest bliss.

Diamond Dagger (Tib.: Dorje Purbha / Skt.: Vajrakilaya): Wrathful embodiment of Diamond Mind and important activity of the Buddhas.

Diamond-holder Power Buddha (Tib.: Channa Dorje / Skt.: Vajrapani): The power and energy of all Buddhas.

Diamond Mind (Tib.: Dorje Sempa / Skt.: Vajrasattva): Embodying the cleansing power of all Buddhas.

Diamond Paunch (Tib.: Dorje Drollö): Wrathful aspect of Guru Rinpoche.

Diamond Sow (Tib.: Dorje Pamo / Skt.:Vajravarahi): The highest wisdom of the Buddhas. The pig represents basic ignorance which is transformed into highest wisdom.

Great Black (Tib.: Nagpo Chenpo / Skt.: Mahakala): The protection power of all Buddhas.

Green Liberatrice: see Liberatrice.

Highest Joy (Tib.: Khorlo Demchok / Skt.: Chakrasamvara / Lit.: Wheel of Highest Joy): Radiant transpersonal joy which is the true nature of space. Blue skin, wrathful. May appear alone or in union with Diamond Sow. Transforms attachment.

Horsehead (Tib.: Tamdrin / Skt.: Hayagriva): Protector of the pure land of Highest Joy.

Liberatice (Skt.: Tara); White Liberatice (Tib.: Dölkar); Green Liberatice (Tib.: Dölma): Female embodiment of the compassion of all Buddhas. She protects against dangers, fears and pain. Helps in finding partners.

Long-life Goddess (Tib.: Tseringma): Main important partner of Milarepa.

Loving Eyes (Tib.: Chenrezig / Skt.: Avalokiteshvara / Lit.: The one whose eyes look at everyone). The love and compassion of all Buddhas.

Medicine Buddha (Tib.: Sangye Menla / Skt.: Bhaisayaguru).

Wheel of Time (Tib.: Dükyi Khorlo / Skt.: Kalachakra): Important Buddha aspect. Transforms ignorance.

White Liberatrice: see Liberatrice.

White Umbrella (Tib.: Dukar): Protective female Buddha. She emanated spontaneously from Buddha's crown.

Wisdom Buddha on a Lion (Tib.: Jampel Maseng / Skt.: Simhasana Manjushri): Much-used meditative aspect in the Kagyu school. The embodiment of the wisdom of all Buddhas.

Glossary

Black Crown: Attribute of the Karmapas. Signifying the power to help all beings, the female Buddhas bestowed this energyfield on Karmapa at his enlightenment several thousand years ago. It is constantly above his head. The replica shown at ceremonies has the power to open the subconscious of those present and permits the Karmapa to exchange his limitless space-awareness for beings' inhibitions and pain. It is a means for gaining liberation through seeing which only a Karmapa can use.

Bodhgaya: Dorje Seat, now a village in north India. The first Buddhas of each Dharma-period manifest full enlightenment there.

Bodhisattva vow: Promise to always work for the enlightenment of all beings. One makes it in the presence of a Bodhisattva and should strengthen the motivation daily.

Bond (Tib.: Damtsig / Skt.: Samaya): The basis for the rapid psychological growth in Diamond Way Buddhism. Through the unbroken connection to teacher, meditation forms and co-disciples, students quickly manifest their potential. Especially the bond to one's first teacher is very important.

Buddha (Tib.: Sangye): The name denotes a state of mind. "Sang" means "perfectly purified" of all obscurations. "Gye" means "perfect unfoldment" of all qualities and wisdom.

Buddha aspects (Tib.: Yidam): The great richness of enlightened mind expresses itself in countless forms of energy and light. By identifying with them in meditation and daily life they rapidly awaken our innate Buddha-nature.

Buddha energies: see Buddha aspects.

Crown Ceremony: see Black Crown.

Dharma (Tib.: Cho): the Buddha's teachings.

Diamond Way (Tib.: Dorje Thegpa / Skt.: Vajrayana): Consequential methods of quick transformation based on the motivation and philosophy of the Great Way (Mahayana). Can only be practiced with the willingness to see all things on the level of purity.

Emptiness (Tib.: Tongpanyi / Skt.: Shunyata): The fact that nothing outer or inner exists through or in itself. Everything arises from conditions, the ultimate nature of which is the potential of space.

Enlightened Mind (Tib.: Chang Chub Kyi Sem / Skt.: Bodhicitta): Has two aspects: the relative means perfecting ourselves through the six liberating actions for the benefit of all beings. The absolute is spontaneous and effortless activity without thought or hesitation. The experience of subject, object and action as a totality makes this intuitive state automatic.

Enlightenment: see Buddha.

Gampopa (1079-1153): Main disciple of Milarepa and teacher of the first Karmapa, Dusum Chenpa. He was prophesized by the Buddha to spread the Dharma widely in Tibet and is the source of the monastic Kagyu transmissions.

Gelug: The latest of the four main lineages of Tibetan Buddhism. This reformed school, founded by Tsongkhapa, puts special stress on studying the scriptures and on the monastic tradition. Though possessing several Tantras, it does not accept the first—Nyingma—transmission of Buddhism into Tibet and often represents itself as belonging to the Mahayana, not the Vajrayana.

Great Perfection: see Maha-Ati.

Great Way (Tib.: Theg Chen / Skt.: Mahayana): Motivation and practice to reach enlightenment for the benefit of all beings. Its very basis is the development of compassion and transpersonal wisdom.

Guru Rinpoche (Tib.: Pema Jungne / Skt.: Padmasambhava, the Lotus-born): The probably Afghan yogi who brought the full cycle of Buddhism to Tibet in the eighth century. He manifested an exciting life and countless wonders and is highly revered in the three non-reformed schools of Tibetan Buddhism. His energy-field is especially present on the tenth day after new moon.

Initiation (Tib.: Wang / Skt.: Abhisheka): A better word is empowerment. Ceremony which introduces the practitioner to the powerfield of a certain Buddha aspect. It may be given as a blessing or at the start of a practice. One also needs a "lung," a reading of the text, and a "thri," the instructions on how to use it. The effectiveness of these methods in developing one's awareness cannot be overestimated.

Jewel Ornament of Liberation: Main philosophical work of Gampopa. It explains the view and path of the Great Way. Excellent introduction to the basic teachings.

Kagyu Lineage: The yogic transmission among the four main schools of Tibetan Buddhism. It encompasses both the old (Nyingma) and the new (Sarma) teachings which reached Tibet. Being heavily practice-oriented, it is called the "oral" or "perfection" school. It was brought to Tibet by the hero Marpa around year 1050 and derives its power from the close bond between teacher and student.

Four major and eight minor schools originated from Gampopa's three main disciples. Today the major ones have all fused into the Karma Kagyu of which H.H. Karmapa is the head. Among the minor ones, the Drugpa and the Drigung Kagyu have strong followings in Bhutan and Ladakh.

Karma (Tib.: Le / Lit.: action): Law of cause and effect. Any outer and inner situation depends on the impressions stored in beings' minds and in the world around them. These are produced by one's physical, verbal and mental actions right now.

The Karmapa Meditation: see Three Lights Meditation.

The Karmapa (Lit.: Activity Man): First consciously reborn lama of Tibet and the spiritual head of the Kagyu lineage. The Karmapas embody the activity of all Buddhas and were prophesized by Buddha Shakyamuni and by Guru Rinpoche. Before his death each Karmapa leaves a letter containing the exact conditions of his next birth. Up until now, there have been seventeen incarnations:

1. Dusum Chenpa, 1110 - 1193
2. Karma Pakshi, 1204 - 1283
3. Rangjung Dorje, 1284 - 1339
4. Rolpe Dorje, 1340 - 1383
5. Deshin Shegpa, 1384 - 1415
6. Tongwa Donden, 1416 - 1453
7. Chodrag Gyamtso, 1454 - 1506
8. Mikyo Dorje, 1507 - 1554
9. Wangchug Dorje, 1556 - 1603
10. Choying Dorje, 1604 - 1674
11. Yeshe Dorje, 1676 - 1702
12. Changchub Dorje, 1703 - 1732
13. Dudul Dorje, 1733 - 1797
14. Thegchog Dorje, 1798 - 1868
15. Khakhyab Dorje, 1871 - 1922
16. Rangjung Rigpe Dorje, 1924 - 1981
17. soon to be officially disclosed

Lama (Lit.: "highest mother"): Teacher. In the Diamond Way he is especially important. Without him, there is no key to the deepest teachings.

Level of Joy: see State of Joy.

Level of Truth: see State of Truth.

Lineage Holders, Four: The heart sons of Karmapa, who carry on the transmission between his lives: Kunzig Shamar Rinpoche, Tai Situ Rinpoche, Jamgon Kongtrul Rinpoche, and Goshir Gyaltsab Rinpoche.

Lung: A ritual reading of texts of the Diamond Way. The mere hearing of the syllables transmits their inner meaning; see also inititaion/empowerment.

Maha-Ati: (Tib.: Dzogpa Chenpo): The "Great Perfection" is the absolute teaching of the old or Nyingma tradition. Essence and goal correspond to the Mahamudra of the Kagyu transmission.

Mahamudra (Tib.: Chagya Chenpo): The "Great Seal" of reality. Buddha's promise that this is the ultimate teaching. It is mainly taught in the Kagyu tradition and brings about the direct experience of mind. Mahamudra includes basis, way and goal and is the quintessence of all Buddhist teachings. See also my book *Mahamudra*.

Mahayana: see Great Way.

Mandala (Tib.: Khyil-khor, Center-circle): Powerfield which arises out of the potential of space. An enlightened mandala manifests from the thirty-seven perfect qualities of Buddhas and Bodhisattvas.

Mantra (Tib.: Ngag): Natural vibration of a Buddha aspect. When used, the Buddha is there. Important part of Diamond Way meditation.

Marpa (1012-1097): The "Great Translator." Travelling to India three times, Marpa was able to rebuild Buddhism in Tibet. His main teachers were Naropa and Maitripa. He was the first Tibetan lineage holder of the Kagyu tradition and became Milarepa's teacher. The lay and yogi transmissions of the Kagyu lineage are often called "Marpa Kagyu."

Milarepa (1040-1123): Main disciple of Marpa and teacher of Gampopa. He is the most famous of Tibetan yogis. Started his career by killing thirty-five enemies of his family. Due to his unshakeable confidence in Marpa, and a willingness to meditate under extreme conditions, he realized the teachings in a single lifetime.

Naropa (1016-1100): Indian Mahasiddha and former professor at Nalanda University. Disciple of Tilopa and teacher of Marpa.

Ngondro: see Preliminary Practices.

Nyingma: The earliest of the four main lineages of Tibetan Buddhism, the "old school." Its origins go back to the first spreading of Buddhism in Tibet in the eighth century. The outer structure and transmission was destroyed by King Langdharma shortly after, but the hidden treasures have remained until today.

Power Circle: see Mandala.

Powerfield: see Mandala.

Preliminary Practices (Tib.: Ngondro): Four are general and four are special. First comes a thorough self-motivation through the understanding of four basic facts about our life: The rarity and preciousness of our present existence, that we can use it to reach liberation and enlightenment. Impermanence, that one should use it now. Karma—cause and effect—that we create our own lives. And the fact that enlightenment is the only lasting joy. The latter are a set of four repetitive but intensely rewarding practices which create masses of good imprints in one's subconscious. These work deeply in our minds, give increasing joy, and remove the causes of future suffering. The Ngondro is the basis for recognizing mind both through its nature as energy and as awareness. See my book *Ngondro.*

Protector: There are three kinds: Unenlightened energy-fields—Jigtenpas— believing in a "self" are better avoided; they may be very difficult customers. If controlled by yogis like Guru Rinpoche and the Karmapas, they become Damzigpas, held positive by the promise not to harm beings. They often look somewhat "unusual" and, gradually becoming Bodhisattvas, manifest a vertical wisdom-eye in their foreheads. The most important protectors are direct emanations of the Buddhas: male Mahakalas and female Mahakalis. They are harmonious in outer appearance and are always from the eighth Bodhisattva-level and up. From the taking of Buddhist Refuge they ensure that every experience becomes a part of the Practitioner's way towards enlightenment.

Puja: Meditation sung in Tibetan. An invocation with ritual offerings.

Pure Realm: A Buddha's field of consciousness. It is experienced as continual blissful growth in a palace of energy and light. This again arises from the thirty-seven perfect qualities.

Realm of Great Joy (Tib.: Dewachen / Skt.: Sukhavati): Pure Realm of the Buddha of Limitless Light.

Refuge (Tib.: Kyab Dro): A reorientation towards values that can be trusted. One takes Refuge in the state of Buddha as the goal, in the Dharma—the teachings—as the way, and in the Sangha—the practitioners—as one's friends on the way. These are called the Three Jewels. To practice the Diamond Way one needs the additional Refuge in the Three Roots, called Lama, Yidam and Protector. They are the sources of blessing, inspiration and protection along the way.

Rinpoche: Honorific title meaning "Precious One." It is frequently given to Buddhist Masters.

Sakya: One of the three old or unreformed lineages of Tibetan Buddhism. There is both hereditary and incarnate succession. This school has contributed some of the most important philosophical commentaries.

Six Teachings of Naropa: Highly effective methods of the Kagyu lineage. Their goal is realizing the nature of mind through its energetic aspect. They consist of the following meditations: Inner Heat (Tumo), Clear Light (Osel), Dream (Milam), Illusory Body (Gyulu), Intermediate State (Bardo), and Transference of Consciousness (Phowa). Basis, way and goal are the Mahamudra.

Small Way (Tib.: Thek Chung / Skt.: Hinayana; today, Theravada): The way of the "listeners" (Shravakas) and "non-teaching Buddhas" (Prateyka Buddhas). Here the focus is on one's own liberation.

State of Joy (Tib.: Long Ku / Skt.: Sambhogakaya): The free play and spontaneous bliss of mind. It manifests from the State of Truth to help sentient beings on their way. See also Buddha aspects.

State of Truth (Tib.: Cho Ku / Skt.: Dharmakaya): The State of Truth is timeless enlightenment itself, the true nature and radiant awareness of mind.

Stupa (Tib.: Chorten): A physical representation of perfect enlightenment. It shows the transformation of all emotions and elements into the five enlightened wisdoms and the five Buddha families. Its symmetrical form is usually filled with relics, mantras, etc.

Tantra (Buddhist): see Diamond Way.

Three Lights Meditation (Tib.: Lamae Naljor / Skt.: Guru Yoga): Meditation on the Buddha in the form of one's teacher. The most direct way to receive his blessing of body, speech and mind is to identify oneself with his enlightened state. This does not mean becoming a carbon copy but resting in the same fearless space.

Three-year Retreat: Traditional education for Kagyu monks or nuns. It takes three years, three months and three days and is done in celebate groups. The places of retreat are positioned in isolation from the outside world.

Tilopa (988-1069): Great Indian meditator or Mahasiddha. He collected the full transmissions of the Diamond Way. Passing them to his main disciple, Naropa, he thus became the originator of the Kagyu lineage.

Tulku (Skt.: Nirmanakaya): State of compassion. A being who is consciously reborn for the benefit of all beings manifesting with the power to open their abilities. May or may not remember former lives. The word means "Illusion-Body," a form which one has and uses, but is not dependent upon.

Vajrayana: see Diamond Way.

Books Recommended
by Kagyu Teachers and Lamas

INTRODUCTION

KALU RINPOCHE (1986). *The Dharma: That Benefits All Beings Impartially Like the Light of the Sun and the Moon.* Albany, NY: SUNY Press.

NYDAHL, OLE (1988). *Basic Dharma.* Nevada City, CA: Blue Dolphin.

BASIC TEXTS

GAMPOPA (Transl. H.V. Guenther) (1986). *The Jewel Ornament of Liberation.* Boston: Shambhala.

KONGTRUL, JAMGON (Transl. K. McLeod) (1987). *The Great Path of Awakening.* Boston: Shambhala.

SHANTIDEVA. *Bodhicharyavatara.*

SITU RINPOCHE. *Way To Go.* Zalendara Publications.

BOOKS FOR PRACTICE

KALU RINPOCHE (1986). *The Gem Ornament of Manifold Oral Instruction.* KDK, 1892 Fell St., San Francisco, CA 94117.

KARMAPA KAKHYAB DORJE, FIFTEENTH. *Commentary to the Chenresig Practice.*

KARMAPA WANGCHUK DORJE, NINTH. *Mahamudra: Illuminating the Darkness of Ignorance.*

KONGTRUL, JAMGON (Transl. J. Hanson) (1986). *The Torch of Certainty.* Boston: Shambhala.

NYDAIIL, OLE.(1990). *Ngöndro.* Nevada City, CA: Bluc Dolphin

NYDAHL, OLE & ARONOFF, CAROL (1989). *Practical Buddhism.* Nevada City, CA: Blue Dolphin.

BOOKS ON MAHAMUDRA

NALANDA TRANSLATION COMMITTEE (1989). *The Rain of Wisdom*. Boston: Shambhala.

NYDAHL, OLE (1991). *Mahamudra: Boundless Joy and Freedom*. Nevada City, CA: Blue Dolphin.

RANGDROL, TSELE NATSOK (1989). *Lamp of Mahamudra*. Boston: Shambhala.

LIFE STORIES

CHANG, GARMA C.C. (Transl.) (1977). *The Hundred Thousand Songs of Milarepa*. Boston: Shambhala.

DOUGLAS, NIK & WHITE, MERYL(1976). *Karmapa: Black Hat Lama*. London: Luzac Publ.

DOWMAN, KEITH (1986). *Masters of Mahamudra*. Albany, NY: SUNY Press.

GUENTHER, HERBERT V. (Ed.) *Life of Marpa the Translator*. Boston: Shambhala.

KALU RINPOCHE (1985). *The Chariot for Travelling the Path to Freedom*. (Out of print, write to Blue Dolphin for photocopy).

KARMAPA, SIXTEENTH. *Dzalendara & Sagarchupa*. Dzalendara Publ.

LHALHUNGPA, LOBSANG (1990). *Life of Milarepa*. New York: NAL-Dutton.

MILAREPA (1978). *Drinking the Mountain Stream*. Novato, CA: Lotsawa.

MILAREPA (1987). *Miraculous Journey*. Novato, CA: Lotsawa.

NYDAHL, OLE (1985). *Entering the Diamond Way: My Path Among the Lamas*. Nevada City, CA: Blue Dolphin.

NYDAHL, OLE (1992). *Riding the Tiger: Twenty Years on the Road: Risks and Joys of Bringing Tibetan Buddhism to the West*. Nevada City, CA: Blue Dolphin.

SITU RINPOCHE. *Tilopa: Some Glimpses of his Life*. Dzalendara.

YESHE TSOGYAL (1983). *Mother of Knowledge*. Berkeley, CA: Dharma Publishing.

BUDDHIST PHILOSOPHY

ASANGA & MAITREYA. *The Changeless Nature*. Dzalendara.

GYAMTSO, KENPO Ts. *Progressive States of Meditation*. Longchen Fou.

HOOKHAM, SHENPEN K. (1989). *The Buddha Within*. Albany, NY: SUNY Press.

MISC.

EVANS-WENTZ. (Transl.). *The Tibetan Book of the Dead*. London: Oxford Univ. Press.

RANGDROL, TSELE NATSOK (1989). *Mirror of Mindfulness: The Cycle of the Bardo*. Boston: Shambhala.

VIDEOS

Tsurphu: Home of the Karmapas
The Lion's Roar
Secret Journey Through Eastern Tibet

TAPES BY OLE NYDAHL

Available from: Sound Photosynthesis, P.O. Box 2111, Mill Valley, CA 94942

AUDIOS

0172-87—(2) *The Tibetan Buddhist Way of Transforming Emotions*, (SV) $18.
0176-87—(2) *Vajrayana Meditation*, $18.
0177-87—(2) *The Yogic Path*, $18.
0271-88—*On Relationships*, $9.
0266-87—*Interview*, (FBVS-F. int.) $9.
0407-89—(2) *The Way Things Are*, (SV) $18.
0408-89—(2) *Principles and Practice of the Yogic Path*, (SV) $18).
0409-89—(2) *Mahamudra Teachings*, $18.
0410-89—(2) *Steps along the Diamond Way—Stages of Meditation*, $18.
0623-90—(2) *Buddhism in Eastern Europe: What We Can Learn*, (SV) $18.
0624-90—(2) *Death and Rebirth: Bardo Teachings*, (SV) $18.
0625-90—(2) *Buddhism in the 90s: Active Compassion*, $18.

VIDEOS

9083-88—*On Relationships*, $35.
9047-87—*Interview*, (FBVS-F. int.) $35.
9066-87—*The Tibetan Buddhist Way of Transforming Emotions*, (SV) $35.
9064-87—*Vajrayana Meditation*, $35.
9065-87—*The Yogic Path*, $35.
9129-89—*The Way Things Are*, $35.
9130-89—*Principles and Practice of the Yogic Path*, (SV) $35.
9131-89—*Mahamudra Teachings*, $35.
9132-89—*Steps Along the Diamond Way—Stages of Meditation*, $35.
9210-90—*Buddhism in Eastern Europe: What We Can Learn*, $35.
9212-90—*Death and Rebirth: Bardo Teachings*, (SV) $35.
9213-90—*Buddhism in the 90s: Active Compassion*, $35.

ONE OF THE YEARLY TEACHING TOURS

—— overland (train and car)
—— flight
● main centers we work with
■ main places of retreat
▲ Kagyu relics have been placed here

AROUND THE WORLD — EARLY 1992*

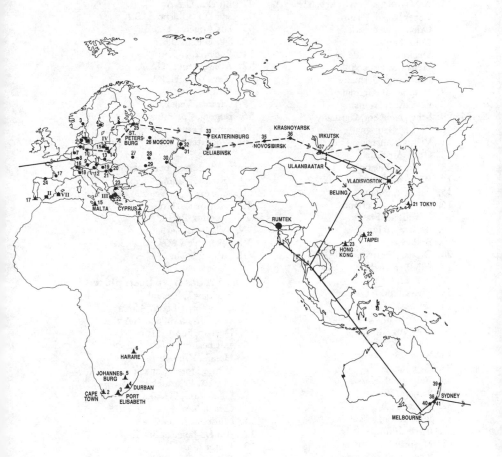

Index to Map

Afterword

The financial help and painstaking work of idealists made this book possible, and I would like to thank them here. After years when I was available around the clock, I would also like to thank the countless students who renounced or delayed private requests to free the necessary time. Here the names of my main helpers:

On the financial side:
My parents
Annemarie Schaerer
Roland Peters
Karen Grillitz
Ira and Jenny Greene
Annie Benett Clark
  and Mike McAnally
Dan & Sandy Bellin
Beate Hengesbach
Lisa Yannios
Katja Oberwelland
Robert Norett
Peter Fairfield
Dechen and Jason Groode
Keico Sano
Peter Wilkie
Tomek Lehnert
and many others

For correcting this English copy:
Carol Aronoff, editor
Jennifer Birkett
Paul Clemens
Adrian Flynn
Linda Maxwell
Helen Williams

For the pictures and maps:
Markus Kuhn
Heike Hoymann
Tomek Lehnert
and the Blue Dolphin staff

List of Tibetan Buddhist Centers

Our groups of the Karma Kagyu Lineage have kept the Tibetan nomad tradition of moving to ever better locations. For that reason I will only give the addresses of a few main places here. They have information about local developments and will be glad to direct you. Greetings from us.

UNITED STATES
Karma Triyana Dharma Chakra
352 Mead Mt. Rd.
Woodstock, NY 12498
(914) 679-2487
Seat in N. America of H. H. Karmapa

Karma Jigme Ling
33 Marne Ave.
San Francisco, CA 94127
Roland Peters: (415) 661-6467
Ole Nydahl's address in USA
Resident teacher: Jesper Jorgensen

Arizona
KTC c/o Erma Pounds
1338 W. 16th St.
Tempe, AZ 85281
(602) 892-1479

California
Karma Dechen Oser Ling
P.O. Box 2426
San Anselmo, CA 94960
Laurel Bellon: (415) 653-9295

Los Angeles KTC
c/o Izabelle Gros
3586 Tacoma Ave.
Los Angeles, CA 90065

Palo Alto KTC
P.O. Box 60793
Palo Alto, CA 94306
(415) 323-7944

Santa Cruz KTC
P.O. Box 8059
Santa Cruz, CA 95061
Lama Dudjom Dorje
(408) 476-0651 / 462-3955

San Diego KTC
904 Edwina Way
Cardiff, CA 92007
(619) 942-2963

Ira and Jenny Greene
P.O. Box 40
Bayside, CA 95524

Colorado
Marianne Marstrand
P.O. Box 339
Crestone, CO 81131
(719) 256-4698 / 256-4694

Hawaii
Lama Tenzin
P.O. Box 1029
Paia, HI 96779

Janet Graves
P.O. Box 296
Kilauea, HI 96754

New Mexico
Bob & Melani Sachs
214 Girard Blvd. NE
Albuquerque, NM 87106
(505) 265-4826

Lama Dorje
751 Airport Rd.
Santa Fe, NM 87501
(505) 474-1151

Norbert Ubechel
P.O. Box 696
El Prado, NM 87529

New York
Lisa Yannios
23-72 36th St.
Astoria, NY 11105
(718) 278-7452

AUSTRALIA
KKDC Sydney
44 Tindale Rd.
Artarmon, NSW 2064
Lama Trijam
+61-2-411-1246

AUSTRIA
Wien KCL
Am Fleischmarkt 16
A - 1010 Wien
+43-222-8285434

Graz KCL
St. Peter-Pfarrweg 17
A - 8020 Graz
0043-316-673135

COLOMBIA
KTC Bogotá
Eduardo Velazquez
Calle 87 #11A-42
Bogotá

DENMARK
Karma Drub Djy Ling
Svanemøllevej 56
DK - 2100 Copenhagen Ø
Tel: +45-31-292711
Fax: +45-31-295733

Karma Tcho Phel Ling
Korterupvej 21
DK - 4920 Søllested
+45-53-916097

FRANCE
Dhagpo Kagyu Ling
Landrevie / St. Léon s/V
F - 24290 Montignac
+33-53507075

GERMANY
Hamburg KCL
Harkortstieg 4
D-2000 Hamburg 50
+49-40-3895613

Wuppertal KCL
Heinkelstr. 27
D-5600 Wuppertal 2
+49-202-84080

Frankfurt KCL
Wielandstr. 37
D-6000 Frankfurt
+49-69-5973263

München KCL
Schweppermannstr. 10
D-8000 München 80
+49-89-493772

Haus Schwarzenberg
Sys Leube
Tel: +49-8366-1696
Fax: +49-8366-1697

Berlin KCL
Mariannenplatz 22
D-1000 Berlin 36
+49-30-6122513

GREECE
Karma Drub Dji Chökhor Ling
Sonierou 15 b, Platia Vathis
GR - 10438 Athens
+30-1-5220218

Karma Berchen Ling
c/o Georgia and Magnus Sandberg
Ioannionon 38-40
GR-16674 Pirnari-Athens

HOLLAND
KDL Groningen
Schoolholm 25f
NL-9711 Groningen JE
+31-50-122588

HUNGARY
Budapest KCL
Buday Lászlou Falags. 1
H-1024 Budapest 11
Istvan & Eva Gruber

ITALY
Karme Chö Ling Brescia
Corso Palestro 35
1-25100 Brescia
+39-30-53782

NEW ZEALAND
Karma Jigme Ling
Manfred and Barbara Ingerfeld
127 Knowles Street
Christchurch 5
+64-3-3555992

NORWAY
KTC Oslo
Björnasveien 124
N-1272 Olso 12
+47-2-2612884

PERU
Ricardo La Serna
Gral. Mendiburu 842-B
Miraflores, Lima

POLAND
Karme Czioe Ling Drobin
Kuchary 57
PL - 9210 Drobin
Gelong Rinchen

Gdansk KCL
P.O. Box 1
PL-80-958 Gdansk 50
Leszek Nadolski

Krakow KCL
PL-32-040 Swiatniki
G218
Karol Sleczek

RUSSIA
Karma Leshey Ling
ul. Kuybysheva, 5-27
Skt. Petersburg 197046
Tel: +7-812-2306828
Fax: +7-812-1220759
Sasha Koibagarov or
Vagid Ragimov

SPAIN
Karma Gön
Atalaya Alta / Apart. 179
E - 9700 Velez-Malaga

SWEDEN
KSDL Stockholm
Hökarvägen 2
S-12658 Hägersten
+46-8-886950

SWITZERLAND
Karma Dorje Ling
Neuarlesheimer Str. 15
CH - 4143 Dornach
+41-61-7018531

Karma Yeshe Gyalthsen Ling
Hammerstr. 9a
CH - 8008 Zurich
+41-1-3820875

UKRAINE
ul. Prichalnaya 11-2
Zaporojle 33067
Vitaly Bocharov

VENEZUELA
KTC Caracas
Apartado 50731
Caracas 1050-A
Iris, Almira, Solvig Hoogesteijn